Routledge Revivals

I0127655

Urban Problems

Urban problems and their resolution represent one of the major challenges for planners and decision makers in the modern world. This
book, first published in 1990, makes a major contribution to the field,
presenting an international and interdisciplinary approach to the challenges presented by the urban environment. The coverage is comprehensive, ranging from the economic and political dimensions of the
capitalist system, to the issues of poverty and deprivation and questions
about housing equity. This is an essential reference guide to social,
economic and environmental problems in urban areas, which is of great
value to students of planning, urban studies, geography and sociology.

Urban Problems
An Applied Urban Analysis

Michael Pacione

Routledge
Taylor & Francis Group

First published in 1990
by Routledge

This edition first published in 2013 by Routledge
2 Park Square, Milton Park, Abingdon, Oxon, OX14 4RN

Simultaneously published in the USA and Canada
by Routledge
711 Third Avenue, New York, NY 10017

Routledge is an imprint of the Taylor & Francis Group, an informa business

© 1990 Michael Pacione

Publisher's Note
The publisher has gone to great lengths to ensure the quality of this reprint but
points out that some imperfections in the original copies may be apparent.

Disclaimer
The publisher has made every effort to trace copyright holders and welcomes
correspondence from those they have been unable to contact.

A Library of Congress record exists under LC control number: 81004455

ISBN 13: 978-0-415-70764-0 (hbk)
ISBN 13: 978-1-315-88665-7 (ebk)
ISBN 13: 978-0-415-70766-4 (pbk)

URBAN PROBLEMS

An Applied Urban Analysis

MICHAEL PACIONE

R

Routledge
London and New York

First published 1990
by Routledge
11 New Fetter Lane, London EC4P 4EE

Simultaneously published in the USA and Canada
by Routledge
a division of Routledge, Chapman and Hall, Inc.
29 West 35th Street, New York, NY 10001

Phototypeset in 10pt Times by
Mews Photosetting, Beckenham, Kent
Printed and bound in Great Britain by
Biddles Ltd, Guildford and King's Lynn

British Library Cataloguing in Publication Data

Pacione, Michael
    Urban problems: an applied urban analysis.
    1. Capitalist countries. Urban regions. Social
    planning
    I. Title
    307'.12'091732
    ISBN 0-415-01392-5

Library of Congress Cataloging-in-Publication Data

Pacione, Michael.
    Urban problems: an applied urban analysis / Michael Pacione.
        p.   cm.
    Bibliography: p.
    Includes index.
    ISBN 0-415-01392-5
    1. Urban policy. I. Title.
HT151.P26   1990
307.76–dc20   89-10337
                                                        CIP

Contents

Preface

The approach to the urban environment employed in this book is based upon the view that the process of urban development in capitalist societies is inherently problematic, being accompanied by conflicts which give rise to a myriad of social, economic and environmental problems. The identification, analysis, and resolution of these problems is the central concern of applied urban analysis which can be defined as the application of cross-disciplinary knowledge and skills to the resolution of urban problems.

The book focuses on urban environments under the capitalist system, with particular reference to contemporary situations in the United Kingdom and North America in the post-war period. It is written for an undergraduate readership and, although designed primarily for students of geography, planning and urban studies, will also be of relevance for courses in the cognate disciplines of sociology, economics, politics, administration, and environmental psychology.

I would like to record my appreciation of the technical assistance provided by Christine Meek, Lorraine Nelson and Jean Simpson who typed the bulk of the manuscript, and Elisabeth Harvey who prepared the illustrations. My wife, Christine, acted as an invaluable sounding board for ideas as well as unpaid proof–reader, while Michael, aged 7, and Emma, aged 5, made their own unique contributions to the progress of the work.

Michael Pacione
University of Strathclyde
Glasgow

Figures

Figures

Tables

Introduction

Growing concern for the future of cities and for the well–being of city dwellers, stimulated by trends in world urbanisation, the increasing number and size of cities, and the deterioration of many urban environments, has led in recent years to great emphasis being placed upon the applied or problem-solving approach to the study of the city. This applied perspective is the thread which runs throughout this book in which we will range widely across the academic terrain to identify appropriate responses to the myriad of problems confronting contemporary metropolitan areas. The complexity of the real world and the fact that urban patterns, processes, and problems cut across many of the traditional academic boundaries emphasise the importance of an inter-disciplinary approach. While each of the social sciences can make an individual contribution to urban analysis a full understanding of urban phenomena must be sought outside the confines of a single discipline.

The diversity of problems encountered in the city is vast, ranging from extreme geophysical hazards such as landslides and flooding to socio-psychological difficulties such as stress and mental illness. This broad spectrum of problems includes social iniquities arising from speculative investment activities, residential segregation, discrimination, displacement and community disruption; problems related to traffic and transportation, and the impact of new retail developments; economic problems of poverty and unemployment, deprivation, and fiscal crisis; issues of residential environmental quality; access to power; and questions of juridical equality, territorial justice and equity in collective consumption. An important distinction can be made between problems *in* the city and problems *of* the city (Herbert and Johnston 1976). The former are general social problems which occur in both urban and rural areas but which are particularly visible in the city because of the concentration of population. The latter are created by the pattern of population concentration and are specific problems of the city. Poverty, for example, though found in most cities, is largely a 'problem in the city'. It may be concentrated there to a greater extent than is the total population because the under– and unemployed are attracted to the potential urban opportunities but the existence of cities does not create under– and unemployment. Two types of urban problems have been characterised as being *of* the city. The first are a consequence of urban size and population density, with an example being the negative influence of the urban environment on criminal and other anti-social behaviour. The second type comprises these problems which result from the internal spatial structure of the city. This affects the cost of providing welfare services and physical infrastructure. It can influence transport and travel patterns and shape networks of social interaction effectively keeping certain groups and individuals in restrictive environments with poor housing, deteriorating services and limited accessibility to employment opportunities. The physical and social segregation of population groups also encourages misunderstanding, increases alienation, and is reflected in the differential distribution of power. Applied urban analysis is concerned both with problems *in* the city and problems *of* the city.

The chief purpose of applied urban analysis is to provide the basis for planning remedial action. This process may be summarised as *description*, *explanation*, *evaluation* and *prescription* leading to *implementation*, followed by *monitoring* (Figure I.1). A note of caution is appropriate at the outset however. No-one should read this book in the expectation of finding simple answers to urban problems. There is none. The cause of any urban problem is multifactorial. Moreover, the varied complexity of urban settings in the modern world and the fact that there is generally more than a single possible solution for every problem makes the existence of a direct relationship between problem and solution rare. A primary objective of this book is to assist the reader to understand the interrelated complexity of contemporary social, economic and environmental problems in urban areas, and to illustrate how applied urban analysis can assist in resolving some of these polemics.

In order to achieve an understanding of the nature and the causes of urban problems we must untangle the Gordian knot of causal linkages which underlie the observed difficulty. In some instances, such as the relationship between ground slippage and building collapse, cause and effect are relatively straightforward. But in the majority of cases the cause of a problem may be more apparent than real. For example, the immediate cause of the problems faced by a poor family in a deprived council estate in Liverpool may be lack of employment opportunities following the closure of a local factory. However the root cause of the social and financial difficulties confronting the family may lie in the investment decisions of financial managers in London, New York or Tokyo. Even to begin to tackle an urban problem we must recognize the real as opposed to the apparent cause. The complexity of modern urban environments, the fact that metropolitan areas are not closed

Figure 1.1 The practice of applied urban geography

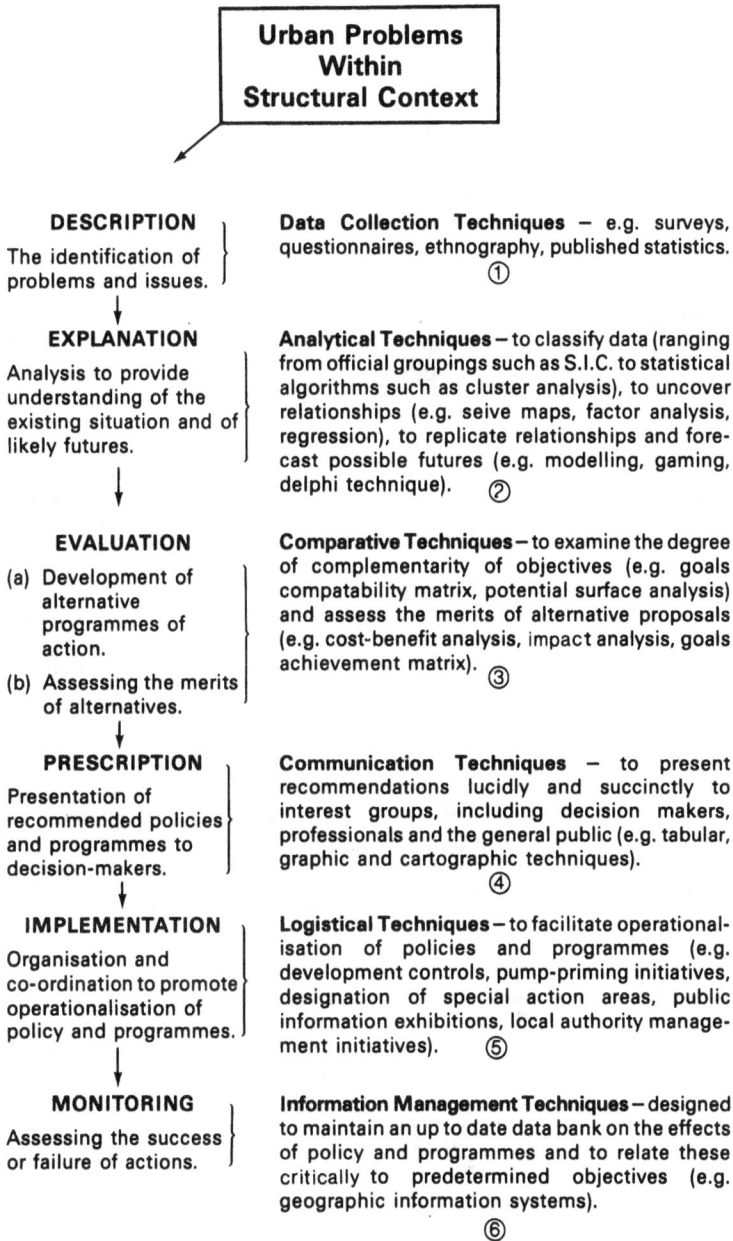

```
┌─────────────────────────┐
│      Urban Problems     │
│          Within         │
│     Structural Context  │
└─────────────────────────┘
```

DESCRIPTION

The identification of problems and issues.

Data Collection Techniques – e.g. surveys, questionnaires, ethnography, published statistics. ①

↓

EXPLANATION

Analysis to provide understanding of the existing situation and of likely futures.

Analytical Techniques – to classify data (ranging from official groupings such as S.I.C. to statistical algorithms such as cluster analysis), to uncover relationships (e.g. seive maps, factor analysis, regression), to replicate relationships and forecast possible futures (e.g. modelling, gaming, delphi technique). ②

↓

EVALUATION

(a) Development of alternative programmes of action.

(b) Assessing the merits of alternatives.

Comparative Techniques – to examine the degree of complementarity of objectives (e.g. goals compatability matrix, potential surface analysis) and assess the merits of alternative proposals (e.g. cost-benefit analysis, impact analysis, goals achievement matrix). ③

↓

PRESCRIPTION

Presentation of recommended policies and programmes to decision-makers.

Communication Techniques – to present recommendations lucidly and succinctly to interest groups, including decision makers, professionals and the general public (e.g. tabular, graphic and cartographic techniques). ④

↓

IMPLEMENTATION

Organisation and co-ordination to promote operationalisation of policy and programmes.

Logistical Techniques – to facilitate operationalisation of policies and programmes (e.g. development controls, pump-priming initiatives, designation of special action areas, public information exhibitions, local authority management initiatives). ⑤

↓

MONITORING

Assessing the success or failure of actions.

Information Management Techniques – designed to maintain an up to date data bank on the effects of policy and programmes and to relate these critically to predetermined objectives (e.g. geographic information systems). ⑥

systems, and the interrelated nature of urban problems must be constantly borne in mind.

As well as describing the nature and explaining the cause of urban problems the applied urban analyst also has a role to play in evaluating possible responses and in prescribing appropriate policies and programmes, which may then be implemented by urban planners and managers in both the public and private sectors. In carrying out these tasks the analyst will be confronted with a plethora of potential remedies for any problem. In this book, for example, we will discuss *structural* policies on the redistribution of wealth, *areal* approaches to urban deprivation, *local* programmes for housing rehabilitation, *psychological* techniques to overcome urban stress, *technical* solutions to transport problems, *political* strategies to resolve the inequitable allocation of power, *physical* responses to geomorphological hazards, *legal* challenges to discrimination, and *architectural* modifications to combat deviant behaviour. Clearly, the selection of appropriate strategy to address a problem is far from straightforward. Choice must be based not only on technical criteria but also on a wide range of conditioning factors which include residents' preferences, available finance, and externality considerations or how the strategy to resolve a particular problem will affect other problems in the city. The fact that the nature and relative importance of the criteria vary between and within cities underlines the importance of focusing on the general principles involved in problem recognition and strategy selection rather than on specific settings *per se*. Consequently, this book is not intended to be a catalogue of urban policies, plans and programmes. Nor does it undertake to examine examples of every kind of urban problem, but rather concentrates on substantive questions of importance in the analysis of urban problems in the modern world. This does not, however, diminish the utility of case studies, and a variety of examples selected from an international range of urban settings is included to illuminate the general principles introduced.

One fundamental conceptual issue which those working within an applied urban framework must address at the outset is encapsulated in the structure–agency debate in social science, and concerns the value of a problem–oriented approach. The structural critique of applied social science, and in particular that voiced by Marxist theorists, dismisses the contribution of applied urban analysis as irrelevant to the resolution of the real problems in capitalist society. This issue is tied to the general question of the ethical and political values underlying research, and it is important to make explicit the position adopted in this book. The view of knowledge as neutral and objective can be rejected. The impossibility of a value–free applied urban analysis is now widely accepted. Johnston (1981), with particular reference to policy analysis, lists three ideological assumptions implicit in applied research. These are that (a) the researcher is prepared to work within the present structure of society, (b) the researcher accepts that because of the difficulty of long-term prediction most of his work will be directed towards the amelioration of current problems, and (c) a strong state system is necessary to implement public policy. This much is unremarkable and acceptable. It is then suggested that in accepting these the applied researcher 'who uses his expertise in policy evaluation and development is apparently committed to the status quo' (p. 216). The relevance of this statement hinges on the interpretation placed on the status quo. At the macro-level applied urban analysts would agree that the orientation of their research is not designed to effect radical change in the structure of society (the social formation or mode of production). Thus, expressed in Marxist terms, most would concur that 'ameliorative policies patch up the present system, aid the legitimation of the state, and bolster the forces of capitalism with their inbuilt tendencies to create inequalities' (p. 217). At the local 'human scale' level, however, applied urban research is most definitely not supportive of the status quo but rather has as its central objective the resolution of real problems and improvement of life quality. The radical contention that participation in policy evaluation and formulation in the short term is ineffective since it hinders the achievement of the greater goal of revolutionary social change (to which many applied urban researchers may be committed) is rejected. Equally, the aim of effecting structural change via emancipatory applied research within a realist philosophy which seeks to educate people as to the real causes of their felt situation (Johnston 1986) is necessarily a long-term goal. To ignore the opportunity to improve the quality of life of some people in the short term in the hope of achieving possibly greater benefit in the longer term is not commensurate with the ethical position implicit in the problem-oriented activity of most applied urban analysts. Neither does the argument that knowledge is power and 'a public commodity which can be used for good or ill' (Barnes 1979: 157) undermine the strength of the applied urban researcher's position. What is problematic here is the extent to which the researcher is responsible for the use to which the knowledge he or she creates is put. Clearly, any knowledge is potentially 'counter-revolutionary' and could be employed in an oppressive discriminating manner to accentuate inequalities of wealth and power, but this is no argument for eschewing research. Access to the expertise and knowledge produced by applied urban research need not be the sole prerogative of the advantaged in society, but can be equally available to pressure groups seeking a more equitable share of resources. As Frazier (1982: 16) remarks, applied research 'involves the formulation of goals and strategies and the testing of existing institutional policies within the context of ethical standards as criteria. This should not imply a simple system maintenance approach to problem solving. Indeed it is often necessary to take an unpopular anti-establishment position, which can result in a major confrontation'. For practical examples of this we need only refer to the pragmatic radicalism practised by the Cleveland city planning commission (Kraushaar 1979) and the recommendations of the British Community Development Projects which advocated fundamental changes in the distribution of wealth and power to combat urban deprivation, and which led to conflict with both central and local government (Community Development Project 1974, 1975, 1977).

The organization of the book

We can now turn to consider how the diverse subject matter of applied urban analysis will be treated in this book. The first point to note is that the range of topics included is selective, but not arbitrary. Given the enormous scope of the subject, it would have been impossible to include all issues which have attracted the attention of applied urban researchers. The overall balance of the book favours social and economic (human) as opposed to environmental (physical) issues. This decision is in keeping with the author's view of the relative importance of these issues, and also reflects the volume of recent research in the field. The preferred epistemological perspective is the realist philosophy of research which accepts the necessity of viewing local events within their structural context. In practical terms this means that applied urban analysts must learn to think globally but act locally.

The book comprises ten main chapters, together with the introduction and a conclusion. The first chapter on land-use issues focuses on the economic dimension of the capitalist mode of production and examines the process and problems of urban development under capitalism. The second considers the complementary political dimension of the capitalist system and analyses the key concept of power and its allocation and use in the local state. Chapter 3 examines the central human issues of poverty and deprivation, while Chapter 4 considers the related concept of territorial justice with particular reference to questions of collective consumption and residential segregation. The theme of urban environmental hazard is examined in Chapter 5 with consideration afforded to both natural and social hazards. Attention then switches to the built environment in Chapter 6 which discusses the concept of urban liveability and the problem of producing a humane urban environment. In Chapter 7 the process and consequences of urban change at the neighbourhood level are addressed, and in Chapter 8 issues relating to housing equity, access, and finance are examined. In Chapter 9 problems arising from the process of change and innovation in the urban retailing system are considered, while in Chapter 10 attention is focused on the question of urban transportation. The book concludes with a set of principles to guide the practice of applied urban analysis.

Chapter one

Land-use issues

Towns and cities are primarily economic phenomena. Although most have occupied the same location for centuries the buildings and other physical infrastructure which comprise the built environment are not fixed but are continuously affected by the dynamic forces of change initiated by public and private development interests. This modification or 'development' of the urban environment occurs at a variety of scales ranging from the residential relocation decisions of myriad individual households, and the restructuring of operational techniques and workforce requirements by firms and industries, to large-scale projects, including public road building programmes and private housebuilding schemes. In addition, to different degrees in different countries, the operation of these market forces is influenced (enhanced or constrained) by state and local planning mechanisms. The net effect of these socio–spatial processes impacts upon the lifestyle of citizens (influencing, for example, journeys to work, access to facilities, and the housing environment), and is most tangibly revealed in patterns of land use and land-use change.

Growth and change in the capitalist city

The limited ability of traditional ecological and neo-classical economic theories to explain the forces underlying the urban development process led researchers to consider the place of the city in the capitalist mode of production. Although many of the earlier interpretations of urban growth and change based on Althusserian structuralism have been superseded, study of the political–economy of urbanization has made a significant contribution to understanding the processes underlying contemporary urban development. In Marxist theory the city is regarded as a particular built form commensurate with the fundamental capitalist goal of accumulation, according to the dictum 'accumulation for accumulation's sake, production for production's sake'. Thus, as well as concentrating the means of production, cities also develop the urban infrastructure which facilitates the geographical transfer of surplus value (profits) – i.e. the circulation of capital. The central role of capital in urban development forms the basis of Harvey's (1985) analysis of the urban process under capitalism. Harvey envisaged three circuits of capital. The primary circuit may be regarded as the structure of relations in the production process. Surplus value (money capital) created in the production process is either reinvested in the primary circuit or is channelled via the capital market into the secondary circuit. In the process of constructing the built environment the mobile 'money capital' is fixed in place and extra value created. The tertiary circuit of capital comprises the investment in science and technology that ultimately leads to increases in productive capacity, together with the social expenditure undertaken by the state as part-contribution to the reproduction of the labour force (including, for example, investment in education and health services, and in mechanisms of law and order). There is a limit to the process of capital transfer from primary to secondary circuits. When this point is reached investments become unproductive and the exchange value of capital put into the built environment is reduced, or in some instances lost completely (which could lead to bankruptcy for some fractions of capital). However, the devaluation of exchange value does not necessarily destroy the use value (the physical resource). This can be used as 'devalued capital' and as such can help to promote renewed accumulation (i.e. the 'use value' of a building can be the basis for further development).

Devaluations of fixed capital provide one of the main ways in which capitalism can check the fall in the rate of profit and speed accumulation of capital value through formation of new capital. There is, therefore, a major contradiction in the capitalist city between the capitalist dynamic of accumulation (provoking urban growth and change) and the inertia of the built environment (which resists urban growth and change). As Harvey (1981: 113) explains 'under capitalism there is a perpetual struggle in which capital builds a physical landscape appropriate to its own condition at a particular moment in time, only to destroy it, usually in the course of a crisis, at a subsequent point in time'. The different forms of crisis which assail capitalist economies have been outlined by Edel (1981). One of these — underconsumption (e.g. due to a fall in market demand) — along with its counterpart, overaccumulation, has been hypothesized as the main cause of post–war suburbanization in North America (Baran and Sweezy 1966). According to this thesis, because of an inability of the domestic market to absorb the industrial surpluses which built up as the war machine returned to peacetime production, other labour and capital absorbing activities were promoted by successive governments in the 1950s and 1960s, including suburban capital formation. By engineering a shift of investment into the secondary circuit the state and specialist financial institutions avoided a crisis of overaccumulation in the primary circuit and simultaneously stimulated new demand for industrial goods in the housing and transportation sectors. While the under-consumptionist thesis provides a convincing foundation for the suburbanization process in USA it has less relevance for the situation in Britain where successive post-war governments have sought to control capitalist tendencies for urban growth through the operation of a planning system which seeks to circumscribe urban development and direct it towards socially desirable goals. The regional specificity of the under-consumptionist thesis serves to underline two important points. The first is that the concrete patterns of development in which the capitalist mode of production is manifested vary considerably between different societies. Consequently a proper understanding of the internal structuring of any city requires an appreciation of the wider framework of national social and economic development. The second point is that while urban areas and their residents are caught up by structural forces outside their control this does not imply an insignificant role for local conditions or human agency in determining the form of the built environment. It is necessary, therefore, to complement a macro-level structural analysis with consideration of the major actors in the production of the built environment.

Major actors in the production of the built environment

The land development industry comprises a variety of builders, sub-contractors, architects, marketing agents, developers, and speculators together with their legal and financial consultants. During the conversion of rural land into occupied housing a plot might pass through the ownership of at least five different actors — a rural producer, a speculator, a developer, a builder, and finally a household. Assisting with land transfers at each stage are a set of facilitators including real estate agents and financiers. Finally at local and central government level planners and officials oversee the development process to varying degrees according to the prevailing social formation. The motives and methods of these participants vary considerably. Bearing in mind the inter-related nature of the land development process we can, in the interests of clarity, examine the operation of several of these individual actors in detail.

The speculators

Property speculators, either individual entrepreneurs, or corporations, purchase land with the hope of profiting from subsequent increases in property values. Speculative activity is a characteristic of capitalist urban development which occurs throughout the urban arena. Speculation in the central city can contribute to the creation of slums, prior to revitalisation of a neighbourhood, either through private sector upgrading or

9

gentrification or publicly-financed rehabilitation. The effects of speculative activity on the residents of the existing built up area can be pronounced, often leading to displacement and the destruction of communities. The impact of speculative development on land use is seen most starkly around the periphery of cities in USA, where the area currently under urban use is over ten million acres but 'twice as much land is withdrawn from other uses because of the leapfrogging which characterizes much suburban growth' (Feagin 1982: 51). Leapfrog development usually occurs as builder-developers try to avoid land which is tied up in complex legal arrangements or is being held by speculators in anticipation of very high profits. Some indication of the level of profits possible is provided by the fact that in Los Angeles, the price of residential land increased at a rate of 40 per cent per year in the late 1970s, in part due to speculative activity. Such inflationary costs are, of course, built into the final purchase price for suburban housing.

On the urban fringe, the effects of land speculation constitute one of the most important impacts on land use. For agriculture speculative land holding can have both positive and negative effects. Beneficial interaction can occur through the rental back to farmers of farmland which has been purchased by non-farm interests. Provided that lease conditions are not onerous, from a purely economic perspective it may be attractive for a farmer to rent land rather than to purchase and encumber the business with a heavy mortgage, thus releasing more of the farmer's capital for improvements. On the other hand, rising land prices and land speculation make farm enlargement costly, and where tax is levied on *land values*, as in USA, sales of surrounding land can push up property taxes. Tax pressures coupled with other urban shadow effects such as pollution, trespass, theft and vandalism may eventually force the suburban agriculturalist to sell out to speculators. The impact of *potential* urban development also affects land husbandry practices in the fringe. Where urban pressures are strong farmers may become active speculators, disinvesting in their farms while anticipating a large capital gain from the sale of their land in the near future. Some farmers may 'farm to quit' or attempt to 'mine' the soil fertility while others may 'idle' their farmland. In the absence of effective land market regulation idle land may be a perfectly rational land use response to the economic incentives created by the urban fringe property market. Berry and Plaut (1978), for example, estimated that for every acre converted to urban uses in the north-eastern USA another was idled due to urban pressures. Farmers living under less intense urban pressures may be involved in a more passive form of land speculation, watching the appreciation of land values with a view to selling for a large profit on retirement.

The real estate agents

Although the principal role of real estate agents is as middlemen between buyers and sellers of property some adopt a broader remit and may operate in the assembly of small land parcels for development or as speculators in the urban land market. Direct involvement in the land market can be particularly profitable during periods of inflation and can lead to manipulation of the land market. Gutstein (1975) found that in a resurgent inner-city neighbourhood in Vancouver in the early 1970s some properties were 'sold' several times in a single year between holding companies with the same owner in order to force up rent levels in the local market. Similar instances of land speculation have been recorded in areas of racial transition (Rapkin and Grigsby 1960) where real estate agents also often play an active role in blockbusting; a process whereby members of minority (black) groups obtain entry to residential areas previously reserved exclusively for the majority (white) population. A real estate speculator who has bought a property in a block is able to resell to a black family for a substantial profit when demand from the minority group reaches a critical level (Foreman 1971). Frequently this initial sale stimulates existing homeowners to sell up (due to fears about falling property prices and/or racial bias) and reduces demand from other majority group buyers (Farley *et al.* 1978). It can be argued that the blockbuster is providing much needed accommodation to groups that are discriminated against in the open housing market but in some cases the blockbuster is guilty of exploiting the anxieties of residents (possibly forcing them to sell below market price) and the housing poverty of minority groups (who are willing to pay above market prices) to realize a significant capital gain. Foreman (1971) estimated that in Chicago during the 1950s and 1960s a small minority of real estate agents triggered the blockbusting of 70,000 white families over a decade. The social costs in terms of racial disharmony, resentment, and harassment are less easy to calculate. More generally, real estate agents can influence the social composition of neighbourhoods by directing people to particular housing areas based on their perception of the market, their partial knowledge of the city, and normal operating territory of their company. As Damerall (1968: 80) observed they have the power to 'steer Protestants, Catholics, Jews, and Negroes into their respective ghettos'.

Financial institutions

These have grown in importance in both Britain and North America with the decline in private rented housing and the growth of home owner-ship. In common with developers, financial institutions seek to maximize profits and minimize risks. Since these opportunities are differentiated over the urban area, financiers adopt spatially discriminating lending practices. This will have a significant impact on the location of new construction as well as on maintenance and improvements to existing structures. Discrimination has also been practised on the grounds of race (especially prior to the Civil Rights legislation of 1968), with bank lending to blacks based on the twin criteria of residence in an established Negro neighbourhood and in a 'good area' (Foreman 1971). Such practices were also stimulated by economic reasons since banks, concerned to protect property values in areas where they had invested, were uncertain about the long term effect on values of racial transition. This inherent need to minimize risk continues to influence the spatial pattern of lending practices. Harvey (1975) has demonstrated how various financial agencies in Baltimore segmented the city into a series of sub-markets on the basis of their individual lending preferences. This practice of red-lining areas perceived as poor risks has also been followed by the insurance industry (Squires *et al.* 1979). Despite the passage of the US Home Mortgage Disclosure Act 1975 which requires lending agencies to disclose the geographic pattern of mortgage awards discriminatory practices continue (Kantor and Nystuen 1982). Given the need for financial institutions to operate within a free market environment it is hardly realistic to expect otherwise.

While, for clarity, we have so far examined each set of actors independently, in practice growth coalitions cutting across private and public sectors operate to foster development. Evidence of power groups managing urban growth led to the formation of the *manipulated city* hypothesis which argues that urban form is the outcome of a conscious manipulation by an alliance of élite interests with social power (Gale and Moore 1975). Although this is clearly not the sole factor behind urban growth and development it does have a role to play. While the reality of élite coalitions has been validated empirically (Gottdeiner 1985), the extent of their effects is more difficult to assess. In Canada in the early 1970s half of the aldermen on the city councils of Toronto, Winnipeg, and Vancouver held occupational connections with development interests and pro-growth parties held control of city hall in each case (Lorimer 1972). In instances of financially weak cities the business–financial community can exercise close to monopoly control (Ley 1983). The fiscal crisis of New York in the mid 1970s is a classic example of how a financial coalition can benefit at the expense of the public. By 1977, 20 per cent of New York's budget was committed to interest payments (Tabb 1978). Similarly, in Cleveland the oligopoly of business interests which formed the Cleveland Trust Company (which has interlocking directorates with major local steel, coal, utility, and banking companies) was able to extract significant economic concessions from the city in 1978 in return for arranging a loan (Cockburn and Ridgeway 1979). In light of such findings it is not surprising to find Harvey (1971) characterizing much of the political activity of the city 'as a matter of jostling for and bargaining over the use and control of the hidden mechanisms for redistribution'. Most significantly, the land use changes which result from these activities lead to a redistribution of net costs and benefits to urban residents.

Clearly, the degrees of freedom which permit growth networks to profit at the public expense are provided by the relative autonomy of the secondary circuit of capital itself. As we have suggested, this freedom varies between countries depending upon the extent of state policy, planning, and land-use controls.

Government land-use policy and planning

The one actor in the urban development process not yet considered is potentially the most influential. The state — central and local government — exercises both a direct (planning regulations) and indirect (taxation policy) influence on urban form.

Planning policy

The detailed history of planning policy in UK and USA has been recounted elsewhere (Cullingworth 1982; Scott 1969). The main planning and related legislation in UK is summarized in Table 1.1.

Table 1.1 Major urban planning legislation, UK

Act	Provisions
1851 Common Lodging Houses Act (Shaftesbury Act)	vestries and boroughs given supervisory public health powers over 'common lodging houses' for the very poor and transients
1851 Labouring Classes Lodging Houses Act (Shaftesbury Act)	vestries and boroughs permitted to raise money on local rates or from Public Works Loan Commissioners for building lodging houses for single *working* people
1855 Metropolis Local Management Act	established Metropolitan Board of Works in London, with wide powers for street buildings, etc; ordered appointments of Medical Officers of Health
1855 Nuisances Removal Act	established minimum standards of housing conditions, gave local authorities duty to close houses 'unfit for human habitation'
1866 Labouring Classes Dwelling Houses Act	Public Works Loan Commissioners empowered to make loans to private companies and local authorities for the erection of labourers' dwellings in populous towns

Act	Provisions
1866 Sanitary Act	'overcrowding' made a statutory nuisance; adoptive powers given to local authorities to make public health regulations and control standards
1868 Artisans' and Labourers' Dwellings Act (Torrens Act)	boroughs and vestries given powers for compulsory purchase of insanitary premises for demolition or improvement
1874 Building Societies Act	building societies given limited company status, establishment of 'Permanent' societies providing investment for savings independent of house purchase
1875 Artisans' and Labourers' Dwellings Improvement Act (Cross Act)	Metropolitan Board of Works and boroughs with population over 25 000 given powers to purchase and clear large tracts of insanitary property and to lease it to bodies willing to build housing
1875 Public Health Act (extends Nuisances Removal Act)	established conditions under which local authorities should take action to purchase premises for clearance purposes
1882 Artisans' Dwellings Act	obligation to rehouse under Cross and Torrens Acts reduced to 50 per cent of those displaced
1883 Cheap Trains Act	railway companies in London area made subject to Board of Trade orders to introduce workmen's trains and fares on lines where working–class housing had been built, in return for remission of passenger duty paid to Board of Trade
1885 Housing of the Working Classes Act	consolidated and amended Shaftesbury, Torrens and Cross Acts; lodging houses redefined to include separate dwellings for labouring classes; interest rates for Public Works Loan Board lowered; severe limitation of compensation to slum owners
1890 Public Health Act	extended 1875 Act; local authorities given power to strengthen sanitary regulations for private houses
1890 Housing of the Working Classes Act	further consolidation of previous housing legislation removal of obligation to rehouse displaced tenants in provincial cities; local authorities allowed to build houses for working class (for disposal within ten years)
1899 Small Dwellings (Acquisitions) Act	local authorities empowered to advance money for purchase of small dwellings by their occupiers
1900 Housing of the Working Classes Act	amended 1890 Act; local authorities given powers to purchase land outside their own jurisdiction for new house building in addition to building on cleared sites

Act	*Provisions*
1903 Housing of the Working Classes Act	amended 1890 Act; extended period of loan repayment from sixty to eighty years; limitations on borrowing reduced
1909 Housing and Town Planning Act	obligation on local authorities to sell their housing stock removed; Local Government Board given powers to enforce local authorities to build housing; powers for slum clearance strengthened
1915 Increased Rent and Mortgage Interest (War Restrictions) Act	rents of private houses with rateable values not exceeding £35 in London (£30 in Scotland, £26 elsewhere) fixed at prewar level (extended to more expensive houses after the war)
1919 Housing and Town Planning Act (Addison Act)	imposed duties on local authorities to survey housing needs in their districts and to carry out building schemes as needed, with approval of Ministry of Health; all losses in excess of a penny rate to be borne by local authority
1925 Town Planning Act	a consolidating Act and the first to be concerned solely with town planning
1932 Town and Country Planning Act	extended planning powers to almost any type of land whether built up or undeveloped. Introduced the practice of interim development control (i.e. once a local authority resolved to prepare a planning scheme for an area any person wishing to build in that area must first obtain permission or risk having the structure removed without compensation if it conflicted with the planning scheme)
1935 Restriction of Ribbon Development Act	designed to control the sprawl of urban development along major roads
1940 Report of the Royal Commission on the Distribution of the Industrial Population (Barlow)	to enquire into the causes of and probable change in the geographical distribution of the industrial population and to propose remedial measures
1942 Report of the Expert Committee on Compensation and Betterment	proposed a comprehensive system of national ownership of development rights in all undeveloped land
1944 Greater London Plan (Abercrombie)	proposed the rehousing of 500 000 people from the metropolitan area into ten New Towns in the surrounding counties.
1946 New Towns Act	underlined the principle of the Greater London Plan and initiated the UK post-war New Town programme

Act	Provisions
1947 Town and Country Planning Act	nationalized development rights. Introduced a new legal framework for planning at both national and local level. The planning scheme of pre–war planning was replaced by the quinquennial development plan and planning authorities were required by law to prepare such a plan for their area
1952 Town Development Act	enabled large cities with congestion problems to arrange overspill schemes with other authorities
1963 Report on Traffic in Towns (Buchanan)	set out principles for reconciling the efficient movement of traffic and.the preservation of a liveable urban environment
1965 Report of the Planning Advisory Group on the future of development plans	proposed a basic change which would distinguish between policy or strategic issues and detailed or tactical issues
1966 Industrial Development Act	provided 85 per cent grants for reclamation of derelict sites in development areas
1967 Civic Amenities Act	required local authorities to identify areas of special architectural or historic interest, and to designate conservation areas
1967 Land Commission Act	introduced a betterment levy to capture for the community part of the development value which arises from granting of planning permission
1968 Town and Country Planning Act	replaced the unitary development plan system with a dual system of structure and local plans
1969 Housing Act	provided for the designation of General Improvement Areas — areas of fundamentally sound housing with the potential to provide good living conditions and unlikely to be affected by redevelopment proposals
1969 Report on Public Participation in Planning (Skeffington)	provided recommendations on the best means of securing the participation of the public at the formative stage in the making of development plans for their area
1972 Local Government Act	increased the level of land reclamation grants to 100 per cent in all Assisted Areas and in Derelict Land Clearance Areas
1974 Town and Country Amenities Act	extended the powers of local authorities in dealing with conservation areas and the preservation of historic buildings
1974 Housing Act	introduced Housing Action Areas — areas of particular stress which can be improved within five years

Act	Provisions
1976 Development Land Tax Act	provided for the taxation of development value
1978 Inner Urban Areas Act	designed to give additional powers to local authorities with severe inner area problems to help them generate economic development — 48 designed areas
1980 Housing Act	attempt to focus on worst housing. Introduced improvement grants (at discretion of local authority), intermediate grants for standard amenities (claimed as of right) and repairs grants for pre–1919 dwellings
1980 Local Government, Planning and Land Act	introduces Enterprise Zones (with tax exemptions and simplified planning procedures). Extended coverage and eligibility of derelict land reclamation grants

Recognition of the need for urban planning emerged in the UK, and in North America during the late nineteenth and early twentieth centuries as a response to the problems of the industrial city. But despite the existence of similar urban problems national responses were different. In the USA an ideology favouring private property rights and local autonomy has limited intervention to zoning and minimum land use control, whereas in the UK the public have accepted the implications of the powerful system of urban planning initiated by the Town and Country Planning Act of 1947. The basic principle enshrined in the 1974 Act was that of private land ownership but public accountability in use, so that landowners seeking to undertake development first had to obtain permission from the local planning authority. The primary objectives of the 1947 system at the city–region scale were urban containment, protection of the countryside and the creation of self-contained balanced communities (e.g. New Towns). Secondary objectives were the prevention of scattered development and the building up of strong service centres. At the local scale the two main objectives were enhancement of accessibility to urban functions, and the promotion of a high level of physical and social environment. These goals were advanced by local authorities through the development plan/development control process, and by central government through the New Towns programme, supplemented in England and Wales by the Expanding Towns scheme introduced by the Town Development Act of 1952. On balance the 1947 planning system has been successful in achieving its stated objectives; post–war urban growth has been contained to the extent that coalescence of adjacent cities has been prevented and good quality agricultural land protected (Hall *et al.* 1973). Green belts around the major cities have halted peripheral sprawl, although they have also contributed to inflation in land and housing prices in existing settlements within the green belt. Although increases in transport technology and in the length of acceptable commuting journey have meant that some residential development has leapfrogged into settlements beyond the green belt, in general, the planning system has been successful in preventing the type of scattered urban development in evidence around cities in North America.

By contrast with the situation in Britain, in the USA there is no system of planning in the sense of a common framework with a clearly defined set of physical, social, and economic objectives. Planning is not obligatory as in the UK and, together with the fragmented structure of local government — in addition to the federal government and 50 states there are about 8,000 counties, 18,000 municipalities and 17,000 townships each with the power to plan or regulate land use, i.e. an average of 760 per state (Moore 1983) — this means that the content of planning is both local and variable from place to place. In principle a range of techniques for controlling urban growth and land-use change are available (Table 1.2) but in practice the major tool employed is land-use zoning.

Just as the early public health and sanitary reform acts in Britain were designed to overcome the deficiencies of the nineteenth-century city so the forerunners of modern land-use zoning in metropolitan America were acts designed to restrict nuisance activities. Extension of the nuisance principle led to the first zoning laws being enacted in Washington (1844), Boston (1904) and Los Angeles (1909) with the aim of restricting land use and building height. The first comprehensive zoning ordinance was passed in New York in 1916. This set specific requirements for land-use districts, area or lot coverage and height of buildings. The judgement of the US Supreme Court in 1926 that zoning did not infringe the Fourteenth Amendment to the Constitution (which protects against property being 'taken' without due process of law) and the subsequent Enabling Act passed by Congress in 1928 led to widespread adoption of the technique. Under this law and similar acts passed by state legislatures the effective control of land use was transferred from the states, which had made little use of their powers to the municipalities and townships which were thereafter permitted to limit the types of development occurring on land within their boundaries (Nelson 1980). In essence, the enabling acts granted control over the height, bulk and area of buildings constructed after enactment of zoning regulations. The purposes of such controls were to minimize the problems of congestion, fire hazard, shading by high buildings, and control of population density; to ensure provision of urban services; and to promote the general welfare of the public. Critics of zoning maintain that (1) it is unnecessary since market forces will produce a 'fair' segregation of land uses, (2) the system

Table 1.2 Techniques for controlling urban growth

Public acquisition	Conventional subdivision regulations
Fee simple acquisition	Zoning/subdivision regulation/
Less than fee simple acquisition	building codes used for permanent
Land banking	population regulation
Compensable regulation	Exclusive nonresidential zones
Public improvements	Exclusion of specified types of
Location of facilities	housing (mobile home, multiple
Access to existing facilities	family, etc.)
Environmental controls	Minimum floor area or lot size
Floodplains, wetlands, slopes, etc.	Height restrictions
Critical areas	Zoning or other off-site regulations/
Developments of regional impact	exactions and other requirements
Pollution controls	Mandatory dedication of land or
Development rights transfer	capital
Restrictive covenants	Low-income housing requirements
Zoning techniques	Tax and fee systems
Conventional zoning	Urban and rural service areas
Conditional zoning	User and benefit fees
Contract zoning	Special assessment
Planned unit development	Preferential taxation
Flexible zoning	Development districts
Performance standards	Annexation
Bonus and incentive zoning	Timing of infrastructure development
Floating zones	(capital programming)
Special permit	Numerical limits and quotas
Variance	Total population goals
Miscellaneous management and planning	Annual limit on building permits
activities	Fair share allocations
Moratoriums and interim controls	
Administrative delays	
Analysis of benefits vs. costs,	
environmental impact, carrying	
capacity, etc.	

Source: Jackson 1981: 149

is open to corruption, particularly in respect of variances or zone changes, (3) it can lead to premature use of resources by owners who fear a zoning change, (4) it is unequal in its effect since a piece of property zoned for commercial uses within a residential area provides its owner with windfall profits at the expense of neighbours who must bear the costs of increased traffic noise and congestion, and (5) zoning may have a negative effect on urban land because of the expectations of land owners. Since some land uses result in a greater return to the owners than others some cities may overzone for certain categories of land use. This is particularly important in the inner city where existing vacant land may be concentrated in areas zoned for commercial or industrial use while the public need is for low–income housing. In Chicago nearly 75 per cent of the 9,000 vacant acres in 1963 was zoned for manufacturing, commercial, and business use at a time when the city had 215,000 substandard housing units (Jackson 1981). The most vociferous criticism, however, has been reserved for the practice of *exclusionary zoning* which refers to the legal regulations adopted by suburban municipalities to preserve their territories against intrusion of less-desired land uses. Thus regulations requiring large lots, three or more bedrooms, excessive floor space or excluding multiple unit dwellings, high density development or mobile homes all serve to maintain high cost housing and effectively exclude lower-income population. Supporters of zoning argue that it is a flexible tool and an effective means of allowing local residents to determine part of the character of their neighbourhood. Certainly its wholesale use during the past half century has largely determined the current land use structure of metropolitan America.

Specific issues

Land conversion in the urban fringe

Considerable debate has ensued over the magnitude and effects of the loss of agricultural land for urban development. Protagonists either take the view that there is no serious threat to future food supplies or open space, or conversely demand controls over the transfer of land out of agricultural use often within the context of a national land-use plan. In the UK, for example, differing interpretations of agricultural and urban land-use statistics have provoked debate between authorities like Coleman (1978: 32) who contends that 'we are taking land unnecessarily, wastefully, blindly, and much faster than we realise' and Best (1978: 13) who considers that 'there is no real land problem in Britain at the moment. Most of the problem is simply in the mind; it is not out there on the ground.' Equally polarized assessments of the land situation are evident in North America. Hart (1976: 15), for example, finds it 'reasonable to conclude that little more than 4 per cent of the nation's land area will be urbanized by the year 2000 and that urban encroachment will not remove significant acreages of land from agricultural production within the foreseeable future'. By contrast Lapping (1974: 394) considers that since the 1960s 'the transfer of huge amounts of productive farm lands to residential, industrial and speculative uses (has) approached ominous proportions'.

The rate of conversion of agricultural land to urban use in UK can be seen in Figure 1.1. Apart from the dramatic effect of the Second World War the pattern exhibits three notable features. First, the scale of urban growth and agricultural displacement was at its greatest in the 1930s. This was a period of suburban expansion at more liberal space standards,

Figure 1.1 Transfer of agricultural land to urban use

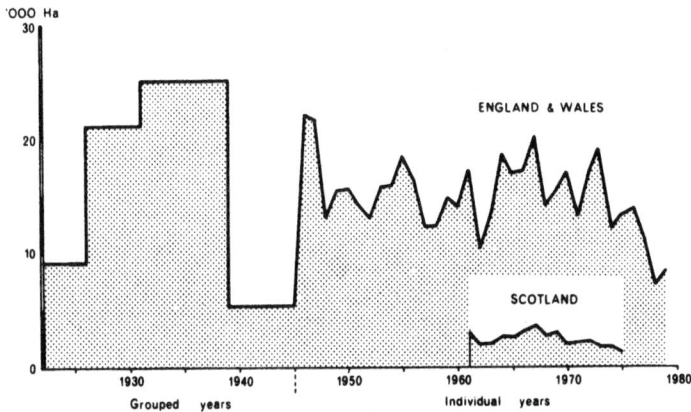

Source: Best 1981

cheap building sites on open farmland, improved public and private transportation, and a virtual absence of planning control prior to the 1947 Town
and Country Planning Act. Second, there has been no sustained increase in
the loss of farmland to urban use in the postwar years. This has been due
partly to the improved economic position of farming since the 1930s, rising
land and property prices during the 1970s, the increased difficulty of
obtaining mortgages, the sharp fall in the birth rate up to the end of the
1970s, the growth of rural preservation groups, and most of all is a result of
the conservation–protectionist ethic which has dominated postwar rural
planning. Third, in Britain as a whole the annual extension of forest and
woodland now often outpaces that of urban growth (Best 1981). Changing
the scale of analysis, however, reveals above average levels of agricultural
land have been taken for urban development in certain parts of the country,
particularly around the urban zone stretching from London northwest
towards Merseyside. Similarly in USA national land statistics mask major
changes in the individual states or multi-county regions and overlook the
loss of land in urbanized regions such as New York, Florida, and California
which produce important vegetables and fruit (Vlassin 1975). The local
importance of urban expansion is highlighted by the fact that in most countries, since many cities developed in the richest agricultural areas, urban
encroachment on rural areas often involves prime agricultural land.

In Britain the major planning instrument exercised to limit and control
the spread of urban development into the countryside is the green belt.

21

Green belt policies have been applied to London since 1938 (Munton 1983) and were encouraged around provincial cities by a government circular in 1955 (Ministry of Housing and Local Government 1955) so that they now cover 4,800 km^2 of the metropolitan green belt. In addition to the green belt legislation two further means of protecting open countryside from widespread development are available. First there is a suite of statutory controls upon land use and changes in land use, often operated by local planning authorities through their normal development control procedures. Second, *publicly owned* land can act as a buffer against unwanted urban and industrial expansion, being more resistant to market forces than land in private ownership.

There is no doubt that green belts have been successful in achieving their protective aims, and without them much greater amounts of agricultural land would have been lost under suburbia. Munton (1981), for example, cites the growth of nonconforming land uses in the approved metropolitan green belt at a comparatively slow rate of 2.0 per cent per decade or 600 ha per annum. The green belt is not, however, an impenetrable barrier, rather it acts 'like a more or less leaky dyke: there is the occasional break, and there is constant seepage through land speculation and blight, but for the most part it holds back a flood' (Hebbert 1981: 22).

The fact that some development has leapfrogged the green belt around most large towns has prompted the criticism that the policy is spreading urban influences and the pressures of 'fringe farming' further into the countryside than would otherwise have been the case. Furthermore, even within the green belt 'urban anticipation' still affects the behaviour of landowners. By reducing the supply of housing land in a desirable residential area, green belts have the effect of raising the value of the small amount of land that is released for development. In a situation of strong demand for development land, as in London's green belt, for the planning system to be *largely* successful in preventing development is not sufficient. The possibility of planning permission is kept alive in the minds of property owners within the restricted zone, who are well aware of the enormous price differences between land with planning permission for residential development and land valued for agricultural purposes, and whose ultimate goal is to realize this 'hope value' of their land. As Munton (1983) points out, what green belt restraint does is increase the risk of planning refusal and in spatial terms to concentrate the prospects of development close to existing settlements located within or just beyond the green belt boundary.

Suburban versus central city growth

As well as protecting good quality agricultural land and preventing urban sprawl policies to constrain suburban development may also be related to the goal of inner city revitalization. In situations where the central city is overcrowded rapid suburban growth can be of benefit in relieving congestion but when the suburban development process has resulted in an overall housing surplus the outmigration of households can undermine the inner city housing market and lead to decay and abandonment in many neighbourhoods. The accompanying loss of employment opportunities shrinks the core city's tax base and reduces the resources it has available to combat decline.

Under these circumstances a case could be made for policies to limit future suburban growth around cities. Several possible growth limiters are shown in Table 1.3 with the first eight in use in at least one US suburban community. Some indication of the response of housing markets to limits on suburban housing construction can be seen by observing the effect of the tightening of housing credit in 1974 and 1975. A 50 per cent fall in new suburban building from 2.4 million in 1972 to 1.2 million in 1975 was accompanied by a major increase in spending on renovation and maintenance of older homes in the central cities (James 1980).

Table 1.3 Possible means of limiting suburban residential growth in order to stimulate inner–city housing demand

1. Limiting new sewer and water systems
2. Establishing yearly maximum permits for new housing units in the entire metropolitan area, with quotas for each part of the area
3. Enforcing very low-density zoning in most vacant, undeveloped land to reduce the number of new housing units potentially competitive with those in the central city
4. Using Environmental Protection Agency regulations for air and water pollution to prohibit or limit growth in environmentally fragile (and other) portions of the metropolitan area
5. Creating green belts (forest preserves or other open space) of vacant suburban land to keep it from being urbanized
6. Purchasing development rights to agricultural land to keep it agricultural
7. Purchasing scenic or other land outside the city with public funds and holding it as open space
8. Shifting the financing of new infrastructures (such as roads, streets, sewer and water systems, street lights, and schools) from general property taxes to building permit fees, development fees, and land contribution requirements charged against the new developments that would use these infrastructures
9. Creating a federal or state building permit tax charged against every new suburban housing unit within those metropolitan areas with significant central city housing surpluses
10. Requiring local governments, through state rules, to develop future land-use and urban development plans for all land within each of their metropolitan areas by using some areawide planning body given the power to execute such plans, at least for transportation facilities, sewer and water systems, and housing
11. Requiring every suburban housing or other developer to prepare and file detailed environmental and urban impact statements concerning the effects of any proposed project before it could be built

Source: A. Downs 1981: 140

In practice, such legislative attempts to control urban growth have a greater chance of success in UK than in USA where (a) planning controls are less powerful, (b) governmental control over land use in most metropolitan areas is fragmented among many small jurisdictions, (c) intense opposition would arise from the building industry, suburban realtors and landowners and even central city residents hoping to upgrade their situation in the future, and (d) the strategy could deflect potential growth further out into unregulated territory rather than generate added demand for housing in older central city neighbourhoods. A more general objection is encapsulated in the alternative view that emphasizes the benefits of suburbanization. According to this 'urban policy should assist cities in all regions and of all sizes and ages to cope with and adjust to continued suburbanization; more households and firms will benefit from accommodating, rather than reversing these trends' (Hicks 1982: 37).

Taxation policy

The state also intervenes to affect land use through its taxation policy. The aim is either to capture development value for the community and/or to influence the pattern of urban growth. In general landowners are affected by revenue taxes (e.g. income tax and corporation tax), capital taxes (capital gains tax and capital transfer tax) and by rates (property tax), each of which can affect decisions over the sale, retention or use of a property. In UK particular controversy has arisen over those taxes specifically designed to capture some of the gain in land value which results from development (betterment) for the public good (Goodchild and Munton 1985). In USA the principle of community gain from land development has not achieved popular acceptability, a major distinction being that the rights of land ownership and development have not been separated as they have in Britain. American experience with the 'unbundling' of property rights has been through the limited use of transferable development rights (TDR) (Rose 1975) and the related strategy of public purchase of development rights. In theory, use of TDR eliminates both wipeouts (e.g. where an individual suffers a loss through his property being zoned for agricultural use) and windfalls (through a re–zoning of property for high-density development). In such circumstances the first owner would have the opportunity of selling the development rights from his property while the owner wishing to develop at high density would have to purchase development rights from other landowners (Jackson 1981). In practice the concept of TDR is alien to the basic American ethic of land as a private right and a source of speculative profit and implementation will have to overcome both this inbuilt resistance by property owners and the land development industry and judicial challenges to the constitutionality of such schemes (Case and Gale 1984).

Vacant urban land

The results of the decisions of individual actors, interest groups and state policies are translated into the land-use mosaic of the city. Houses, schools, shops, offices, roads, and factories all compete for locations. In many cities however the non–use of land is equally striking. The Civic Trust (1977) reported 250,000 acres of dormant land in England (an area that could accommodate housing for five million people) while Nabarro *et al.* (1980) estimated that one acre in fifteen in Britain's older metropolitan areas lies vacant. Studies of individual cities have found high rates of dereliction — 10 per cent of central Liverpool, 6 per cent of the urban area of Cardiff (Bruton and Gore 1980), 5 per cent of London, and 12 per cent of the inner area of Glasgow (Burrows 1978). In terms of ownership, there is clear evidence that most of the vacant urban land is owned by the public sector and in particular by local authorities. Wilson and Wormsley (1977) found that Liverpool city council owned more than half the vacant land in the city and over 75 per cent of vacant land in one area, most of which had been acquired in the course of slum clearance. While some amount of vacant land is both desirable and inevitable during the course of redevelopment, many sites have been left fallow for several years as a result of revisions in the housing and road-building programmes of local authorities since the economic crisis of 1973. Such prolonged periods of vacancy may encourage a stock rather than flow perspective on behalf of local authorities further reducing the prospects for redevelopment (Nicholson 1984). The incidence of vacant, derelict or 'dead' land throughout the urban area is a feature of urban development under capitalism. Such areas represent a misuse of land resources, contribute to environmental degradation, underline the imperfections in the land market, and illustrate the limited influence of planners to *positively manage* the built environment. Some of the major reasons for the presence of vacant urban land are shown in Table 1.4. A combination of these factors can affect most sites and it is not impossible for all to be experienced by one site. As a result many urban sites have remained vacant for over a decade.

Clearly the fundamental issue is that of land value. While the actual and potential development value of land on the edge of the built-up area stimulates demand the challenge for planners in the more central locations outside the CBD is to create a level of values sufficient either to encourage owners to market their land or to attract private investors and developers. In an attempt to stimulate use of local authority owned vacant land in UK the government introduced a system of partial land registration under the provisions of the Local Government, Planning and Land Act 1980. This gave the Secretary of State the power to order the registration of all land held by public authorities that was surplus to their operational needs and to direct any owner of registered land to dispose of its interests in it (Stungo 1984). It was hoped that registration would make owners realize the development potential of any land holdings and, since much was in the older inner city, redevelopment would serve the dual purpose of improving the local environment and reducing pressures on greenfield sites. A major difficulty is that land is placed on the register not because it is of prime development quality but because it is surplus to the requirements of its public sector owners. Some of it is unsuited for any development. In addition, the cheap cost of holding on to vacant land does little to encourage authorities to market the property. It may be that a more stringent taxation (rating) system is required to precipitate action. In a similar vein tax reliefs could be employed to persuade owners to improve the appearance of vacant sites.

Table 1.4 Reasons for the presence of vacant urban land

---

1. Land is not available for current development.
    (a) land held for future use, e.g. public and private sector land banks and operational land of statutory undertakings.

    (b) land held speculatively as a hedge against inflation, aided by income from temporary uses (e.g. car parking) and low holding costs.

    (c) until recently some local authorities have not been favourably disposed towards private sector development on ideological grounds, especially where development was seen to be in conflict with the councils' own industrial and housing programmes.

2. Land is not in demand, due to —
    (a) physical constraints such as location, size, shape, ground conditions or a poor surrounding environment which make the site more costly to develop than a greenfield site.

    (b) land price does not reflect the potential user's valuation of the site.

    (c) uncertain future, e.g. if the site is blighted by future development proposals.

3. Land is in the process of redevelopment but implementation is delayed.
    (a) development deferred, e.g. lack of resources for housing or highway scheme.

    (b) design stage delays, e.g. problems between authorities, departments and developers on proposals, or planning appeals and enquiries.

    (c) development procedure delays, e.g. site acquisition problems, rehousing.

For investors the question of confidence is of paramount importance (Cadman 1979). Development will only take place if sites are attractive enough, in financial and environmental terms, to generate confidence in the future of the area. In London and other cities, areas of dereliction and blight lie within sight of major private sector urban development projects. The difference is between prime investment sites in the central area and high-risk sites in the surrounding inner city. To attract investment to off-centre sites will require government pump-priming initiatives to raise the value of the land. Public efforts to increase the development value of land either through fiscal incentives to new land users or by reducing the cost of redevelopment through derelict land and urban development grants are essential to the revitalization of the inner city. It is also clear, however, that even in large-scale public initiatives such as the GEAR project in Glasgow (Pacione 1985) the private sector has an integral role to play in the regeneration of derelict urban areas.

Externalities

Cities would not have grown up if the *collective* effect of land-use decisions was not beneficial. However, many of the effects of spatial decisions are negative in that they impose dis-benefits on some users of urban land. These adverse effects or negative externalities can take a variety of forms. They may, for example, arise from commercial invasion of residential areas or from the continued intensification of central city land use causing traffic problems, or from the process of urban sprawl. As well as being unpriced, externalities are unplanned (in the sense that their extent and impact is not predetermined by a public agency) but they are not always unintended since, for example, the pollution of atmosphere or an urban river by a factory is usually a deliberate attempt to transfer part of the real cost of production from the producer to society at large. Indeed, according to Harvey (1973: 58), 'much of what goes on in a city (particularly in the political arena) can be interpreted as an attempt to organize the distribution of externality effects to gain income advantages'. Once the externality problem reaches a critical level it is likely to provoke a public response in the form of planning intervention, the aim of which is to influence the market mechanism 'so that either prices are adjusted to reflect full social costs or outputs are controlled to a socially optimal level' (Walker 1981: 76). Frequently local urban governments have to carry the costs generated by negative spillovers as, for example, in the demands made on municipal exchequers by the peripheral expansion of cities and the consequent need for infrastructural investments to maintain minimal residential standards (Pacione 1987). Such financial strains played a major contributory role in creating the fiscal crisis which has affected central city administrations in North America.

Another land-use problem which is related to the question of externalities is the free-rider issue. A free rider is defined as an individual who refrains from any active initiatives but who benefits from the actions of others. This can be illustrated with reference to its consequences for urban blight. Once any neighbourhood starts to decline in status individual property owners will frequently, and quite rationally in individual cost-benefit terms, choose to do nothing in the face of the deterioration of their property, waiting instead for someone else to undertake improvements from which s/he will obtain positive externalities. Unfortunately the normal effect is that private renewal is postponed indefinitely as individual property owners await the windfall gains that, in practice, have little likelihood of appearing unless government rehabilitation programmes are enacted.

Chapter two

Power and politics in the city

In our discussion of capitalist urban development in the preceding chapter we saw how different individuals and interest groups attempt to manipulate social, economic and political forces to produce an environment most suited to their own particular requirements within the CMP. The common denominator underlying such manoeuvres is power. The uneven distribution of power and influence is a crucial factor underlying a host of social, economic and environmental problems in the modern city. Definitions of power abound but basically it refers to the possibility of imposing one's will upon the behaviour of others. As we saw in Chapter 1 this may be achieved through the economic system. Here we consider the equally important relationship between power and the political system. The study of power and politics in the city is essentially the study of the ways in which individuals and groups seek to satisfy their interests at the expense of others, that is, the process of 'who gets what, when, and how' (Lasswell 1958). A fundamental position in the power–politics complex is occupied by the state. For applied urban analysis special importance attaches to the nature of the relationship between central and local government, and in particular the degree of autonomy of the latter.

Central constraints on local government

Writers such as Dear and Clark (1981) see the actions of the local state as highly constrained by central government whereas others such as Dunleavy (1980) assign significant discretionary powers to the local level. A basic fact we must bear in mind is that the local state is a creation of the central state. It exists to further the aims of the state apparatus, has no independent existence and may be dissolved by the superior authority, the most recent case of the latter action being the abolition of the English metropolitan counties in 1986.

   The main channels along which central government directs its attempts to constrain local government are via legislation, circulars, planning and finance.

1   **Legislation** — the unitary system of government in Britain allows central government to impose specific duties and powers on local authorities. Application of the principle of *ultra vires* means that the lower tier can only undertake activities specifically approved by Parliament. This framework suggests strict legislative control over local government, but in fact there is considerable discretion in some areas. In the USA the system of legislative control over local government is markedly different largely because of the federal organization of the state. Urban managers in US local governments receive their authority from the relevant state government not from the federal authority. To ensure that local managers adhere to the rules of practice laid down in each state's written constitution there is a system of state courts which can interpret both managerial (e.g. zoning) and legislative actions (e.g. passing new laws). Where required, for example if an action is challenged by a citizen, interest group or even the state, the state legal system can be activated to oversee the operation of the local state. In addition to the state legal structure there is also a federal system of courts, the apex of which is the Supreme Court. As with the state courts the federal courts only become involved in civil issues if an individual or group brings a case to them. As Johnston (1981) has shown the American legal system has been centrally involved in adjudicating on issues of *discrimination* in legislation and local government practice.

2   **Circulars and guidance** — in an effort to clarify central government intentions and legislation a constant flow of circulars links the two levels of government, supplemented by a range of informal contacts between central departments and local government officers. The main method of communication is the circular which may instruct or may be merely advisory or explanatory. Among the defects of this communication system are (a) the balance between coercion and advice varies widely with the result that the status and purpose of many communications is unclear, (b) the communication process has tended to be one-way, (c) many central government communications emphasize uniform national policies and ignore specific local circumstances which influence the effectiveness of policy implementation, (d) central government often involves itself needlessly in the detail of local government administration, (e) central government guidelines focus attention on the provision of services but give insufficient consideration to the effectiveness of different levels of provision, and (f) central government tends to take an individual view of different services instead of examining the inter-relationships between different policies and programmes at the local level (Hambleton 1978).

3   **Planning processes** — the role and efficacy of planning has been the subject of considerable debate since the structuralist or neo-Marxist

critique of normative planning. In effect Marxism and planning are antithetical concepts. Marxists consider urban planning in capitalist coun-tries to be part of the dominant mode of production, supportive of the status quo and therefore counter–revolutionary (Scott and Roweiss 1977). Most planners would not accept the conspiratorial undertones of this view nor the impotence of their efforts to promote beneficial social change. Nevertheless, planning is a state activity and central government lays down a number of planning processes which control and influence the work of local authorities.

4   **Finance** — the fourth way in which central government exerts control over local government is through finance. The lower tier's funding is derived from local taxation (a major source being property tax in the US and rates in Britain), public borrowing on money markets, charges for services rendered (e.g. council house rents), and government grants. In UK the majority of local authority income stems from the last of these, in the form of the Rate Support Grant. In the late 1970s this contributed over 60.0 per cent of the total income of local governments. Until 1981 this was structured so that there was a negative relationship between an authorities fiscal resources (rateable values per capita) and size of grant, and a positive relationship between its needs (the demand for services) and the grant. The formula was altered by central government in 1981 as part of its general attempt to reduce local government spending. Now, a target expenditure for each authority is set according to its centrally-perceived needs and a grant towards that expenditure is provided. Should the local government seek to spend over the target it is penalised by withdrawal of all or part of the Rate Support Grant. This clearly has major implications for local autonomy.

So far our discussion has been concerned with structural macro-scale 'top–down' constraints and influences on the local state. We must recognize that power is also distributed unevenly *within* local jurisdic-tions, and that the power struggle is waged between a host of formal and informal groups, each seeking to influence the nature and activities of the local state. A major division is between agents operating within the prevailing local government structure, including both (a) informal (and occasionally illegal) influences and (b) formal 'top–down' public participation; and (c) more radical 'bottom–up' pressure groups or social movements.

Informal community influence

Informal networks of influence exist outside the representative input mechanisms and serve to channel the influence of particular sections of the local population to policy-makers in local government. Dunleavy

(1980) has identified three areas in which informal influence networks are significant.

1   Local party organizations play an important role in linking council groups to party-affiliated interests. This occurs partly via formal party structures (e.g. the trade union involvement in the Labour party), partly through overlapping memberships (such as between the Conservative party and the local Chamber of Commerce), and partly via the social organizations (e.g. political clubs and women's organizations) associated with local parties. All of these serve to structure access to local political elites. Given the prevalence of one-party control in local government this can result in the real definition of 'insider' and 'outsider' interest groups in particular localities.

2   Patronage represents the second main line of informal influence. In most localities it is possible to identify a 'burgher community' composed of major party council members, some party activists and members of partly affiliated interests, cemented together by a middle-class bias and overlapping membership of local government and other state agencies (e.g. regional and area health authorities). The influence of this community extends widely through the social structure because of the prevalence of political nominations for positions such as Justice of the Peace and membership of school management boards. In addition to bodies on which politically affiliated elites are formally specified, the influence of the burgher community can extend to other groups such as voluntary welfare agencies, which are often dependent on council grants and hence keen to please on policy and appointments.

3   Some degree of corruption (e.g. favours for friends in council house allocations, or planning permissions) is inevitable, and at an individual level does not have a great impact on public policy. A more fundamental threat to the legitimacy of local government is posed by the direct economic exploitation of the system by large corporations (e.g. in the determination of land and property values and construction of public infrastructure) with corruption networks often organized by local politicians (Pinto–Duschinsky 1977). In the city of Birmingham, for example, a regional building firm maintained a 'Christmas list' of two thousand local authority employees, including a corrupt city architect, and in the period 1966–1973 received £110 million worth of public housing work.

Public participation

In most Western nations the twin processes of globalization (Beer 1973) and professionalization (Lee 1963) of decision-making have reduced the power of local electorates and led to calls for public participation and local democracy. The basic dilemma stems from the perpetual tension between the need for effective administration and the need for maximum accountability. While the former invokes centralist tendencies in urban government, the latter demands greater decentralization. Proponents of citizen involvement in government decision-making envisage the concept being operationalized in the (a) democratization of resource allocation strategies, (b) decentralization of service systems management, (c) deprofessionalization of bureaucracies, and (d) demystification of planning and investment decisions (Pacione 1988). These sentiments are at the same time anathema to many elected officials who question the value of participation. Nevertheless, over the last two decades the principle of citizen participation as a necessary component of governmental decision-making has been generally acknowledged.

A key question in the participation debate is the amount of power that is devolved to citizens. Several classifications of the power relationship between decision-makers and public have been advanced including Arnstein's (1969) ladder of citizen participation, the eight rungs of which can be grouped into three broad categories relating to

(a) non-participation forms which merely give an illusion of power.
(b) degrees of tokenism based on one-way 'top–down' strategies of informing, consultation and placation, and
(c) degrees of real citizen power (Figure 2.1).

Figure 2.1 A ladder of citizen participation

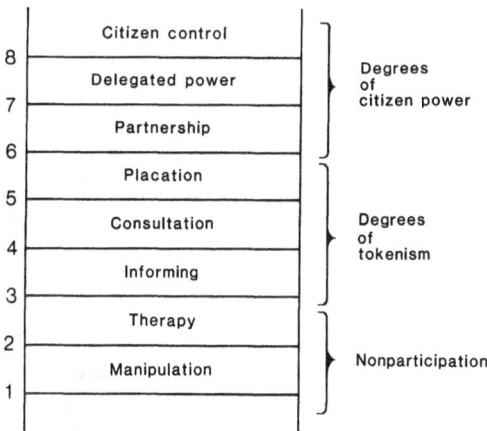

Source: Arnstein 1969

A similar categorization has been advanced by Alterman (1982) (Figure 2.2). In practice many of the conventional methods utilized have advanced

Figure 2.2 Alternative forms of the power relationship between citizens and planners/decision-makers

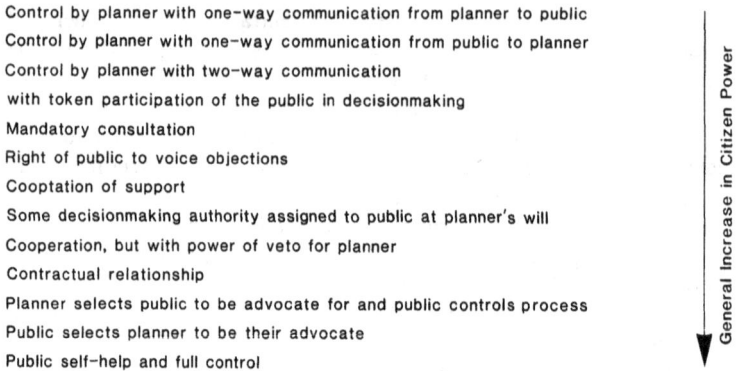

Control by planner with one-way communication from planner to public
Control by planner with one-way communication from public to planner
Control by planner with two-way communication
with token participation of the public in decisionmaking
Mandatory consultation
Right of public to voice objections
Cooptation of support
Some decisionmaking authority assigned to public at planner's will
Cooperation, but with power of veto for planner
Contractual relationship
Planner selects public to be advocate for and public controls process
Public selects planner to be their advocate
Public self-help and full control

General Increase in Citizen Power

Source Alterman 1982: 307

the cause of citizen participation only slightly, being more concerned with deseminating information. Such techniques include (a) exhibitions, (b) public meetings, (c) publication of surveys and reports, (d) media publicity, (e) ideas competitions, (f) referenda, and (g) public enquiries (Fagence 1977). Approaches with more potential for citizen involvement have occurred in the spheres of area management policies, neighbourhood councils, advocacy planning and pragmatic radicalism.

The neighbourhod area approach to urban management

Underlying this approach is the notion of public learning whereby local governments develop an enhanced ability to perceive and understand the inter-related and changing nature of problems in a community (problem recognition) as well as an adaptive capacity to respond to these changing difficulties in a timely and effective manner (problem response). In relation to this concept, the local democracy or neighbourhod area approach has the twin aims of (a) bringing local government closer to the people and (b) tuning actions to the needs of particular areas within a city. In short 'area approaches involve gearing the planning and/or management of policies to the needs of particular geographical areas within the local authority and may involve delegating administrative and/or political responsibility for at least part of this work to the local level' (Hambleton 1978; 71). A number of local authorities in Britain, Western Europe and USA have enacted area management schemes. Particular attention has been attracted by Boston's little city halls programme, but similar area management experiments have been carried out in other cities such as Dayton Ohio and New York (Washnis 1972), as well as in British cities including Stockport and Liverpool (Webster 1982).

In UK the reform of local government in the early 1970s greatly reduced the number of authorities, increased the population of the basic local government units and thereby, inevitably, served to distance the citizen from the decision-making process. To counter this trend local government reform in Scotland incorporated a statutory form of local participatory body, the community council (Scottish Development Department 1974, Pacione 1982). These bodies are not seen to be a third tier of local government, below the region and district levels. Community councils do not have statutory responsibility for delivery of services, nor the power to raise revenues by taxation. Their general objective is to ascertain, coordinate and express the views of local communities to the relevant public bodies. Despite problems of the representativeness of the bodies arising from low voter turnouts at elections and a middle-class bias in membership the community council idea had spread to most parts of the country within a few years of local government reorganiza-tion. Interpreted in pluralist terms the extension of community councils represents a widening of political accessibility but this is clearly taking place within constraints set from above. A structuralist understanding of the phenomenon would emphasize the lack of any real delegation of power to the local level and view the scheme as merely a useful means of social control by which grassroots pressure for social change may be diverted into a concern with amenity and the immediate environment rather than with social justice (Coit 1978).

Increased citizen participation has also been a subject of concern in the countries of Western Europe where a variety of initiatives have been introduced (Susskind and Elliott 1981). These range from schemes which are essentially paternalistic (e.g. citizen involvement in the design of local traffic schemes) to others which involve a greater degree of local autonomy. An example of the latter is the co-production strategy employed in cities such as Rotterdam and Madrid. Here a degree of power-sharing is involved in the decentralization of responsibility for public services and joint preparation of urban development plans. Moves toward effective neighbourhood government have been particularly strong in Italy where experiments with various forms of urban decentralization began in the early 1960s in some communist controlled areas, such as Bologna (Nanetti and Leonardi 1979; Nanetti 1985).

Advocacy planning and pragmatic radicalism

The roots of advocacy planning have been traced to the growing rate of delinquency and vandalism in the US city of the late 1950s, which

35

several analysts attributed to citizen alienation and anomie. For Cloward and Ohlin (1960) anomie resulted from the disparity perceived by low-income youth between their legitimate aspirations and the social, economic, political and educational opportunities made available to them by society. The solution lay in reforming society with the involvement and participation of low-income citizens, and the major agent for this change was seen as the planning professional. When urban riots erupted in the 1960s these arguments were adopted by government and translated into the Economic Opportunity Act of 1964 which embraced the principle of 'maximum feasible participation' (Heskin 1980).

In essence advocacy planning means the provision of professional planning expertise and services to minority groups lacking the financial ability to purchase such services. The concept was popularized by Davidoff (1965) who envisaged a plural form of planning (as opposed to, for example, a unitary master plan) in which all the special interests of society would be represented by planners who meet 'in the political arena' with their clients' proposals so that the best plan would emerge. This perspective recognizes that 'the public interest' is not a matter of science but rather a matter of politics. Advocacy planning, in its various forms, is an attempt to move citizen participation forward from merely reacting to agency plans to proposing their own concepts of appropriate goals and future action. The limited power of the advocacy strategy has been criticized however (Hatch 1968) and in general fundamental system change has proved to be beyond the powers of even the most successful advocacy planners (Breitbart and Peet 1974). Despite its limitations, however, advocacy planning continues particularly in relation to community and economic development (Perlman 1976).

Some supporters of advocacy planning have suggested that it should be undertaken by planners operating within the established city planning system without the necessity of a client group. This approach has been referred to as *pragmatic radicalism* (Kraushaar 1979). This theoretical framework is constructed on the basic assumption that the normal workings of the capitalist system produce hardship for the working class. Concerned professional planners must therefore assume the interventionist role of politically committed activists to protect the interests of the urban poor and working class in the face of the profit-driven economic development and land-use decisions of major economic and political interests. These conflict planners seek to alter the shape of the commercial and financial decisions that have created urban social problems – such as redlining by banks, neighbourhood disinvestment, suburban relocation by industry and business, and socially costly redevelopment schemes. An example of this philosophy in practice is the activity of the Cleveland City Planning Commission (Krumholz *et al.* 1975) whose explicit goal is to promote 'a wider range of choices for those

Cleveland citizens who have few, if any, choices' (p. 299). The agency combines activism, class advocacy and policy planning on behalf of the city's poor and its existing neighbourhoods. Thus, for any proposed redevelopment project the planning staff would undertake a social impact analysis to examine questions such as whether it will provide more jobs at liveable wages for city residents, the effect on the level and quality of public services, and whether it will support neighbourhood vitality or contribute to its deterioration. Projects which fail to meet these distributive criteria would be opposed by the Commission. This approach is a radical interpretation of the concept of 'planning gain'.

Populist politics

In Britain where local politics are closely tied to the national party structure the formation of new political groupings to contest local elections is not common. By contrast, in North America the dominance of non-partisanship in municipal government allows independent interests to enter the political arena more easily, as demonstrated by the election of a populist/liberal majority on the Santa Monica city council in 1981 (Shearer 1984). Non-partisanship in US cities most often exists where the structure of 'reformed' government has produced a commission or city-manager form of administration. In many of the large North American cities, however, the apparent independence of politicians disguises a conservative business-oriented outlook. Under particular circumstances social and economic trends can combine to generate a momentum which is sufficient to give rise to a popular alternative political movement as a challenge to the status quo. One example of such an event is the emergence of The Electors Action Movement (TEAM) in Vancouver. This liberal urban reform party was founded in 1968 and assumed political control of the city between 1972 and 1978. Based on an ideology of producing a liveable city TEAM challenged and temporarily replaced the prevailing growth boosterism basis of Vancouver politics (Ley 1980).

To date, however, most significantly in the US city the struggle between citizen interests and those inherent in the capitalist urban development process has been an unequal one. To redress the balance and advance the cause of participatory democracy requires greater commitment to a form of political management favourably disposed to local self-government, administrative decentralization and citizen participation. Practical measures which seek to enhance the use value of urban amenities include a housing policy based on rehabilitation and maintenance rather than on extensive new development, schools that open in the evenings and weekends to serve the wider needs of the community, private offices that become tax-deductable cultural centres in the evening, and a land-use plan that encourages conservation and maximization of uses and that eliminates land speculation. In short, even with the same budget and similar legal instruments 'many reforms are possible *if there is a firm political will* and a clear planning policy based upon the principle that the existing city and its gradual development have to be preserved and managed as a collective use-value, rather than made obsolete before time and submitted to privately appropriated exchange-value' (Castells 1983: 15). The problem which has confounded most attempts at municipal democratization has been that in most instances a level of influence rather than power has been redistributed.

The lack of ability to exert a meaningful influence on urban decision-making through formal channels of participation (i.e. representative democracy and government-mandated citizen participation) has resulted in the rise of radical 'bottom–up' protest groups and urban social movements.

Radical urban movements

Concensual community participation — gaining 'inside' access to policy-makers — offers a direct formal route to government officials but also raises the possibility of co–optation. For urban protest groups there are clear advantages in operating outside the formal system via a strategy of *conflictual participation*. These include the strengthening of internal group solidarity, and an ability to gain concessions from government through fear, sympathy or successful mobilization of public groups to which elites are normally attentive. Viewed in this context participation and resistance are dialectically linked and represent a combination which may offer the best hope of success to alienated neighbourhoods. This is illustrated in a study of the political impact of Community Action Agencies in the USA. These stemmed from a federal initiative, launched in 1964, to promote neighbourhood-based services and community organizing with at least one–third representation of the poor on CAA governing boards. Austin (1972) in a survey of twenty cities found that only in the one-third of agencies where neighbourhood participation was adversary was there any relationship between resident action and urban change. Direct action to obtain decisions favourable to disadvantaged groups and neighbourhoods is often necessary because as Reidel (1972: 219) notes 'no one gives up power to others unless he no longer needs it, can no longer sustain it for personal reasons, or is forced to do so'. Barring a fundamental transformation in social structure or political consciousness in western society direct action by neighbourhood protest movements will generally be required to push political elites unresponsive to demands for political equity and social justice.

The urban social movement phenomenon has shown a remarkable

growth in the last two decades although as the case of the Glasgow rent strike of 1915 (McLean 1974) indicated radical protest movements have long been a response of the poor to the inequities of the capitalist system. More recent urban social movements include tenants' associations opposed to council-house rent increases (Baldock 1982), ratepayers organizations keen to promote private sector provision of urban services (Nugent 1979), groups to defend local schools and small hospitals against rationalization, movements against urban redevelopment programmes and motorway schemes which threaten stable communities, and the squatters movement seeking to effect a more equitable use of housing (Wates and Wolmar 1980). Urban social movements are now present in every western society including, for example, Spain (Castells 1978), Italy (Lagana *et al.* 1982), Netherlands (Anderiesen 1981), France (Castells 1978), West Germany (Katz and Mayer 1985), and Australia (Camina 1975) as well as Britain (Lowe 1986) and USA (Friedland 1982).

The crucial importance of pluralism, government accountability, local autonomy and widespread citizen participation in urban politics was emphasized by Alinksy (1969) who advocated the mobilization of community groups using confrontational tactics to strengthen their voice in the decision-making process. Assessments of Alinsky-inspired community organizations (Lancourt 1979) conclude that while they have failed to achieve a significant re–ordering of the distribution of power in urban government, locally important gains have been recorded over a range of issues such as redlining, utility rates, senior-citizen benefits, property tax assessment, and citizen involvement in programme planning. In addition, there is the less tangible benefit of educating people on how power and politics actually operate.

Table 2.1 Characteristics of successful grassroots groups

1. Full-time, paid, professional staff
2. Well-developed fund-raising capacity
3. Sophisticated mode of operation, including:
a. Neighborhood street organizing
b. Advanced issue-research capacity
c. Information dissemination and exposé techniques
d. Negotiation and confrontation skills
e. Management capability in the service delivery and economic development areas
f. Policy and planning skills
g. Lobbying skills
h. Experience in monitoring and evaluating government programs
4. Issue growth from the neighborhood to the nation
5. A support network of umbrella groups, technical assistants, action-research projects, organizer-training schools
6. Expanding coalition building with one another, with public-interest groups, and with labor

Source: Perlman 1978: 71

Generally, in order to develop a political voice at the national level where major policy decisions are made it may be necessary for individual social groups to broaden their perspective and seek to initiate coalitions with other single-issue interest groups, such as state-level trade unions, senior citizen, environmental and women's organizations. The example of the Australian Green Ban Movement (an alliance between residents' actions groups opposed to certain types of development and the Builders Labourers Federation demonstrates the potential power of broad-based social movements (Camina 1975). Forming alliances without surrendering identity and penetrating the political system while reserving the right of direct action are among the major requirements (Table 2.1) for a shift from grassroots *pressure* to grassroots *power* in the shaping of urban policies.

Chapter three

Poverty and deprivation

Despite the social legislation of the post-war era, poverty remains the daily experience of large numbers of people in western societies. A key factor in the debate over the extent of poverty in urban society is the distinction between absolute and relative poverty. The absolutist or subsistence definition of poverty derived from that formulated by Rowntree (1901: 186) contends that a family would be considered to be living in poverty if its 'total earnings are insufficient to obtain the minimum necessaries for the maintenance of merely physical efficiency'. This notion of a minimum level of subsistence and the related concept of a poverty line exerted a strong influence on the development of social welfare legislation in post-war Britain. The system of National Assistance benefits introduced following the Beveridge Report (1942) was based on calculations of the amount required to satisfy the basic needs of food, clothing and housing plus a small amount for other expenses. If, however, we accept that needs are culturally determined rather than biologically fixed then poverty is more accurately seen as a relative phenomenon. The broader definition of needs inherent in the concept of relative poverty includes job security, work satisfaction, fringe benefits (such as pension rights), plus various components of the 'social wage' including use of and access to public property and services, as well as satisfaction of higher-order needs such as status, power and self-esteem (Maslow 1970). The absolutist perspective carries with it the implication that poverty can be eliminated in an economically–advanced society, while the relativist view accepts that the poor are always with us.

According to the Bureau of the Census, in 1983, 15.2 per cent (35 million people) of the US population lived below the poverty line (which is based on the minimum amount of money families need to purchase a nutritionally adequate diet, assuming they use one-third of their income for food). For blacks the incidence of poverty rose from 31.4 per cent in 1973 to 35.7 per cent in 1983, and for Hispanics the respective rates were 21.9 per cent and 28.4 per cent. In the central cities the average poverty rate was 19.9 per cent in 1983 while in 'poverty areas' within

the central cities the incidence of poverty increased from 34.9 per
cent in 1975 to 45.6 per cent in 1982 (US Bureau of the Census
1984).

In UK up to 1988 the official extent of poverty was indicated by those
living on supplementary benefit (approximately 40.0 per cent of average
net earnings). Despite regular upward revisions of supplementary benefit
rates there is ample survey and case–history evidence (Townsend 1979)
to indicate that there are many people in Britain who have neither enough
to eat or sufficient clothing, or who lack adequate furniture or other
household equipment (Table 3.1). As Figure 3.1 shows, since the
initiation of a national scheme in 1948 the size and composition of the
claimant population has changed significantly. While the proportion of
pensioner claimants has remained consistently high, most significant has
been the increase in number of unemployed claimants from the late 1970s

Table 3.1 Lack of necessities as a result of shortage of money among supplementary benefit claimants

Twenty-two standard-of-living necessities in rank order	Households on supplementary benefit		
	Pensioners	*Families*	*Others*[a]
	% not having items because can't afford it		
Heating	11	25	24
Indoor toilet	12	5	8
Damp-free home	15	23	34
Bath	10	5	10
Beds for everyone	3	3	3
Warm water-proof coat	33	28	20
3 meals a day for children[b]	—	15	—
2 pairs of all-weather shoes	19	41	30
Sufficient bedrooms for children[b]	—	12	—
Refrigerator	11	5	5
Toys for children[b]	—	13	—
Carpets	1	19	7
Celebrations on special occasions	8	21	15
Roast joint once a week	11	23	30
Washing machine	18	21	15
New, not secondhand clothes	24	24	29
Hobby or leisure activity	3	29	25
2 hot meals a day (adults)	8	17	11
Meat/fish every other day	9	41	20
Presents once a year	13	24	16
Holiday	27	67	54
Leisure equipment for children[b]	—	46	—

Source: Mack and Lansley 1985
[a]These include some families with children over 16 and households with more than one claimant.
[b]Families with children under 16 only.

onwards. The other major change has been the rise in number of single–parents claiming supplementary benefit, this figure doubling between 1973 and 1983 to reach 450,000.

Figure 3.1 Supplementary benefit claimants by client group

UNITED KINGDOM

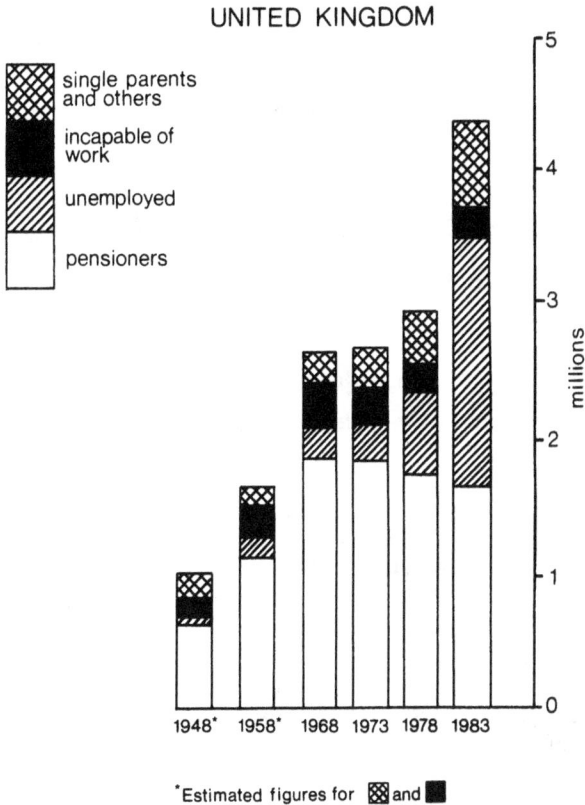

*Estimated figures for ▨ and ■

Source: Mack and Lansley 1985

In addition to those on supplementary benefit any definition of the poor must include those low-paid workers whose income is insufficient to provide a decent standard of living. As well as the direct income effect of low pay on a family, low pay influences poverty indirectly in two ways. First low pay at one time may contribute to poverty in later life. This is most clearly demonstrated by poverty in old age, low pay during working life preventing the acquisition of property or accumulation of savings. Second, low-paid workers, referred to by Marx as the reserve army of labour, are more likely to become unemployed and less likely to enjoy fringe benefits such as sick pay schemes. In brief, inadequate life-time earnings, job insecurity, sickness and ill-health correlate with low pay and contribute to poverty. Evidence from a number of investigations (Townsend 1979, Mack and Lansley 1985) suggest that 15 million people (27.5 per cent) in UK are living in or on the margins of poverty. According to Townsend (1979) those who run the highest risk of being in poverty are:

1   those in a household of a man, woman and three or more children where the occupational status is that of unskilled manual worker (93 per cent of this group were in poverty).
2   being aged 80 years or over (82 per cent).
3   having an appreciable or severe disability and being of pensionable age (82 per cent).
4   being a child (aged 0–14 years) with parents of unskilled manual status (77 per cent).
5   having an appreciable or severe disability (74 per cent).
6   being retired or living alone and aged 60 years or more (70 per cent).

Thus the factors found to be associated with poverty are the familiar ones — unskilled manual work, old age, disability, childhood, fatherless or single-parent families, few years of education, and unemployment.

Poverty is a central component of the multi–dimensional problem of deprivation in which individual difficulties reinforce one another to produce a situation of absolute disadvantage for those affected. Significantly, the complex of poverty-related problems such as crime, delinquency, poor housing, increased rates of family breakup, homelessness, increased mortality and mental illness have been shown to exhibit a spatial concentration in cities. Such a patterning serves to accentuate the effects of poverty and deprivation for the residents of particular parts of cities.

The ghetto

Some of the most visible concentrations of deprivation are found in ethnic ghettos. The spatial segregation of particular groups on the grounds of race, religion or national origin has its roots in the process of in-migration. The degree of perceived social distance between the host community and migrant groups is a critical determinant of the degree to which assimilation occurs. Assimilation is a temporal process which takes place at different rates for different groups. It is not, however, an inevitable process and the level of segregation of some ethnic groups (e.g. American blacks) can remain high. Blaut (1983: 37), with reference to the black ghettos of Harlem in New York and Chicago's South Side, states that 'few ghetto-dwellers have the opportunity to move out of the ghetto . . . almost every family that lived in these old ghettos in the 1920s is living there still'. Although not all ghettos are slums (Ford and Griffin 1979) generally such areas are characterized by inferior living conditions and severely restricted economic opportunities (Rose 1971).

Residential segregation can serve a variety of functions both for capitalist society in general, by creating a 'super-exploited' sector of the working class (Blaut 1983), and for the ethnic groups. For the latter the functions of the ghetto include the defensive (e.g.physical security), supportive (as refuge in an unfamiliar environment), conservative (preservation of cultural heritage), and as a power-base from which to launch attacks on the prevailing social formation. While the negative social and economic conditions in most ethnic ghettos continue to demand attention the positive potential of ethnic concentration is also being recognized. Spatial concentration can, for example, enable an ethnic group to elect its own representatives who can carry group arguments into the local and national political arena. For some, such as Petticrew (1969: 63), 'the democratic objective is not total racial integration and the elimination of the ghetto; the idea is simply to provide an honest choice between separation and integration. . . . The long term goal . . . is the transformation of those ghettos from today's racial prisons to tomorrow's ethnic areas of choice'.

In addition to ethnic ghettos several researchers have drawn attention to the growth of *service-dependent ghettos* in the modern city (Dear and Wolch 1987). These comprise people such as the low-income elderly, the mentally-handicapped, the physically disabled and the chronically unemployed who rely on cash income transfers from government and services-in-kind for their support. Studies of these non-labour force groups in USA have shown that up to one-half of their income consists of the cash value of services-in-kind targetted for them by various public and private agencies (Massey 1980). The centrifugal population movements of the post-war era have meant that in the US city these disadvantaged groups have increasingly been left behind in poverty-ridden central neighbourhoods. The same degree of central-city concentration is not apparent in Britain where public urban renewal policy has served to disperse the service-dependent poor. However, many have been relocated onto peripheral housing estates, the most deprived areas of which have been characterized as 'cashless societies'. In the US community opposition towards deinstitutionalization of the mentally handicapped, prisoners, juvenile delinquents or those with drug or alcohol abuse problems (Dear and Taylor 1982) and exclusionary local zoning aimed at service-dependent groups and facilities operate to ensure the continued spatial segregation of such groups. The concentration of service facilities attracts other populations in need of the services provided to

45

these 'poverty-zones', initiating a cycle of co-location that can ultimately result in the ghettoization of those who depend on publically provided services. This can have adverse effects both for those trapped within the area and, through negative spillover effects, for the surrounding non-dependent populations. Clearly a geographically informed social policy sensitive to the environmental impact of programmes is required to obviate such difficulties (C. Smith 1981). Ethnic and service-dependent ghettos are, of course, particular elements of the more general 'inner-city' problem.

Unemployment

Unemployment is the single most important cause of poverty and is therefore the main target for those seeking to alleviate urban deprivation. As Table 3.2 shows the number of 'unemployed claimants' in UK increased steadily between 1961 and 1985. By September 1985 there were 3,346,000 unemployed in UK representing a national rate of 13.8 per cent. In 1984, regional unemployment ranged from 9.5 per cent in the South East to 18.3 per cent in the north of England while within regions local rates reached over 40.0 per cent in some housing estates. The growth of long-term unemployment has been particularly serious. While total unemployment in UK increased by 5.0 per cent between July 1984 and 1985 the number of long-term unemployed increased by 7.0 per cent. At the latter date 800,000 people (25.0 per cent of unemployed claimants) had been unemployed for more than two years.

The fact that unemployment is concentrated in metropolitan areas

Table 3.2 Unemployed claimants: annual averages for U.K.

| | UNITED KINGDOM | | | |
| | Unemployed (thousands) | | | Unemployment rate |
	Males	Females	Total	%
1961	231	61	292	1.3
1971	647	104	751	3.3
1976	1,006	296	1,302	5.5
1979	930	366	1,296	5.3
1980	1,181	484	1,665	6.8
1981	1,843	677	2,520	10.4
1982	2,133	784	2,917	12.1
1983	2,219	886	3,105	12.9
1984	2,197	962	3,160	13.1
Year ending mid-1985	2,268	1,003	3,271	13.5

Source: CSO 1986: 71

does not, of course, indicate that it is a problem *of* the city. Urban unemployment arises from a combination of local and non-local or structural forces. A major reason behind the current high levels of unemployment in many urban areas of Britain has been the process of deindustrialization in the UK economy over the last two decades. In general British manufacturing industry has failed to maintain its international competitiveness (Singh 1977). There are several reasons for this. First is the obsolescence of plant and equipment. The second refers to under-investment. Finance capital has flowed out of manufacturing into areas offering greater profit, including pension funds and speculative booms like the office boom of the early 1970s. In addition, the leading sector of British industrial capital has sought to retain its competitiveness by operating internationally rather than by expanding from a secure home base. Evidence of a similar trend in USA is offered by Bluestone and Harrison (1980). This has led to the relocation of production facilities to the low-wage countries of the Third World (the new international division of labour). The third reason is declining productivity partly as a result of the lack of new investment and partly due to the defensive economic power of the organized labour movement. The result of these forces has been bankruptcy of industrial firms, factory closures and heavy job losses in manufacturing. This general decline of employment in manufacturing firms has had a disproportionate effect on the cities which were traditional centres for such activity. Within metropolitan areas the inner cores have suffered the most severe job losses. Most large urban areas in the advanced market-economies are experiencing similar trends of stable or declining metropolitan-area population combined with intra-metropolitan decentralization of people and manufacturing employment, and a change in industrial structure from manufacturing to service employment.

Deprivation in the inner city

The range of deprivations affecting the major conurbations and urban cores in the UK was recognized during the late 1960s and 1970s. A government White Paper identified four basic components of the inner city problem (Department of the Environment 1977):

1 First was the economic decline and unemployment associated with the decentralization of population and industry, and the national problem of deindustrialization manifested in the run-down of traditional inner-city activities. One explanation suggested for the acute decline of manufacturing employment in the urban cores is that it stems from an adverse industrial structure, essentially an overrepresentation of depressed industrial sectors. However this proposition is not supported by shift-

share analyses (Danson *et al.* 1980). Inner-city locations have lost manufacturing largely as a result of changing comparative costs in favour of non-central locations. This has occurred because of factors such as shifts to long-production runs, the internalization of economies of scale, a reduction in the relative costs of transportation and communication in metropolitan areas, and the growth of technologies which require a high land to output ratio. Such processes have reduced the traditional demand for centrality. This tendency has been accentuated by the relatively high costs of industrial land and taxes in the inner city (Keeble 1978), by a shortage of suitable premises, by problems of inadequate access and limited opportunities for expansion (McIntosh and Keddie 1980), by the economic costs of using obsolete premises (D. Smith 1977), and by labour constraints, notably a shortage of female workers and, possibly, greater union activity in cities. The cumulative effect of these processes has been to encourage the decentralization of manufacturing activities and the overall decline of employment in the inner areas.

This centrifugal movement of firms comprises actual physical relocation and the net effect of closure of inner city operators and the birth of new plants on the periphery. In general evidence suggests that the death of inner city firms has been of greater significance than relocation (Elias and Keough 1982). In this context, the impact of planning policies, and in particular urban redevelopment strategy, on job loss has been exaggerated. While between a quarter and a half of firms displaced by comprehensive redevelopment disappeared the significance of this for employment has been overstressed since (a) displaced firms were mainly small, (b) many that disappeared were operating at very low levels of profitability and would have died eventually. Those equipped for growth survived and moved into new premises, and (c) while insensitive redevelopment caused the loss of many small firms employment losses were mainly the result of the closure of large firms.

Another key factor in the demise of urban industrial employment has been the rationalization undertaken by multi–plant companies which has resulted in the closure of branch plants and the failure of many small dependent firms in an area. Paradoxically government economic policies since the mid-1960s have actively encouraged company mergers and rationalization in the private sector through the work of agencies such as the Industrial Reorganisation Corporation, and similar measures have been taken to increase productivity in the nationalized industries (Massey and Megan 1976). There is little doubt that these policies reinforced the processes of job loss in the inner city. The dominant position of national and international multi-plant companies in some urban economies signals the potential impact of rationalization strategies on a local economy. In inner Liverpool in 1975 almost half of all manual workers were employed in just twelve companies (Lloyd 1979). Clearly, corporate structure is of direct relevance to urban employment and the ability of policy-makers to influence employment change. On the supply side, the inability of firms to respond efficiently to changing market circumstances has also contributed to urban economic decline. This raises questions over the quality of management, organizational structure and capital investment strategies.

2   A second highly visible feature of many inner city areas is the physical dereliction and absence of amenities. A basic reason for such decay is age. Most of the inner areas of UK cities were built over a century ago and have not benefited from the continued investment and improvement which has been directed to the retail and commercial areas of the CBD. Environmental dereliction has also been exacerbated in many cities by public sector activity. Land has been cleared then left vacant for long periods as a result of inflated estimates of local authority needs and the stop–go nature of public sector financing which has affected the continuity of local authority development plans and cast a pall of planning blight over large parts of the inner city. Of particular concern in inner areas is the condition of housing which because of age and neglect often lacks modern amenities and suffers structural decay.

3   Social disadvantage was the third component of the inner city problem identified by the 1977 White Paper. It characterizes those who are poor (the unemployed and low-paid) as well as many of the infirm, elderly and ethnic minority groups. Social disadvantage is collective however, and affects all residents including those in employment and with satisfactory homes. It arises from a general sense of decay and neglect which pervades the whole area and can be related to a decline of community spirit and incidence of anti-social activities such as crime and vandalism.

4   The demand for labour, primarily in manufacturing industries and public services, in some British towns during the 1950s and 1960s led to a marked increase in immigration, first from the West Indies and later from the Indian subcontinent. In the twenty years following the Second World War the non-white population of Britain increased eightfold to reach 595,000. Many of these immigrants were attracted to the low-cost housing areas of the inner city. This has added a fourth dimension to the underlying economic, physical and social difficulties in cities such as London, Birmingham, Wolverhampton, Bradford and Leicester (Redfern 1982). Ethnic minorities in inner cities are affected by the same kind of disadvantage and deprivation experienced by all who live there but as a visually and culturally identifiable group they are open to discrimination in the job and housing markets and are easy targets for those seeking simple causes and scapegoats for the country's or city's economic decline. Although the race problem is less widespread in UK

than in USA the disadvantaged position of ethnic minorities is well documented and conflicts which have occurred in urban Britain in recent decades (Hamnett 1983) indicate the dangers of increased alienation between the various ethnic groups and the host society.

The complex of problems experienced in the inner city represents a major challenge for applied social scientists. While many of the difficulties can be attributed to industrial decline and unemployment, others relate to personal factors such as age, infirmity or ethnicity. Still others stem from the deteriorating physical environment and affect the standard of provision of housing, education, transport, health, and other social services. It is necessary to reiterate, however, that although these problems are most apparent in inner areas this does not mean that the underlying causes are geographical or that they are exclusive to the inner city. There is increasing evidence both from UK (Pacione 1986a) and USA (Masotti 1973) that the incidence of poverty and deprivation is growing in suburban locations.

The outer city

In USA distressed suburban communities are products of the income disparities and forces of discrimination and exclusion which guide residential choice within US metropolitan areas. With few exceptions those suburban communities that display greatest distress have become minority ghettos. As Culver (1982: 10) explains 'the existence of inexpensive housing, the proximity of crowded black core city residential areas, the immigration (both legal and illegal) of sizeable numbers of Hispanics, displacement from inner-city neighbourhoods, racial/ethnic steering and panic peddling by real estate agents and white fright and flight have been important factors in the transformation of suburban communities'. On all measures of distress (per capita income, unemployment, size of poverty population or crime levels), these suburbs differ little from the poverty areas of the central city. In Britain evidence from the 1971 census suggested that non-central concentrations of multiple deprivation were emerging in cities such as Liverpool (Department of the Environment 1977c), Hull (Davidson 1976) and Newcastle (Barke 1977). This has been confirmed by more recent evidence from the 1981 census (Pacione 1986b) which has suggested that the broadening spatial basis of urban deprivation may be a continuing process.

Policy responses to poverty

National policies to combat poverty and deprivation in UK stem from the late 1960s when the experience of riots in US cities, concern over the possible growth of an urban racial problem in Britain, and the 'rediscovery of poverty' focused attention on urban social problems as opposed to the physical deficiencies which had been the concern of the earlier comprehensive redevelopment strategy. Reports on specific issues including housing (Milner-Holland 1965), social services (Seebohm 1968) and education (Plowden 1967) served to increase government concern.

Between 1965 and 1977 the Urban Aid Programme formed the main plank of the government's anti-poverty policy, with the primary objective being to direct supplementary funds to deprived communities. Of greater significance for the future development of urban policy, however, were the Community Development Projects. These were a series of twelve neighbourhood-based experiments to investigate new ways of meeting the needs of people living in areas of high social deprivation. The underlying assumption was that after five years' work the CDP would be in a position to correct many of the local problems through 'better field co-ordination of the personal social services, combined with the mobilization of self-help and mutual aid in the community' (Edwards and Batley 1978: 227). Significantly, however, the final inter-project report rejected the prevailing 'social pathology' view of deprivation and concluded that 'there might certainly be in those areas a higher proportion of the sick and the elderly for whom a better co-ordination of services would undoubtedly be helpful, but the vast majority were ordinary working class men and women who, *through forces outside their control*, happened to be living in areas where bad housing conditions, redundancies, lay-offs and low wages were commonplace' (Community Development Project 1977: 4). This structural interpretation of the underlying cause of urban poverty was supported by the three Inner Area Studies conducted in Liverpool (Toxteth), Birmingham (Small Heath) and London (Lambeth).

The 1977 White Paper on the inner cities marked a turning point in urban policy separating an earlier period of urban policy experiments from a series of more permanent initiatives. Based on the findings of the CDPs and IASs the White Paper emphasized the economic foundations of urban problems and recommended the revitalization of inner urban areas through a programme of economic assistance and co-ordinated aid by central government in association and partnership with local authorities. The subsequent Inner Areas Act 1978 established seven partnership areas in which central government in partnership with other appropriate public bodies (notably local authorities) formulated programmes of action designed to improve the economic, physical and social structure of the inner areas concerned. The three guiding principles behind the partnership authorities were to concentrate limited resources on some of the worst problem areas, to co-ordinate action for dealing with the complex inter-related problems faced by these areas, and to tailor policies and actions to local needs. Just such a co-ordinated approach to inner-city regeneration had been anticipated in the Glasgow Eastern Areas Renewal (GEAR) project (Leclerc and Draffan 1984, Pacione 1985).

We should note that a major conceptual debate has ensued over the value of the spatial approach to urban deprivation. Critics have identified the problem of ecological fallacy pointing out that the concentration of deprived individuals in 'deprived areas' is often quite low (Holtermann 1975, A. Evans 1980), as well as the limited explanatory power of a spatial perspective (Hamnett 1979). As we have seen, there is now a sufficient body of evidence to indicate that the underlying causes of local concentrations of deprivation in cities are structural (for example, economic decline and the inadequacy of welfare support) rather than spatial, being related to more general social and economic forces operating within the capitalist system. This does not, however, eliminate the operation of an 'area effect'. The important influence of the local environment was identified by the inner area studies which concluded that 'there is a collective deprivation in some inner areas which affects all the residents, even though individually the majority of people may have satisfactory homes and worthwhile jobs. It arises from a pervasive sense of decay and neglect which affects the whole area. . .' This collective deprivation amounts to more than the sum of all the individual disadvantages with which people have to contend' (Department of the Environment 1977a: 4). This argument has formed a key element of the government's response to urban deprivation. The spatial approach can also be supported on other grounds. First is a recognition that the identification of spatial patterns is an essential starting point in understanding the local incidence of social disadvantage. Such analyses can also be used to identify spatial concentrations of particular population groups each of which can have policy implications. These may include the elderly and the young (with implications for the provision and use of geriatric and paediatric services respectively), unskilled workers (location of industry), and households without cars (transport route planning). Second, although the long-term ideal may remain a fundamental political–economic restructuring to tackle the roots of inequality in society, area-based policies of positive discrimination can provide more immediate benefits which enable some people to improve some aspects of their quality of life. Justified criticism of a policy based solely on area-based action should not overshadow the benefits of community-scale activities. Finally we cannot ignore the fact that for much of the post-war period, in both the USA and UK, government anti-deprivation policy has been focused on sub-areas within cities (Lawless 1986).

The Conservative governments elected in 1979, 1983 and 1987 continued the partnership concept initiated by their Labour predecessors but emphasized the need for greater cooperation with the private sector. This perspective underlay a number of new initiatives introduced by the 1980 Local Government Planning and Land Act, the most significant of which were the concepts of enterprise zones and urban development corporations.

The enterprise zone

The rationale behind the enterprise zones introduced by the Conservative government was to remove the tangle of planning controls and regulations which, in their view, was stifling private initiative and discouraging new investment in declining urban areas. Within the EZs new and existing firms would enjoy a range of benefits including (a) exemption from development land tax, (b) exemption from general rates on commercial and industrial property, with local authorities reimbursed by Exchequer grants, (c) simplified planning procedures, and (d) minimal requests by government for statistical information. Eleven EZs were in operation by the end of 1981 (Corby, Dudley, Hartlepool, Isle of Dogs, Newcastle–Gateshead, Trafford–Salford, Speke, Swansea, Wakefield, Clydebank and Belfast) with the experiment intended to operate for ten years.

Central to an assessment of the effectiveness of the EZ strategy as an instrument of anti-poverty policy is the crucial issue of employment creation versus economic development. While both are desirable goals within any economic policy they are not necessarily mutually compatible. Indeed with the substitution of labour by capital in many sectors these objectives may become contradictory. Evidence from the first eleven EZs indicates that they have been more successful in attracting firms to the zones than in generating a net job gain for the local or national economy (Catalano 1983, Lawless 1986). As currently formulated EZ policy runs the risk of falling between two stools. If economic growth was the main objective this would require the selection of more favourable areas, the expansion of newer industrial sectors, additional financial support, and a more thorough dismantling of controls. Alternatively, pursuing a principal goal of employment creation would necessitate control over incoming companies to ensure they were leading to a net increase in employment, were job-intensive and were assisting the less skilled who form the majority of the urban unemployed.

Urban partnerships

A major shortcoming of UK urban policy has been the limited degree to which private investment has been attracted to participate in the development process. This is in marked contrast to USA where public–private partnerships have operated for several decades (Fosler and Berger 1982). In USA public sector intervention is seen as a vehicle for 'leveraging' private investment. The underlying assumption is not simply that economic regeneration can only take place with the active involvement of the private sector but that the private sector is the main source of regenerative funds and of continuing employment, and that its performance can be enhanced in the inner city through the selective use of public financial incentives. In short, 'the function of the public sector is to catalyse development rather than to either carry out the development itself, or leave the development entirely to the private sector' (Hart 1980: 11). The federal government has promoted private-sector involvement in the inner cities by means of several financial strategies:

1 under the 'new towns in town' programme the federal government used its community development block grant (CDBG) to fund urban development in anticipation of complementary private investment.

2 the Housing and Community Development Act (1977) introduced urban development action grants (UDAGs) as complements to the CDBG, designed to lever finance from the private sector for joint public–private schemes. Local authorities can apply for a UDAG if they have appropriate levels of distress on at least three of six indicators (low per capita income, low population growth, high unemployment rates, low employment growth, old housing stock and high proportions of poverty). The purpose of the grants is to help offset the higher risk and development costs on inner city as opposed to green field sites (Schwartz 1979). Typically, private sources such as local banks would supply 80.0 per cent of the funds for a project and the remainder would be provided by a combination of the city involved and a UDAG. The grant is loaned at a low interest rate to a private developer to carry out the project. The city benefits in two ways: private investment is stimulated by the initial grant and future economic development efforts are endowed from the loan repayments (including, for example, improvement of neighbourhoods impacted by UDAG developments). By late 1981 the Department of Housing and Urban Development had made 1,136 awards to economic development projects in 629 distressed cities under the UDAG programme. At a cost of $2.1 billion these projects generated $12.7 billion of private investment and 298,000 new permanent jobs (Myers 1982). The selection of project is of key importance and here US practice contrasts with UK urban policy to date. In order to effectively lever capital from the private sector the area under consideration must demonstrate some potential for economic recovery. This contrasts with the British practice of concentrating on the worst areas first which Americans see as unpractical and wasteful of resources. As Hart

(1980) concludes economic profitability calculations are necessary if joint venture activities are to be anything other than limited expressions of social concern by the private sector.

3 the Urban Growth and Community Development Act 1970 provides federal mortgage guarantees to encourage the financial institutions to use mortgage-fund capital to fund urban development projects. Joint venture public–private urban development corporations active since the 1970s include the Philadelphia Development Corporation and the Greater Hartford Corporation. The latter has undertaken large scale redevelopment and improvement and is an initiative comparable with the British inner-city partnerships but with a greater private sector financial involvement (Home 1982).

4 the voluntary or community sector has also been more active in inner-city regeneration in USA than in UK, largely because ethnic minority grops are older established and form a larger proportion of the total population in the USA. Such groups have long practised self-help within their own communities and since the ghetto riots of the late 1960s US community development initiatives have proliferated with and without government assistance (Newnham 1980).

By comparison progress towards greater private sector involvement in urban revitalisation in UK has been limited. In an attempt to emulate the US model a system of Urban Development Grants was introduced in 1982 to provide 'pump-priming' funds for local authorities with schemes to attract private sector financed developments. A second initiative has been the formation of the Financial Institutions Group consisting of twenty-six managers from the private sector to make recommendations on how the private sector could best become involved in inner-city development. Among the most important recent government initiatives have been the establishment of urban development corporations with the clear remit of producing an environment conducive to the needs of private capital.

Urban development corporations

Both the London Docklands Development Corporation and the Merseyside Development Corporation were established in 1981 and in 1987 five others were set up for Trafford Park Manchester, Cardiff Bay, Teeside, Tyne and Wear, and the Black Country.

The new urban development corporations were given wide powers to acquire, assemble, reclaim, develop, sell, or lease land and to provide necessary infrastructure, a central objective being to create an environment attractive to private-sector investors. Although appearing to be one of the most interventionist urban strategies, the role of the London Docklands Development Corporation is essentially that of a catalyst seeking out and co-ordinating private sector investment. Reflecting the approach embodied in the American UDAGs the hope is that by being responsive to the demands of the market a long-term development strategy geared to the needs of capital would be implemented and self-perpetuating growth sustained. This economically dominated approach has led to criticism of the limited social content of the development proposals (Newman and Mayo 1981). Some observers have characterized the UDCs as anti-democratic institutions imposed on local community by central government. The counter argument is that the UDC is needed to implement a broad development plan without the inevitable delays, conflicts, compromises, and possible lost investment that arise from normal democratic processes and the involvement of community interests at each stage. These contrasting political–economic philosophies have been evident in the proposals for the London docklands. The London Docklands Strategic Plan prepared by the local authorities in the area (Docklands Joint Committee 1976) emphasized the need to stem existing job losses, to bring new jobs which would match the resident skills, to use the vacant land to tackle the acute housing problem of east London and to improve the general environment. This may be characterized as a comprehensive 'needs-based' approach to planning typical of the 'total approach' to inner-city renewal employed in GEAR. The incoming Conservative government in 1979 favoured a 'demand-led' approach with an emphasis on creating a new local economy attractive to firms and prospective residents from outside the area. The differing priority attached to local and regional–national needs in the two approaches is clearly demonstrated by housing and employment policy. In terms of employment, introduction of the UDC has switched emphasis from attempting to provide manufacturing jobs towards office and warehousing schemes and retail complexes. In the field of housing, emphasis has been put on the private sector construction of owner-occupied dwellings although waiting lists for council housing have risen (e.g. from 3,650 in 1981–82 in the Borough of Newham to 9,112 in 1984–85).

This central–local conflict is, of course, most marked where the respective governing authorities are of different political complexions. In some areas it has led to suggestions of alternative development strategies, or local economic initiatives, more attuned to local needs and less compliant with the demands of capital.

Local economic initiatives

Radically-oriented local economic initiatives seek to moderate the impact of uneven development within the depressed urban regions by focusing attention on the social costs associated with the unfettered ability of corporate capital institutions to move investments to global locations in search of maximum profit. This new form of municipal socialism (Cochrane 1986) envisages a greater executive role for local authorities which may include.

1   The creation of enterprise boards to generate an investment programme which produces long-term local benefits (Hasluck 1987).
2   equity financing which would enable local authorities to take a shareholding in individual firms to provide funds and exercise influence over decision making.
3   the negotiation of planning agreements between local authorities and companies. These would detail the financial assistance to be made available in return for corporate guarantees covering employment, wage levels, working conditions, and trade-union recognition. For example, companies proposing to close a plant within a fixed time period may have to pay some of the social costs involved.
4   the identification and promotion of 'socially-useful production' i.e. products that satisfy un-met local needs. Examples include the production of entry-phones for council flats by a workers co-operative in London following the closure of a multinational plant.
5   a direct role in the economy for the local authority which is often a major employer and purchaser. In Sheffield, for example, the local authority employs over 30,000 people (five times as much as the largest private sector employer) and spends 25.0 per cent of its annual total expenditure (£40 million in 1985) on the goods and services of 900 local firms.

However, while these local initiatives are innovative and wide-ranging it is clear that they alone cannot resolve the economic problems confronting disadvantaged city dwellers. As Rees and Lambert (1985: 181) conclude, of themselves 'they are unlikely o make a substantial contribution to the alleviation of the immediate problems confronting inner-city residents; and any contributions that they make are likely to be swamped by the contrary tendencies originating from the central state and from capital itself'. To be effective local economic initiatives require the support of sympathetic national strategies. Some of the more radical of these include a National Investment Bank, the nationalization of the banks to ensure a socially aware attitude to credit allocation, and control of investment to prevent the continued outflow of funds from the UK. Whether a government committed to such radical intervention can be elected within the advanced capitalist states is problematic however. Supporters of the new municipal socialism who acknowledge its economic limitations argue that the main significance of the approach is educative and ideological. It demonstrates that there are alternatives to the economic strategies of the New Right and, equally important, it represents a political challenge to existing policies and priorities which establishes the debate on the national political agenda.

Poverty, wealth and inequality

Accompanying the economic decline of urban economies in recent decades has been the equally dramatic and related increase in poverty and deprivation. Government anti-poverty policies have had two broad objectives — either to reduce unemployment and/or to provide income support for needy families through the social welfare system. *Employment strategies* have sought to increase the supply of jobs (e.g. through job creation and job subsidy projects, and a host of economic development initiatives that may create additional employment), to reduce the supply of labour (e.g. through job sharing or early retirement schemes), or to improve the fit between the skills of the labour force and those required in industry (e.g. by training programmes). A hybrid between the employment- and welfare-based approaches is the *workfare* system which operates in some US states. Increasingly, urban policy has emphasized economic development as central to area regeneration and less emphasis is now attached to comprehensive strategies addressing social and physical as well as economic issues. Initiatives are now primarily designed to lever private sector industrial and commercial development, the assumption being that such activity equates with urban regeneration for local residents. In practice the effect of this policy redirection has been a concentration on areas of economic potential and the neglect of those areas, such as the large peripheral estates, where poverty and deprivation are most pronounced. As a result many of the council estates of urban Britain have become 'pools of immobile surplus labour' (Moore and Booth 1986: 364). In the field of public *social welfare policy* there is evidence that an important cause of acute poverty is the failure of some people to receive their full complement of benefits (Alcock 1986). This problem may be addressed by establishing local centres to advise on welfare rights, and through take-up campaigns targetted on particular vulnerable areas. These ad hoc approaches, however, are unlikely to reduce poverty to any significant extent.

The effort directed towards employment and welfare policies in the attempt to alleviate poverty must not obscure the fact that the disadvantaged position of the urban poor is inextricably related to the privileged position of the wealthy. What is required is a more interventionist approach which addresses the fundamental question of the distribution of poverty and wealth in society. The Royal Commission on the Distribution of Income and Wealth (1975) revealed that the top half of income recipients received 76.0 per cent of total income. The top 20.0 per cent had over seven times the share in total income of the bottom 20.0 per cent (42.7 per cent against 5.8 per cent). In a review of the impact of progressive income tax the Commission concluded that any shift in relative income was slight and that there was no indication of any consistent trend towards greater equality in the distribution of incomes. Recent figures for the UK indicate that between 1976 and 1983 the distribution of income revealed an *increase* in inequality. Similarly, in terms of wealth there has been little change over the last decade with the richest 1.0 per cent and 10.0 per cent of the adult population owning 20.0 per cent and 54.0 per cent respectively of marketable wealth in 1983 (Central Statistical Office 1986). If poverty and inequality are to be significantly reduced the institutions and principles governing the allocation of resources must be reconstructed. Put simply, in order to improve the situation of the poor it is necessary to reduce the power, privilege and affluence of the rich. For Townsend (1979) an effective redistributive policy to tackle poverty would include a statutory definition of maximum permissible earnings and wealth. Such a radical strategy is unlikely to gain acceptance in advanced capitalist societies however. More realistic is the suggestion to alter the means of financing the social security system which, at present, largely involves a horizontal redistribution from the occupied (principally middle aged and employed) to the unoccupied (unemployed, ageing and old) members of the labour force. The alternative is to effect a vertical redistribution — i.e. improve the standard of living of the poor by reducing that of the wealthy, possibly through the operation of the taxation system. No single approach whether based on employment or social welfare initiatives will resolve the complex of urban social and economic problems that stem from poverty. To approach this goal will require a complementary programme comprising 'people policies' operating over a long term at the structural scale (e.g. to achieve wealth redistribution in society) and more immediate local level 'place policies' to improve the current position of the disadvantaged.

Chapter four

Territorial justice

A major paradox in modern societies is revealed by contrasting the popular support for the doctrine of egalitarianism and the pervasive inequalities that characterize most populations. In this chapter we will focus on inequality in relation to (a) collective consumption, (b) exclusionary zoning, and (c) electoral geography. The underlying theme is that of territorial justice, a concept which is essentially a spatial extrapolation of Marx's dictum 'to each according to his needs'.

Collective consumption

Collective consumption refers to all collectively organized and managed services consumed via non-market mechanisms and at least partly paid for from the public purse. The importance of collective consumption in contemporary society is considerable. As Tietze (1968: 36) observed, 'modern urban man is born in a publicly-financed hospital, receives his education in a publicly-supported school and university, spends a good part of his life travelling on publicly-built transportation facilities, communicates through the post office or the quasi-public telephone system, drinks his public water, disposes of his garbage through the public removal system, reads his public library books, picnics in his public parks, is protected by his public police, fire and health systems; eventually he dies, again in a hospital, and may even be buried in a public cemetery. Ideological conservatives notwithstanding, his everyday life is inextricably bound up with governmental decisions on these and numerous other local public services.' Households with limited personal resources (i.e. access to *private* consumption goods and services) and mobility may well gauge their quality of life in terms of the public goods and services available locally. For them the question of territorial justice in service distribution is of paramount importance.

The justness of patterns of collective consumption may be measured by comparing the distribution of resources among political or administrative units with some normative criteria. The choice of criterion can range from locational efficiency to equity based on social need. The specification of these terms is fraught with difficulty however. Bradshaw (1974), for example, recognized four different ways of defining 'need'. The meaning of equity in public service provision must also be clarified. Some argue that equity is enhanced when services are distributed in proportion to taxes paid, while others contend that equity requires allocation of services in proportion to need. What is clear is that equity should not be confused with equality. The difficulty is that citizens are not equal in their service needs or preferences. Thus, demonstrating that they receive equal services indicates little about how well they are served (the effectiveness of the system). The concept of equity employed here stems from the idea that 'one of the more important purposes of government in contemporary western society is to offset the burdens imposed on some groups by the operation of the market economy, so that a greater equality of life chances is achieved. An equitable arrangement is then one which promotes greater equality of condition. Services are equally distributed when everyone gets the same services. They are equitably distributed when citizens are in a more nearly equal life circumstance than before' (Rich 1979: 152). Further, in order to gauge equity we must focus on outcome rather than output measures of services. Put simply, while the latter are the products of agency activities (e.g. the number of public transit passengers carried) outcomes are the changes in relevant social conditions brought about by a service.

A major issue in public service provision is the degree to which justness has to be traded off against efficiency. As the history of the public sector in Britain and USA testifies the importance attached to each of these concepts varies with the economic and political climate. In USA the criterion of economy and efficiency of urban services prevailed in the immediate post-war era, while equity and social justice at the local level were important goals of public programmes in the 1960s. Since the election of 'New Right' governments in Britain and USA 'value for money' has re-emerged as a central measure of public service provision. Agencies responsible for various aspects of collective consumption have been encouraged to find ways of 'load shedding' most of which have amounted to various forms of privatization (Savas 1982). The advantages of privatization initiatives include the enhanced involvement and more positive attitudes of citizens toward government, and increased production efficiency (i.e. lower costs). A major negative and socially regressive consequence stems from the fact that some citizens are better able than others to supplement reduced public services or replace those transferred to the private market. Further, the services which the city continues to provide may be in a form that is more costly to consume or simply not accessible for some citizens. Particular problems are experienced by those living in the service-dependent ghettos of North

American inner cities, and the 'cashless society' of some UK public housing estates where the disadvantaged survive on welfare payments and the cash value of services-in-kind targetted to them.

As Warren (1986) contends, what is required in considering the equity-efficiency relationship is a broader understanding of the costs factor. The efficiency of a public service is usually measured in terms of agency production costs. Inclusion of the costs borne by citizens attempting to acquire and use the service, however, radically alters the meaning and measurement of efficiency and introduces the concept of equity into the calculation. This 'equality of access' perspective takes the view that no matter how low the unit cost of an urban service this is not an adequate measure of efficiency if the service is not accessible except at additional cost, or is unusable by citizens for whom it is intended. Citizen costs, apart from tax contributions to public service production costs, are of two types. First, are *participation costs* represented by the time, effort and money expended in influencing community decision-making. Federal government attempts to provide for 'maximum feasible participation' of low-income and minority groups in policy making were designed to reduce such participation costs. Second, *consumption costs* are those that a potential user must pay to obtain the service. Completing innumerable forms or travelling long distances are simple examples. Neither equity nor efficiency can be determined adequately without considering the type, amount and distribution of consumption and participation costs which it may be necessary for citizens to incur before having effective use of a service.

Some degree of unjustness in the provision of collective services exists in all cities at all times not least because the relationship between needs and resources is a dynamic one and the equation is only rarely in balance. Given the inevitability of some unjustness the crucial question is whether this exhibits a systematic pattern in relation to the social geography of cities. Several hypotheses have been examined including the 'underclass hypothesis' which suggests that economically disadvantaged groups and areas are actively discriminated against in terms of service provision. As articulated by Lineberry (1977) this subsumes three overlapping hypotheses — the existence of a power elite capable of manipulating the distribution of public resources, the 'race preference' hypothesis which posits discrimination against blacks, and the 'class preference' hypothesis which indicates discrimination against low-income communities in general. While some qualified support for the underclass hypothesis has been found in the distribution of some services in some cities (Weicher 1971, Mladenka and Hill 1977), the general weight of evidence points to a situation of 'unpatterned inequality' with most urban communities favoured by some service delivery patterns and disadvantaged by others. Thus Levy *et al.* (1974) in Oakland found that library resources and roads tended to favour the upper-income areas while black areas tended to receive preferential treatment in relation to teacher supply. However, the fact that the more skilled and experienced teachers moved to the richer areas when vacancies became available indicates the difficulty of including measures of service quality in such analyses. Lineberry (1977) on the basis of a study of San Antonio suggested that within given total levels of provision the decision rules adopted by local bureaucrats are the most significant single factor in the distribution of local public services. These decision rules almost inevitably favour some groups over others but each rule may favour a different group so that there is no consistent bias against any group or area across services. The fact that such empirically identified 'unpatterned inequality' does not relate well to the all too evident disparities in life quality within cities is clearly attributable to differences in the *private* wealth of the inhabitants. This is particularly the case in the American city where a significant number of services are purchased in the private sector.

Adopting the broader definition of costs which brings equity and efficiency considerations together reveals several circumstances which affect the capacity of groups and individuals to consume public goods. These include situations in which mandated public services are (a) not produced, (b) provided in smaller quantities or are of lower quality than available in other areas or to other groups, (c) not consumable, and (d) not accessible without additional costs that may not be equally distributed among areas or groups and may be prohibitively high for some. Each of these cases underlines the importance of the study of *outcomes* for policy analysis.

A notorious incidence of the failure to provide services and of discrimination in delivery was revealed in the court case of *Hawkins v the Town of Shaw, Mississippi* (1971). In this small town 97.0 per cent of the homes without sanitary sewers were black dwelling units and 98.0 per cent of all houses fronting on unpaved streets were in black neighbourhoods. There were also significant disparities in the provision of fire hydrants and stop lights (Anderson 1972). Similar patterns of service inequalities have been judicially recognized in other communities (Warren 1986). Not all cases are so clear cut however. In the 1972 *Beale v Lindsay* case the US Appeals Court ruled in favour of the City of New York against citizens of a Puerto Rican district who contended that the park in their area of the Bronx was in significantly greater disrepair than three others in white neighbourhoods. The city's argument that it had actually allocated more resources to the park in question and that its poor condition was due to vandalism was accepted by the court which concluded that the city was constitutionally responsible only for equal input among neighbourhoods and not equal output (Rossum 1980). This decision carries the implication that the vandalism which reduced the utility of the facility was the responsibility of the area residents and was not, therefore, the outcome of the city's failure to provide adequate levels of other services such as law enforcement.

Services may be made available but not used by citizens because they are either 'non consumable' or too costly. Until recently, most public transport was largely unusable for handicapped citizens (Rosenbloom 1982). The US Head Start programme acknowledged that the standard education package was not consumable by children from poor and minority families entering the first grade. Similarly, the Supreme Court in the case of *Lau v Nichols* found that the rights of Chinese-speaking children in San Francisco to an education could not be met without having classes in Chinese. Consumption costs can assume a variety of forms, physical, financial, and psychological. Most apparent are the physical costs, in terms of time and effort, involved in obtaining welfare-related services. Further examples include the increased financial costs of rehabilitated houses in urban renewal schemes which effectively priced-out original residents. Other consumption costs attached to some public housing projects include the disruption of friendship ties, administrative restrictions and stigmatization. MacDonald (1977) has also noted how the procedures required to obtain and use US food stamps gives rise to stigma costs for recipients, while Page (1984) in England and Ringeling (1981) in Netherlands refer to the psychological costs of consuming unemployment, sickness or supplementary benefits.

During times of resource scarcity and political conservatism in the public sector strategies adopted by public officials to reduce production costs are likely to increase consumption costs, particularly for politically and economically marginal groups. A socially just distribution of public goods and services must recognize the interrelationship between the criteria of equity and efficiency and must be based upon a proper assessment of all of the costs involved.

To date, most effort in applied urban research has been directed towards solving the quintessentially spatial problem of the optimum location for a public facility.

Public facility location

The chief physical component of public facility costs is that attached to overcoming the friction of distance. Public facility planners seek locations which minimize production and distribution costs and maximize accessibility to citizens. For consumers, accessibility to public facilities confers opportunity and choice, enhances the use value of a residential property, minimizes travel costs thereby releasing more household income for expenditure on consumption and can increase the exchange value of a property. Lack of physical accessibility can carry penalties above those arising from the cost and inconvenience of travel. Inaccessibility to health care facilities has been shown to have an effect on therapeutic behaviour with people living beyond a convenient distance (often as little as 0.75 km) from their family doctor tending to make light of symptoms or endure discomfort and uncertainty (Knox 1979). Specific sub-groups in the city, the elderly, handicapped, ethnic minorities, the young and women have particular accessibility-related difficulties (Muller 1976).

Applied social scientists have studied this location-accessibility problem in relation to a range of individual services including shopping (Bowlby 1979), police protection (Bloch 1974), primary medical care (Knox 1978), dental care (Bradley *et al*. 1978), social services (Savas 1979), recreational facilities (Robertson 1978), educational resources (A. Kirby 1979) and public libraries (Cole and Catrell 1986).

Two main approaches to resolving the location-accessibility problem have been employed. The first, focusing on *personal accessibility* involves the identification and manipulation of space–time prisms based on the activity patterns of different population sub-groups. The second based on a modelling approach to *locational accessibility* involves measures which weight units of separation (such as distance) against the number of destinations available.

Personal accessibility

The time–space approach to personal accessibility studies the environment of resources and opportunities which surrounds each individual. The basic premise is that evaluation of accessibility levels should concentrate not on what people do or are likely to do but on what they are able to do. Each individual has his own 'action space' which limits the activities s/he can engage in. The time–space budget of any individual can be depicted grapahically by representing distance along a horizontal axis and time along a vertical axis; the *effective* action space of a person during the day is then described by a prism. As Figure 4.1 shows the shape of the prism depends on the available mode of transport. The time–space budgets of some population sub-groups will permit more effective access to opportunities than will those of others. One group particularly vulnerable to time-related constraints are women. For certain periods of the day she may be confined to the home — until 9.00 by sleep and family commitments, from 12.00 to 13.00 by family lunch time, from 16.00 to 18.00 when she welcomes children from school and prepares tea, and after 22.00 when she again prepares for bed. The challenge for accessibility planning is first to determine the dimensions of the action space of population sub-groups, and secondly to expand it or to place more opportunities within it.

65

Figure 4.1 The space–time realm of a housewife

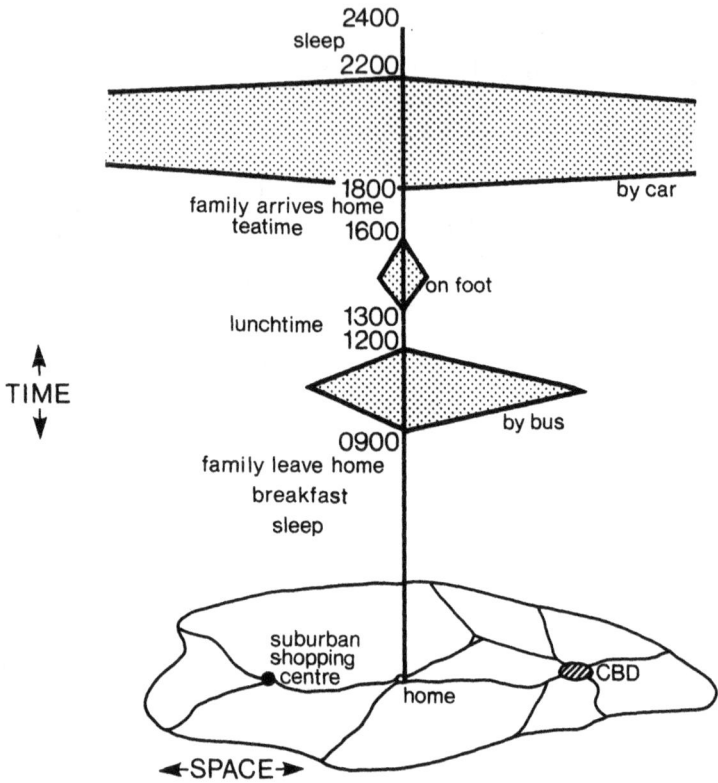

2400
sleep
2200

1800
family arrives home
teatime   1600

on foot

lunchtime   1300
1200

TIME

by bus

0900
family leave home
breakfast
sleep

suburban
shopping
centre
home

CBD

◄SPACE►

Source: adapted from Moseley 1979

Locational accessibility

Although the final decision about the allocation of all public resources
is a political one locational optimizing models can play a useful role by
(a) affording a means of evaluating different combinations of equity and
efficiency, and (b) providing evidence of 'better' solutions to support
a case against inefficient or inequitable proposals. The outcome of an
optimizing model depends on its objectives and constraints (e.g. to
minimize travel cost, maximize demand or maximize equity). Examples
of some possible algorithms are provided by Hodgart (1978). The general
aim of a location pattern for a set of public facilities is (a) to be as near

as possible to the demand in order to reduce transport costs and (b) to keep the cost of establishing the facilities as low as possible both by choosing low-cost locations and by reducing the number of facilities to be established. Some trade-off is usually necessary between these two goals and the task of an optimum location model is to suggest a pattern which best satisfies these, or any other set of required goals. Examples of models which seek to resolve the equity–efficiency trade-off are provided by ReVelle *et al.* (1970, 1976). The particular problem of designing educational catchments illustrates the utility of multivariate modelling techniques which can accommodate questions relating to the location of individual school zone boundaries, the adjustment of enrolments at various schools to eliminate overcrowding, selecting the best locations for new schools and for new classrooms at existing facilities, rationalization of educational systems in view of population change, and delimiting catchments to eliminate racial segregation (Bailey 1982, Woodall *et al.* 1980, Thomas and Robson 1984, Sutcliffe and Board 1986, Pacione 1989).

Exclusionary zoning

Problems stemming from the practice of exclusionary zoning arise in USA as a direct result of the political organization of metropolitan areas. In contrast to the strong degree of central control exercised over the structure of urban local government in UK, local government is more complex and fragmented. Another important difference is that in the American context central government relates to the state governments and not to federal government which has no direct control over local government. The basic element of local government in almost every state is the county. Within this, municipalities may be incorporated to govern defined areas provided they meet threshold requirements of population size and density. The process of incorporation has been of particular importance in determining the social-economic composition of the American metropolis. Generally incorporation follows a petition to the state legislature from the residents of an area and a referendum of all residents. Most importantly, once incorporated a municipality acquires certain statutory powers including that of land-use zoning. This administrative independence conveys several advantages to suburbanites. These include:

1 Local governments raise taxes on local property values and residents must pay taxes only to cover the costs of services within their own municipality. Affluent suburban residents can therefore avoid sharing the costs of social consumption for the inner city poor.
2 Residents of independent municipalities can insulate themselves from the political activities of larger places in which their interests may be outvoted.

3   The land-use planning powers of municipalities enable residents to manipulate zoning schemes to exclude undesirable land uses and users (e.g. industry, the poor, and blacks).

Figure 4.2 Municipalities of the Denver urban area

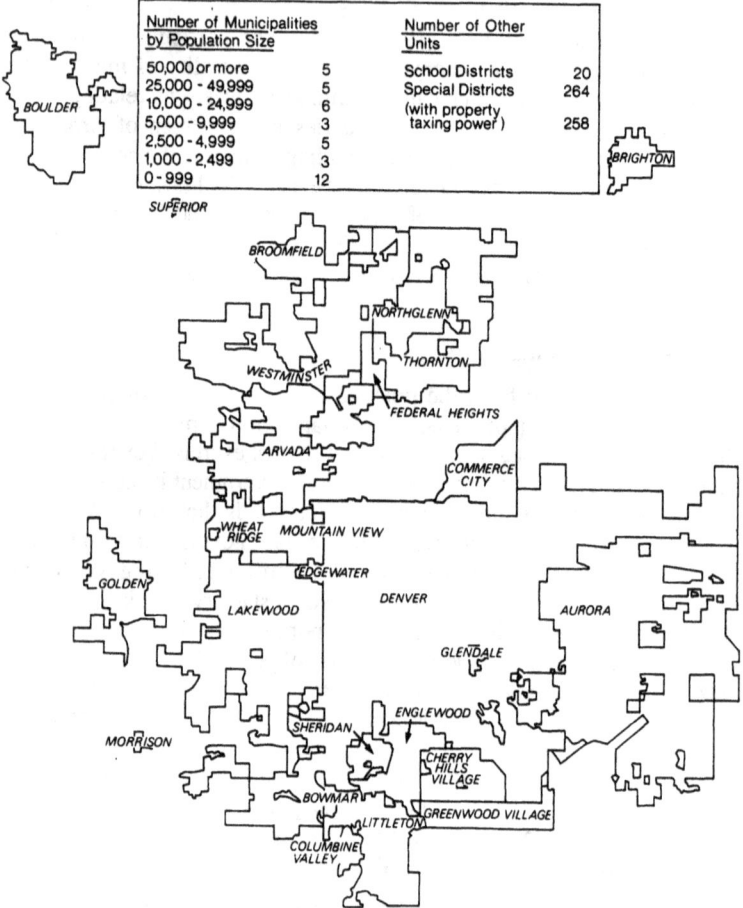

Number of Municipalities by Population Size		Number of Other Units	
50,000 or more	5	School Districts	20
25,000 - 49,999	5	Special Districts	264
10,000 - 24,999	6	(with property	
5,000 - 9,999	3	taxing power)	258
2,500 - 4,999	5		
1,000 - 2,499	3		
0 - 999	12		

Source: adapted from Johnston 1982b, p. 230–2

In 1977 there were 18,862 municipalities in USA, 6,444 of which were in the 272 SMSAs. Most of these were small with 3,241 having populations of less than 2,500 and only 392 (including the central city of most of the SMSAs) having more than 50,000. The Chicago SMSA alone had 261 municipalities. The political geography of the Denver SMSA is shown in Figure 4.2 which also serves to illustrate the impact of *differential zoning*. Small exclusive residential suburbs inhabited by high-income families and zoned for a single land use to dominate are represented by Bow Mar, Columbine Valley, Greenwood and Cherry Hills. As Figure 4.3 shows most of Cherry Hills is zoned for a minimum building lot of 2.5 acres and very little of the municipality is zoned for a density of less than one acre per house. Not all exclusive residential municipalities are zoned for such low densities and, therefore, high income residents. Glendale is zoned almost entirely for apartments. Federal Heights has large areas zoned for mobile homes, and Mountain View is occupied by medium-income groups (with an average dwelling value of $11,000 compared to $54,000 for Cherry Hills). The larger middle-income suburbs to the west of Denver seek to attract, rather than repel, non-residential land uses in order to use their contributions to the property tax base to hold down residents' tax bills and subsidise the provision of municipal services. In this they are competing for property tax revenue both with each other and with the central city. The administrative fragmentation of suburbia is accentuated in most states by the existence of other local government institutions, notably school districts. The separate existence of these single-function authorities is a major attraction for suburbanites wishing to control the social and demographic character of school catchments.

In 1977 there were 15,174 school districts in the country. The Chicago SMSA had 315, of which 75 operated one school only. The mosaic of administrative units is completed by ad hoc special districts set up to carry out a particular function, e.g. volunteer fire districts or districts set up to avoid constitutional limitations on municipal revenue-raising in order to finance certain desired services. The multiplicity of local government units in American urban areas, particularly the suburbs is a key element in their social and economic geography. Attempts to overcome the social and economic problems arising from metropolitan fragmentation and the practice of exclusionary zoning have taken a variety of forms. The legality of exclusionary zoning has been challenged in the courts, with mixed success. Particular attention has been focused on the issues of residential segregation and schooling.

1   Residential segregation — Most legal challenges to *exclusionary zoning* in USA have been brought under the 'equal protection clause' or Fourteenth Amendment of the American Constitution. In general, however, the Supreme Court has refused to hear such cases, arguing that zoning is a right granted to local governments by *state* constitutions and not by the federal constitution. The Court has indicated that it is

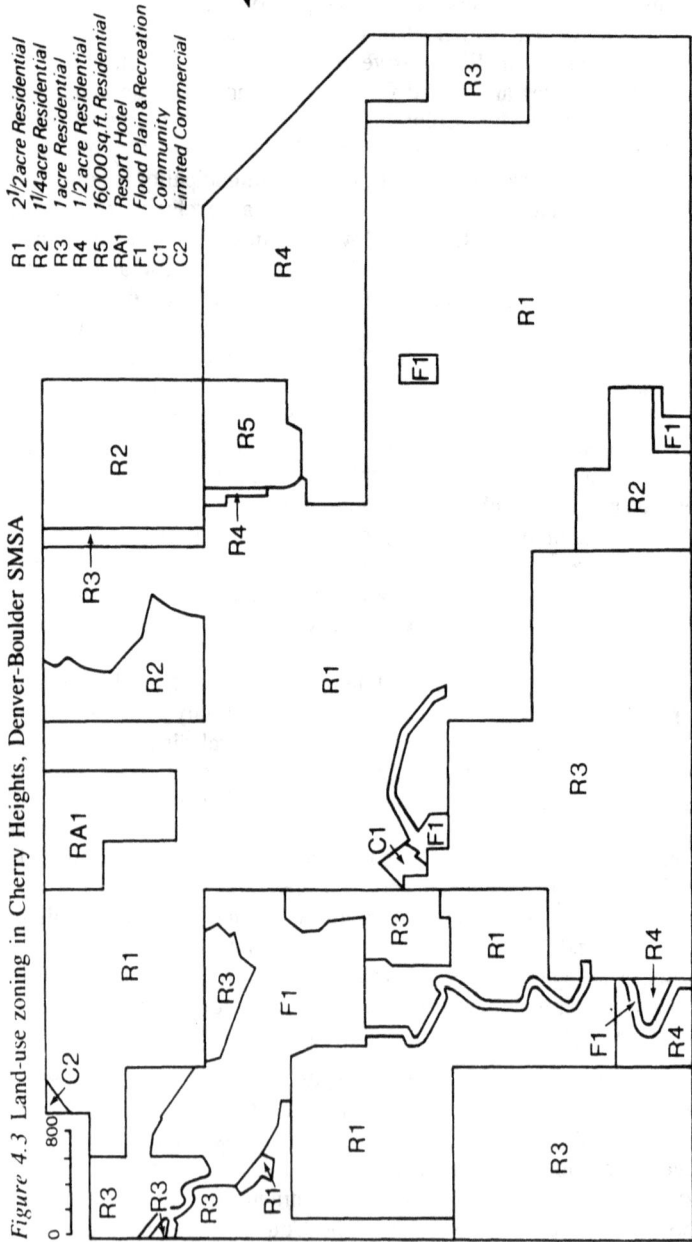

Figure 4.3 Land-use zoning in Cherry Heights, Denver-Boulder SMSA

R1	2½ acre Residential
R2	1¼ acre Residential
R3	1 acre Residential
R4	1/2 acre Residential
R5	16000 sq. ft. Residential
RA1	Resort Hotel
F1	Flood Plain & Recreation
C1	Community
C2	Limited Commercial

Source: Johnston 1984: 32

prepared to intervene where legislation contradicts 'fundamental rights' or where it has drawn 'suspect classifications' between sets of individuals. Fundamental rights are those explicitly or implicitly protected by the US constitution. Explicit rights include freedom of assembly, speech and religion. Examples of implicit rights are the right to travel and to privacy. The major disputes have centred on the range of implicit rights. The case of *Lindsey v Normet* (1971) found that decent housing was not a constitutional right, and generally the Supreme Court has adopted a relatively narrow definition of fundamental right. The Supreme Court's decisions on 'suspect classifications' has also worked against those seeking access to suburban housing. In cases, such as *James v Valtierra* (1971), the Court has refused to accept wealth as a suspect classification and has dismissed claims that discrimination by wealth is *de facto* racial discrimination. The difficulty of seeking redress by means of the Fourteenth Amendment was emphasized by the finding in *Arlington Heights v Metropolitan Housing Authority* (1977) that 'proof of a racially discriminatory motive, purpose, or intent is required to find a violation of the Fourteenth Amendment' (Mandelker 1977: 1236) — in other words, differential *impact* is insufficient evidence of *intent*. One further hurdle, demonstrated in the *Warth v Seldin* (1975) judgement, restricts the use of the court to those individuals and corporate bodies able to prove personal injury as a result of the claimed discriminatory acts. The purpose of the 'standing' doctrine is to ensure that the courts are not bogged down with frivolous suits but an effect has been to exclude third parties. In the Warth case, a number of plaintiffs alleged that the zoning ordinance of Penfield, New York excluded persons of low and moderate income from the town. However, they personally had not been rejected by the town in applying for a building permit and the developers whose rights may have been violated had not applied for building permission because on past evidence they 'knew' the application would be denied (Pearlman 1978). In general, therefore, the 'voice' strategy via the Supreme Court has failed to alter the social geography of suburban USA.

An alternative source of redress for non-resident black plaintiffs denied low-income housing in suburban municipalities is the Fair Housing Act (1968). The important difference between the standards of proof of discrimination under the Fourteenth Amendment and the Fair Housing Act are documented by Clark (1981). Most significantly, whereas the former requires evidence of *intent* the latter requires only a demonstration of discriminatory *effect*. However, although the 1968 Fair Housing Act outlawed discriminatory practices it has achieved little 'opening up of the suburbs'. Eliminating discrimination does nothing to overcome the basic economic inability of blacks to afford suburban housing. If the aim is integration then positive action to provide low-income housing is required. Some progress in this direction was made by the Housing and Community Development Act (1974) This makes the granting of Community Development Block Grants contingent upon a community submitting an acceptable Housing Assistance Plan (HAP) which assess the needs of low-income persons residing or expecting to reside in the community as a result of existing or projected employment opportunities (Clark 1982). Clearly though small affluent municipalities may decide to forego federal aid rather than meet these conditions. Until 1982 the HAP was also used in allocating Section 8 low-income housing certificates among suburban communities receiving block grants (Clark 1984). In all cases evidence of underrepresentation of low-income or racial groups allows the Court to require remedial action ('complex relief'). Wherever complex relief is granted a judgement must be made regarding the amount of housing to be incorporated in the zoning ordinance or constructed. The key question is how many low-income persons would be 'expected to reside' within the municipality in the absence of discrimination. One of the most successful examples of affirmative relief is the case of *United States v Parma* (1980). Parma, one of the largest suburbs of Cleveland, was found to have engaged in a systematic attempt to exclude blacks by blocking the construction of new low-income housing. To this end the city had refused to co-operate with the regional housing agency, denied building permits, passed ordinances setting restrictive height limits, required public referenda on all low-income housing proposals and submitted an HAP which the Department of Housing and Urban Development rejected because it indicated no additional low-income housing was needed. Citing HUDs estimate of the city's need at 2,669 units the Court directed Cleveland to begin building them — at a rate of 137 per year.

More successful challenges to exclusionary zoning have been made in the state courts which may interpret their own constitutions differently from Supreme Court interpretations of the federal constitution. Pennsylvania rejected exclusionary zoning in a series of cases between 1965 and 1975; and, in the Mount Laurel decision (1975), New Jersey required expanding communities to accept their 'fair share' of regional low- and moderate-income housing needs. Legislation to counter the effects of exclusionary zoning has also been passed in New York (Davidoff and Davidoff 1971) and Massachusetts (Krefetz 1979) although, as elsewhere, dogged resistance by suburbanites has reduced its impact. Between 1969 and 79 only 3,600 low- and medium-income units were actually built under the 'anti-snob zoning' law in Massachusetts with, significantly, most designed for elderly as opposed to family housing. A negative 'stick' approach such as the threat of state intervention clearly is not sufficient to overcome resistance. Positive 'carrots' such as state or federal guarantees to cover the local costs of servicing such developments, thereby relieving pressure on the municipal property tax, are necessary. Such strategies, however, will not overcome racial prejudice or fears over possible reduction in the exchange-value of middle-class housing in the affected suburbs.

2 Schooling — A similar general belief that multi-racial schooling would have a regressive effect on white children has led to several means of preserving the white public school system being employed. These include —

(a) The provision of 'separate but equal' school systems.
(b) Use of a 'neighbourhood schooling' policy and delimitation of catchments which given the residential segregation of blacks, ensured that most black or white children attended a school dominated by their own race.
(c) The creation of separate suburban school districts whose racial and social charcter can be controlled via the zoning mechanism.

The first of these strategies was employed widely in the southern states until it was successfully challenged in the case of *Brown v Board of Education of Topeka* (1954). Although this decision required school boards to remedy the situation as soon as practicable there was considerable 'playing for time' and it was not until 1971, in the case of *Swann v Charlotte-Mecklenburg Board of Education*, that busing was ruled as necessary to achieve desegregation in areas with little spatial mixing of the races (Lowry 1973). The two other strategies have been employed particularly in northern metropolitan areas. Figure 4.4 illustrates ways in which the combination of the neighbourhood schooling principle and judicious arrangement of catchment areas could affect the racial composition of school areas. Actions to eradicate such practices have generally been brought under the Fourteenth Amendment clause which meant that plaintiffs must prove not only that such practices were in existence but that they had been enacted with intent to discriminate on racial grounds. The first important decision was in 1973 when segregation in part of Denver was found to be a deliberate result of school board policies. Subsequent decisions of the Supreme Court have ruled as unconstitutional many of the local managerial practices that had been operated to segregate black and white pupils. This has not, however, prevented the development of other practices which did not infringe the constitution. Two examples illustrate the point.

If a school district is ordered to desegregate, parents who do not wish their children to attend integrated schools can either transfer them to the private sector or migrate to another school district. The resulting central city to suburban movement ('white flight') means that racial integration in metropolitan schools can only be effected by amalgamating separate school districts. This was the basis of the plaintiffs argument in the case of *Millicken v Bradley* (1974) which

Figure 4.4 Promotion of de facto school segregation. (a) Pre-existing locations of schools with catchments conforming to neighbourhood school principle. (b) Location of a fifth school with catchment conforming to neighbourhood shool principle. (c) Location of a fifth school with catchment conforming to neighbourhood school principle and three schools with substantial racial mixing.

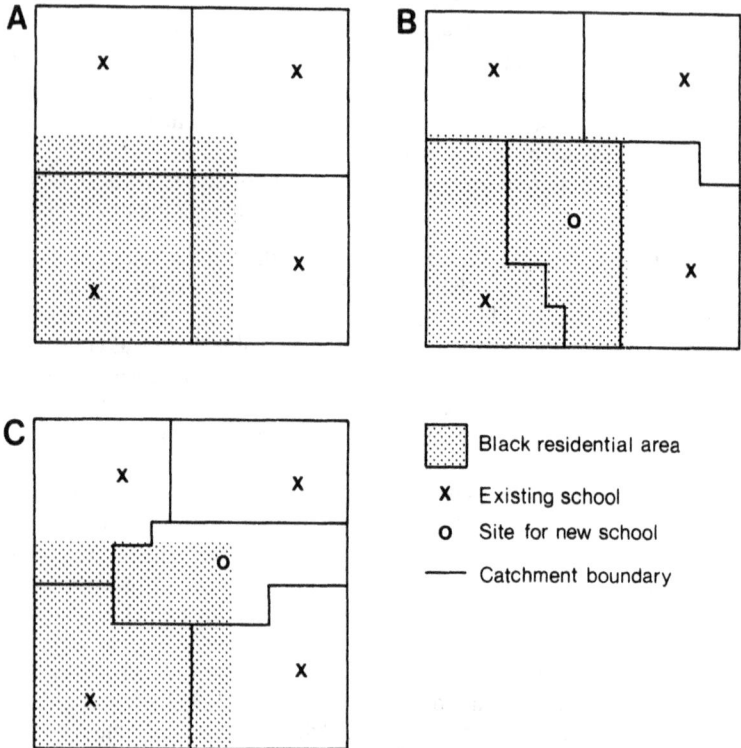

Source: Johnston 1984: 117

referred to the Detroit metropolitan area. The Court ruled against such a solution, however, deciding that local autonomy was more important than its segregation consequences. The Supreme Court's stance against inter-district solutions has protected the position of those involved in white flight to the suburbs in order to avoid integrated schools. The Court has also declined to intervene in regard to inter-district disparities in school financing. This can result in major discrepancies in the quality of education received since there is ample evidence that white middle-class pupils receive higher quality teachers and more capital equipment than schools with lower class and/or black enrollments (Cox 1979). Recently the Court has also questioned the appropriateness and effectiveness of the busing strategy (Johnston 1984). The second example refers to resegregation. The Supreme Court decision in *Swann v Charlotte-Mecklenburg* noted that neither school officials nor district courts are constitutionally required to make regular adjustments of the racial composition of student bodies once the affirmative action to desegregate has been accomplished and racial discrimination through official action eliminated from the system. This was reaffirmed in *Pasadena Board of Education v Spangler* when it was decided that the segregation effects of normal patterns of human migration did not infringe the principle of integrated schools.

Clearly, any strategy which fails to address the structural problem of the political balkanization of suburban USA can be only a partial solution to the social, economic and fiscal difficulties of disadvantaged residents and municipalities. While some moves in this direction have been made via inter-governmental transfer of functions and services, and inter-municipal co-operation (Barlow 1981) progress towards consolidated metropolitan government has been slow, not least because a unified governmental structure would remove most of the economic and social advantages enjoyed by most suburban municipalities.

Electoral injustice

All electoral systems contain biases and so are susceptible to manipulation by those who wish to ensure that the biases work in their favour. The two main methods of engineering electoral injustices are by malapportionment and gerrymandering. Electoral malapportionment is the deliberate creation of constituencies of different sizes for the benefit of one party. The English 'rotten boroughs' of the early nineteenth century where the M.P.s occasionally outnumbered the voters were the most notorious examples. As the hypothetical situation in Figure 4.5 illustrates deliberate malapportionment involves devaluing an opponent's votes by creating above average constituencies in areas where your opponent has an electoral majority and below average constituencies where you are powerful, thus maximizing your opponent's 'excess' votes (Johnston 1979).

Gerrymandering has been a relatively common strategy to bias the democratic process in favour of a ruling party. Busteed (1975) has noted how it has been used to dilute Catholic political strength in Londonderry, while Figure 4.6 provides a graphic illustration from a 1971 proposal

Figure 4.5 Hypothetical example of malapportionment showing: (a) The distribution of votes for parties X and Y in 25 areas; and (b) a set of five constituencies designed to maximize seat-winning for Y

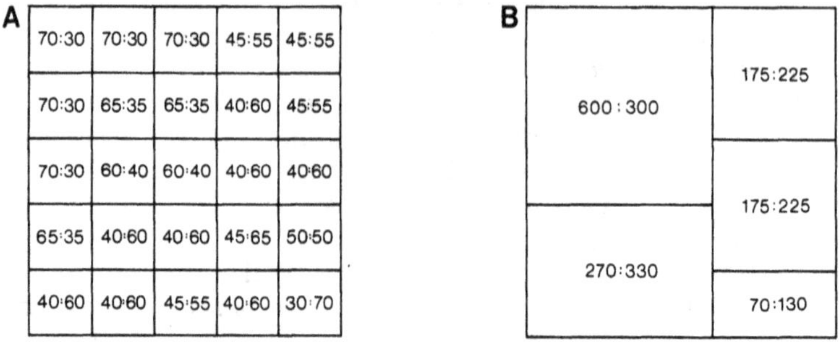

A				
70:30	70:30	70:30	45:55	45:55
70:30	65:35	65:35	40:60	45:55
70:30	60:40	60:40	40:60	40:60
65:35	40:60	40:60	45:65	50:50
40:60	40:60	45:55	40:60	30:70

B

600 : 300	175:225
270:330	175:225
	70:130

Source: Johnston 1979: 159

by the majority Democrats for a reapportionment of electoral district boundaries in Philadelphia. While each district conforms well with the equal population criterion the irregular geography was designed to produce a partisan electoral result. For example, district 196 in the north of the city runs for 4.5 miles in the clear intent to submerge the Republican vote of the inner suburbs beneath the Democratic strength in the inner city. Perhaps the most blatant example of partisan cartography was the attempt by the town of Tuskegee, Alabama to disenfranchise black voters by rearranging the town boundaries from a square shape to a twenty-eight sided figure.

The main problem with gerrymanders is that while the result is usually apparent the intent is difficult to prove. The Tuskegee case apart, legal challenges to electoral district boundaries on grounds of racial vote dilution have frequently failed because plaintiffs were unable to show evidence of discriminatory intent on the part of the redistricting authorities, and because no accepted measure of gerrymandering has been developed. One possible solution is to remove the districting process from the political arena and entrust the task to an independent non-political body, as in UK. However, partisan solutions can still arise in two ways. The first entails a process of benign neglect or 'silent gerrymandering' under which no action is taken on the committee's recommendations if redistricting would be disadvantageous to the party in power. The second stems from the fact that although the neutrality of bodies such as the English Boundary Commission is beyond doubt the rules under which they operate are politically defined and may introduce biases to the procedure. Even use

Figure 4.6 Gerrymandering in proposed re-apportionment of electoral district boundaries in Philadelphia, 1971

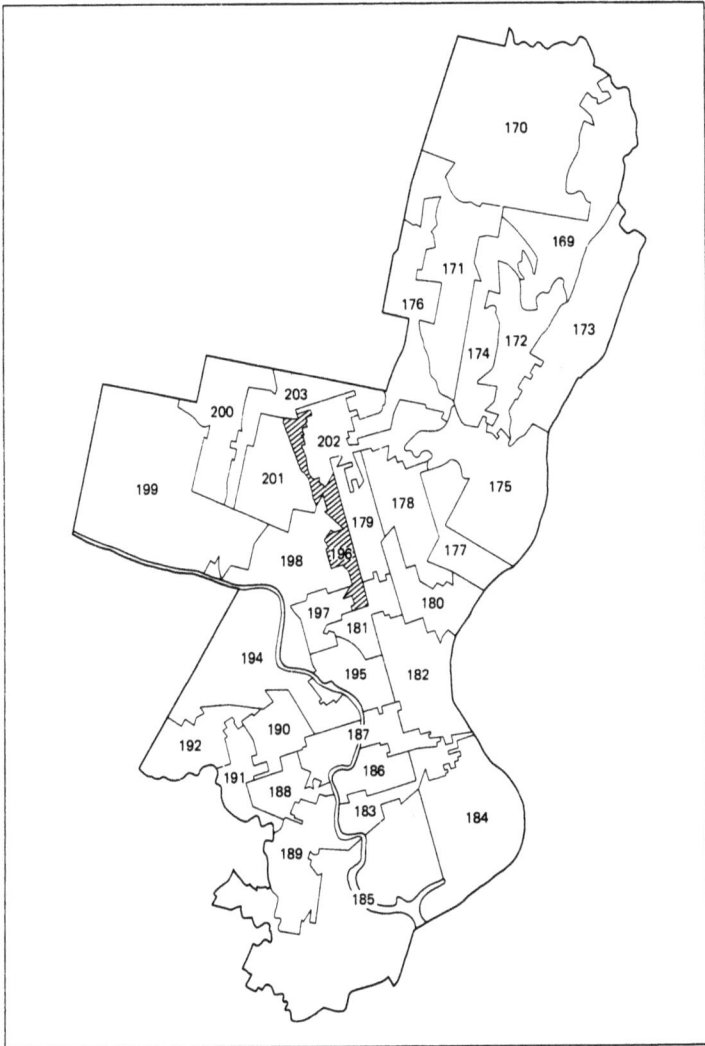

Source: Ley 1983: 364

of 'scientific' algorithms does not exclude subjective influences (Norcliffe 1977). Computer-based redistricting systems (Thompson and Slocum 1982) are powerful tools for designing a set of feasible redistricting plans, but they do not resolve the question of whether they are politically acceptable.

Chapter five

Environmental hazards

The urban environment is a complex social, economic and biophysical system produced by the interaction between a man-made fabric and the physical characteristics of the landscape. In this chapter particular attention is focused on the hazards of urban living contingent upon the physical geography of the city. These vary with the site and location of a city but can include a host of events such as hurricanes (Baker and Patton 1974), flooding (Platt 1982), wind storms (Miller *et al.* 1974), drought (Heathcote 1974), earthquake (Terwindt 1983), snow (Earney and Knowles 1974), landslides (Fleming *et al.* 1979) and ground subsidence (Holzer and Johnston 1985), as well as pollution in its various forms. Here we will examine the incidence of and human response to eight specific urban hazards.

Landslides

While geological surveys are relatively easy to carry out prior to construction or on a green field site, in already built-up areas it is more difficult for the urban geomorphologist to obtain an accurate view of the underlying conditions. In those areas of northern Europe and North America affected by quaternary glaciations many cities are built on glacial drift material. Subsurface water can move at the interface between the drift and underlying rocks or at discontinuities between the products of different phases of glacial deposition. Should urban development take place on a steep hillside under these conditions the consequent alteration in sub-surface hydrology and in the pressures between the different materials in the glacial drift can result in land slipping. Various estimates of the direct and indirect costs of landslides (e.g. loss of tax revenues and reduced real estate values in affected areas, and loss of industrial production due to interruptions to operations and regional transportation) have been made. Krohn and Slassen (1976) estimated the annual direct costs of landslide damage to private buildings and their sites in the US to be $400 million in 1971 dollars. Including indirect costs

Schuster (1978) has calculated the cost of slope failures in the US to be in excess of $1 billion a year. More detailed cost appraisals can be obtained for individual landslide episodes. Particular efforts have been made in California where Taylor and Brabb (1972) estimated the cost of slope movements in nine Bay Area counties during the winter of 1968–69 at at least $25 million. Other studies have attempted to project the costs of landslides for forward planning purposes. Based on the assumption that loss reduction practices in operation in 1970 would remain unchanged, Alfors *et al.* (1973) predicted that the cost of slope movements in California between 1970 and 2000 would be nearly $10 billion or an average of over $300 million per year. Although individual landslides are not as costly as other natural catastrophies such as earthquakes, major floods or tornadoes they are more widespread and the total financial loss due to slope failures is greater than for most other geologic hazards. Much of the damage associated with earthquakes and floods is actually due to landslides triggered by ground shake or water infiltration. In addition to the economic losses, significant loss of human life can result from slope failure, as illustrated by the disasters in Saunders, West Virginia (Davies 1973) and Aberfan, South Wales (Millar 1974).

In planning urban growth, therefore, it is necessary to assess slope stability and to identify situations where human intervention is likely to trigger mass movement. This may require detailed field work to supplement the evidence from geological mapping. For example, planning authorities in the San Francisco region have prepared slope stability maps to indicate the relative extent of landslide hazards. Landslide susceptibility maps are not infallible but they can help to avoid the planning of residential developments in high–risk areas and minimize the remedial cost for the community. More precise guidance on where to locate an individual house, school, hospital or road can be provided by detailed geomorphological maps which show landform features, types of mass movement, breaks of slope, bedrock, sediments, drainage characteristics and slope angles. These are of particular value within a complex geomorphological regime.

The physical production of a geomorphic map, however, is only the first stage in the hazard reduction process. Social science also has an important role to play since the full procedure requires transmission of the research knowledge to planners and decision-makers in local government and eventually action by individuals, community groups or government agencies. As Fleming *et al.* (1979) observe, 'the political implementation of an orderly system designed to reduce hazards and damages is perhaps a more formidable problem than the technical one'. The implementation of technically sound measures is dependent upon the response of various pressure groups which can include those opposed to any regulation on land use (e.g. property developers and real estate interests), and those who do not consider landslides a serious enough problem to justify the effort and cost of a mitigation programme.

While applied urban analysts can act as advocates and expert witnesses in such debates their primary task is to provide the technical information and make recommendations as to the action which can be taken by individuals and government bodies who wish to reduce the hazard. In the USA action commonly takes the form of zoning often with regulations that require geological analysis of the site before, during and following construction. Over the last thirty years the city of Los Angeles has developed a successful landslide reduction programme (Fleming *et al.* 1979). In general, however, a significant gap often exists between identification and public notification of a hazardous locale, and the adoption of appropriate behaviour. As we shall see later this is well illustrated by the experience of the mandated disclosure procedure introduced to reduce the earthquake hazard in California.

Subsidence

Extraction of resources (such as ground water, oil, gas or coal) and/or the compaction of clays and gravels by the weight of building can lead to subsidence in urban areas. Problems due to subsidence include (a) an increased risk of flooding of coastal areas by tides and storm surges necessitating expensive flood control works, (b) regional tilting of land which can affect the functioning of structures, such as canals and sewers, that rely on gravity for their operation, (c) well casing failure which reduces and commonly destroys the productivity of water wells, (d) where subsidence occurs at shallow depth and buildings are founded on firm materials beneath compacting layers, utility connections may be broken, and building access and structural integrity affected, and (e) subsidence may lead to ground failure seen in tension cracks and reactivated faults as in the Houston area of Texas (Holzer *et al.* 1983).

Nelson and Clark (1976) describe how subsidence of up to 10m occurred in the Wilmington oil field Long Beach, Los Angeles. Between 1937 and 1962, 913 million barrels of oil, 484 million barrels of water and 832 billion cu. ft. of gas were extracted from the underlying sediments to a depth of 6,000 ft. As the area was only a few metres above sea level costly sea dykes, drainage systems and elevation of harbour walls was required until subsidence was eventually halted in 1966 by restoring the underground pressure by pumping salt water to replace the oil extracted. Around Phoenix, Arizona extraction of groundwater for irrigation and domestic use (including filling swimming pools) has resulted in subsidence of up to 4m in places. In Cheshire, England salt extraction (initially by rock salt mining and later by brine pumping) has created subsidence problems in adjacent towns as far as 8kms from the production site (Douglas 1983). Similar problems have been experienced in many large cities throughout the world (Holzer and Johnson 1985; Nakano 1975; Pacione 1985a).

Earthquake

Earthquakes are among the least predictable and most intense geographical hazards. On a global scale the seismic events which affect Britain are of minor significance — the most severe on record was centred on Colchester, Essex in 1884 and inflicted damage to 1,200 buildings and caused three deaths. Most British earthquakes are associated with small movements along fault lines. Nevertheless the construction of sensitive structures like nuclear power stations and the need to find geologically stable locations for the storage of radioactive wastes mean that even such minor seismic disturbances are of concern to resident populations. In addition to fault related earthquakes, locally significant tremors which cause property damage and reduce housing values are common in mining areas as a result of subsidence, while minor earthquakes may be artificially induced through the filling of large reservoirs.

The earthquake hazard is more serious in Japan and western USA which are part of the Pacific seismic belt responsible for about 80 per cent of the world's earthquakes. Nearly 90 per cent of the seismic activity of the continental USA occurs in Western Nevada and California, the latter state being an area of pronounced immigration and population growth in recent decades. Several major earthquakes have affected California over the last century including the 1906 San Francisco earthquake which (at 8.3 on the Richter scale) caused 700 deaths and losses of $1.6 billion at 1958 prices. Experts are agreed that the main question is *when* rather than if another major earthquake will occur. According to Mukerjee (1971: 10) 'between 1971 and 2000 we may expect a major earthquake in the San Francisco Bay area of magnitude around 8 Richter and duration of more than a minute. The expected damage to assets would run to 25 billions of dollars at 1970 prices, and loss of life may be in the hundreds or thousands depending on the time of day the quake strikes and the adjustments that are made prior to the disaster and afterwards.' Given the high probability of another major seismic event and the postulated gap between human awareness of a risk and positive action it is instructive to examine the attitudes and response of residents within the California earthquake hazard area.

Several US laws require that environmental information be provided to consumers. For example, the federal government requires that lenders notify prospective buyers that property is located within a flood hazard area as defined by the Federal Insurance Administrator when communities are part of the federally subsidized flood insurance programme. The California mandated disclosure legislation is part of this genre and was introduced in 1975 in an attempt to reduce earthquake risks by providing residents with information on the location of fault rupture zones. Specifically, the Alquist-Priolo Special Studies Zones Act required disclosure to prospective buyers if the location of a property (developed or undeveloped) was within one-eighth of a mile of a fault trace. In theory, based on the assumption that most human behaviour is risk aversive, such information should lead to an appropriate mitigation strategy by home-buyers — e.g. avoidance of the area or at least an attempt to reduce the risk through purchase of insurance. In an empirical survey of two earthquake hazard zones in Berkeley and central Contra Costa County, Palm (1981) found that the disclosure legislation (based on maps prepared by the state geologist) had little measurable impact on buyer or market behaviour. The explanation for such seemingly irrational behaviour must be sought in the value systems of buyers, the role of information agents (the property developers or real estate agents), and the nature of the disclosure legislation. For most buyers, the risk from an earthquake (as well as from other hazards) was considered to be a relatively unimportant factor in making a property purchase, the prime considerations being investment potential and house price. Since most buyers intended to remain in a house for a relatively short time (3–5 years) the decision to locate within a Special Studies (hazard) Zone and to forego mitigation measures is seen as rational from an individual viewpoint. Generally as Palm (1982: 273) observed, 'unless environmental hazards become translated into economic risk to individuals, hazard warnings not followed by severe disasters will probably not be heeded'. A second contributory factor related to the purveyors of information is that real estate agents may provide misinformation concerning the Special Studies Zones (possibly because of a genuine misunderstanding of the nature of the SSZ) or reinforce wishful thinking on the part of the buyer ('all California is earthquake country!'). Finally, failure of the disclosure legislation to specify the exact method and timing of the disclosure made it possible for agents to minimize the impact of disclosure on buyers. Real estate agents were found to be disclosing at the least sensitive time (at the time of contract signing rather than at the initial viewing of the property) and to be using methods which conveyed the least amount of information about the zones. The findings from behavioural studies of this kind carry a number of policy implications. Most important is the recognition that 'mere provision of environmental information to homebuyers who are constrained by other aspects of the purchase process is insufficient as a hazard mitigation or consumer protection measure' (Palm 1981: 399). An effective response requires direct action by local authorities in the shape of zoning or land-use regulation, more comprehensive definition of and transmission of information on earthquake hazards, and in some cases compulsory acquisition of dwellings in particularly hazardous environments. A key factor is that while the definition of hazard zones is essentially a technical matter, enaction of appropriate policy responses is an economic and political question.

Urban climate

As a town develops its presence exerts an influence upon the atmospheric environment which it eventually dominates. It then becomes possible to identify the urban climate as a distinct type of mesoclimate. On average temperatures in the city are usually about 1 °C higher because of waste heat from houses, transport and industry, and the relatively low albedo (heat reflecting properties) of buildings and paved surfaces (i.e. the urban heat island). Rainfall is also 5–10 per cent higher in the city because of greater air turbulence above urban areas and a higher concentration of dust particles (the urban dust dome) which can serve as hygroscopic nuclei. The incidence of cloud cover and of fogs is also higher over cities. On the other hand, because of friction around buildings average wind speeds tend to be lower, although extreme gusts can be caused by groups of buildings, and sunshine duration is on average 5–15 per cent less.

The task of the urban analyst and planner 'is partly that of preserving the advantages of the urban climate, which are few, and of suppressing the disadvantages, which are many' (Parry 1979: 202). Among such disadvantages are problems arising from urban-induced rainfall including automobile accidents, by-passing of sewage treatment plants by run off, and higher costs of water management. Although the effect of urban areas on local climate seems destined to increase as the numbers of vehicles and fossil-fuelled power plants rise and urban growth proceeds, little has been done by public officials to manage urban weather anomalies or to adjust to their impacts. This is in part because social problems such as crime, poor housing and transportation present more pressing and more readily identifiable targets for action, and partly because, undeniably, it is more difficult to modify an existing built environment than to plan anew. But several initiatives are possible in established urban areas. Amelioration of the urban heat island effect in summer can be aided by provision of trees for shade, sprinkling of streets to increase evaporative cooling, and increasing the albedo by employing light coloured paint on roofs and replacement of open parking lots by garages. The utility of vegetation to improve urban climate is also widely acknowledged. As well as increasing cooling in summer by evapotranspiration, trees and other plants reduce run off and, if judiciously planted, will reduce particulate concentrations and noise pollution. Some of the undesirable wind eddies created by the tall buildings of the urban canyons can be avoided by sympathetic planning of street widths and orientations and by employing appropriate building design. In cities where snow and ice are common winter problems the channelling of waste heat under foot-paths and streets, at least at critical points in the urban traffic system (such as bridges, slopes and pedestrian crossings) would be beneficial in combatting the effects of snowfall and glaze storms (in which super-cooled water falls onto a surface with temperature below 0°C and freezes on impact) which can paralyze a city. As yet however few urban plans explicitly take climatic considerations into account.

Air pollution

We can envisage pollution in general as the adverse environmental effects of the processes of production, consumption and growth. Four main pollution sources are (1) the generation of energy from fossil fuels, (2) the agricultural and industrial production process, (3) household con-sumption activities (e.g. space heating and transportation), and (4) the spatial pattern, density and use of urban land.

Atmospheric pollution *per se* is caused by gaseous (oxides of sulphur, nitrogen and carbon, hydrocarbons and ozone) and particulate (smoke, dust, and grit) wastes emitted into the air. Particulates vary from unburnt carbon to complex substances like lead and radioactive compounds. Given adequate dilution and disperson in the atmosphere urban and industrial emissions of common pollutants may not be considered as giving rise to significant adverse effects. Pollution emerges as a problem when the waste assimilation capacity of the environment is exceeded by the volume of residuals output. Air pollution episodes during which concentrates reach socially unacceptable, economically costly and unhealthy levels may last for a few hours or several days. As Elson (1983) explains, such episodes are typically of two types — smoky sulphurous smogs and photochemical smogs. The former, which was the most common form of air pollution in the UK up to the mid 1950s, result from the burning of fossil fuels. During cold anticyclonic conditions in winter emissions of pollutants increase as the demand for space heating of buildings rises but the atmosphere, characterized by only light winds and a restricted mixing layer, has limited capacity of dispersing and diluting the emissions. The present of large quantities of hygroscopic nuclei leads to the formation of fog as temperatures fall and relative humidity increases. During the worst conditions in cities like London the droplets of dilute suphuric acid were covered by a film of oily impurities which gave the urban fog its particular taste and colour ('the pea-souper'). Although pollution concentrations within the smog largely emanate from local point sources the urban wind circulation can spread the pollutants throughout the city. This occurs because of the urban heat island over the city centre which produces rising air (a low pressure area) into which cooler air from the outskirts is drawn. The smog will remain for as long as the anticyclone persists.

While stationary sources of pollution are the main causes of smoky-sulphurous smogs the automobile is held chiefly responsible for photochemical smogs which are a product of the action of sunlight on hydrocarbons and oxides of nitrogen present in vehicle exhausts. The photochemical smog is composed of ozone, aldehydes and peroxy-acetylnitrate (PAN). Collectively referred to as oxidants these cause eye irritation and coughing, reduced visibility and damage to vegetation. The photochemical smog was first identified in Los Angeles in the 1940s by the 1970s it had emerged as a problem in other cities such as London, Tokyo and Sydney as vehicle ownership rates increased. The motor vehicle is also the chief cause of lead pollution in the urban atmosphere. Lead is extremely toxic and accumulates in the body more rapidly than it is excreted, leading to damage to kidneys. It has also been implicated in slow learning problems in children. Between 20.0 and 50.0 per cent of the lead entering the body comes from the air we breathe and people living near roads typically exhibit higher levels of blood lead than elsewhere in a city. Many governments have now introduced legislation to reduce the lead content of petrol. There is however a range of other metals (e.g. mercury, zinc, chromium and cadmium) whose potentially damaging effect on human beings has yet to be adequately examined.

In Los Angeles, since 1974, the California Air Resources Board has imposed an emergency warning system for high pollution concentrations. The first stage alert (peak hourly concentrations of oxidants exceeding 20 parts per hundred million) is a health warning, but if levels exceed 35 p.p.h.m. (a second stage alert) active measures are taken to control emissions. During a second stage alert in Los Angeles on 14 July 1978 all industries which produced hydrocarbons and oxides of nitrogen were required to reduce their output by 20.0 per cent, households were requested to switch off electrical appliances to reduce demand for power, residents were advised to avoid strenuous outdoor exercise, and commuters were asked to share car transport. The third stage alert or emergency situation (set at oxidant levels of 50 p.p.h.m.) during which industry could be closed down and traffic halted, has not yet been called. Such emergency measures are examples of *reactive* rather than *normative goal-orientated* planning. While current conditions in many cities requie e such ameliorative action the real solution to the problem of urban air pollution lies in long term *control strategies*. These are basically of three types, (1) managerial, (2) emission standards, (3) effluent charges (Thornes 1979, Rosencranz 1981). The first seeks to manage or regulate the amount, location and time of pollutant emissions to meet an established level of ambient air quality. Proponents of the second approach argue that since air quality management requires calculating the emission levels needed to achieve air quality standards it is more sensible to directly instruct *all emitters* to adhere to a technology — determined 'good practice' standard. The third approach is based on neo-classical economic principles and would require emitters to pay a tax or fee per unit of emission. The source (e.g. factory) decides upon its level of pollution by comparing the effluent charge with the marginal cost of control. In principal, higher charges lead to greater control. A related 'economic' strategy is the use of emission offset policy, under which a pollution source cannot move into an area unless it first arranges for a greater reduction of emissions from existing local sources either by purchasing an old plant and closing it down, reducing emissions from its own plants already in the area, or through purchasing transferable discharge permits from other sources (Tietenberg 1980). To date, most attention has been given to the use of emission standards although all three strategies possess positive and negative attributes.

Flooding

The process of urban development carries with it a variety of hydrological consequences. In particular urbanization increases the magnitude of floods and reduces the average interval between serious flooding. The major mechanisms which cause this include:

1   the greater proportion of impervious surfaces which tend to increase the total volume of storm run off and reduce the amount of water that infiltrates into the ground.
2   the artificial 'improvement' (e.g. paving and straightening) of stream channels which reduces the time lag between rainfall and channelled run-off.
3   landscaping and subdivision of the land into building sites which usually shortens the distance over which water flows before reaching a drainage way.
4   human settlement of flood plains which reduces the space available for storing flood waters in the valley bottom so that water is forced to rise and flow more rapidly.

Urban areas differ greatly in the causes and combinations of flooding problems they experience but, in general, the problem of floodplain encroachment is more serious in North America than in Britain where extensive floodpain development has been prevented by the land use regulations contained in the 1947 Town and Country Planning Act. The other three problem factors identified (collectively referred to as catchment urbanization) represent the major cause of inland urban flooding in Britain. Parker and Penning-Rowsell (1982), for example, have described how urbanization of the river Frome catchment upstream of the city of Bristol has contributed to a growing flood problem which affects the city centre including a new shopping precinct, large commercial district and a residential quarter. The culverts used in the last century to channel the river Frome underground (to permit development) now suffer from silting and lack of maintenance just as flood flows due to upstream urbanization are increasing. In addition, as in other British cities (where the storm water and sewage systems are normally combined) the sewage disposal drains were built by the Victorians and are now of insufficient capacity and liable to collapse due to age and inadequate maintenance. In major cities like Liverpool and Manchester there is a twenty year backlog of maintenance work. The rehabilitation and maintenance of water distribution systems is also a continuing concern in older US cities.

In Boston 16km of water main must be replaced annually if by the year 2000 no water main is to be more than 100 years old, while in Chicago the replacement cycle is over 200 years. Failure of man-made structures such as dams and canals which run through urban areas also represents a potential flood hazard. Coastal settlements and towns on the tidal reaches of rivers are under the additional threat from sea flooding. This hazard is particularly acute on the south and east coasts of England where due to isostatic re-adjustment of the land and rising sea levels cities such as London are increasingly open to the danger of flooding. The threat of flooding as a result of the combination of high tides and storm surge conditions in the Thames estuary prompted the construction of the Thames barrier (Horner 1979).

The impact of an urban flood is likely to be complex and in addition to the hydrological characteristics of the event (depth, speed and volume of water), will depend on the particular site, situation and morphological structure of a town. Apart from the human costs in loss of life, economic losses due to flooding in towns include damage to buildings and their contents and losses accruing from disruption of economic activities and communications beyond the immediate flood-affected areas. As Perry (1981: 87) observes 'from an economic point of view flooding can be regarded as a kind of tax exacted by nature'. Central to the economic study of flooding is the acquisition of information on flood damage. This can be obtained either by empirical collection of survey data in the early post-flood period or via a theoretical approach which costs likely damage from flood events based on accumulated experience. The latter approach was developed by White (1964) in the USA and the concept of the depth-damage curve has subsequently been widely applied. The curve seeks to relate potential damage in a property to depth of flooding. An inherent assumption is that different types of property will be affected differently. D. Smith (1981), in a study of the town of Lismore, New South Wales, employed the depth–damage curve technique to calculate the actual and potential flood damage to various land use types (Table 5.1). Analyses of this kind (a) permit the estimation of flood losses either in terms of specific heights and frequencies or in terms of mean annual

Table 5.1 Calculation of depth-damage relationships for different land uses, Lismore NSW

Gauge height (m)	Residential	Commercial	Industrial	Total
	Estimated total actual direct flood damage in relation to gauge height			
13.0	1 118 900 (21.6)	3 699 800 (71.8)	337 800 (6.6)	5 156 500
12.5	625 900 (17.1)	2 842 600 (77.6)	193 000 (5.3)	3 661 500
12.0	328 000 (14.0)	1 922 300 (82.7)	77 800 (3.3)	2 350 100
11.5	137 000 (10.8)	1 092 900 (86.4)	35 600 (2.8)	1 265 500
11.0	74 500 (10.8)	600 000 (87.2)	13 800 (2.0)	688 300
10.5	20 300 (19.1)	84 400 (79.5)	1 500 (1.4)	106 200
10.0	6 800 (12.8)	45 600 (85.7)	800 (1.5)	53 200

Figures in parentheses are percentages of damage sustained by each sector at specific gauge heights. All damage values are in Australian dollars at 1974 prices.

Gauge height (m)	Residential	Commercial	Industrial	Total
	Estimated total potential direct flood damage in relation to gauge height			
13.0	2 139 000 (8.3)	18 824 000 (73.5)	4 667 000 (18.2)	25 630 000
12.5	1 155 000 (6.2)	14 990 000 (80.4)	2 489 000 (13.4)	18 634 000
12.0	598 000 (4.7)	10 702 000 (84.0)	1 435 000 (11.3)	12 735 000
11.5	263 000 (3.6)	6 134 000 (83.5)	953 000 (12.9)	7 350 000
11.0	130 000 (4.4)	3 324 000 (91.9)	139 000 (3.7)	3 614 000
10.5	38 000 (7.1)	417 000 (77.9)	80 000 (15.0)	535 000
10.0	14 300 (4.9)	221 000 (76.0)	56 000 (19.1)	291 000

Figures in parentheses are percentages of the total potential damage, by sector, at specific gauge heights. All values are approximate 1974 prices.

Gauge height (m)	Residential	Commercial	Industrial	Total
	Proportion of actual to potential direct damage for the various sectors in relation to gauge height			
	Actual damage as a percentage of potential damage			
13.0	52.3	19.6	7.2	20.1
12.5	54.2	19.0	7.8	19.7
12.0	55.0	18.2	5.4	18.5
11.5	52.1	17.8	3.8	17.2
11.0	50.0	18.0	9.9	19.1
10.5	53.4	20.1	1.8	19.8
10.0	47.6	20.4	1.4	18.1

Source: D. Smith 1981: 34-7

drainage, (b) give an indication of the minimum actual damage levels that could be attained, (c) facilitate comparisons with other flood prone settlements with different levels of flood mitigation systems, and (d) provide cost-benefit information for planned flood alleviation schemes.

Human response to the flood hazard can be private, public or more usually some combination of the two. Individuals can either adopt a fatalistic attitude and accept the losses which are incumbent upon a flood-prone location or can take action to reduce the effects of the hazard. This can range from short term adjustments such as sandbagging or moving furniture upstairs to longer-term strategies to spread the loss, such as insurance. Generally however studies have found that a large proportion of floodplain dwellers consistently underestimate the risk of flood. Harding and Parker (1974) in a study of flood hazard awareness in Shrewsbury found that only 45 per cent of households interviewed acknowledged that there was a flood problem in their area. Infrequent hazards such as floods are typically soon discounted by most people and even in cases of repeated flood experience many foodplain dwellers ignore or play down the risk despite the opinions of experts. The general position in both Britain and USA is of considerable indifference to flooding which is perceived as an infrequent nuisance rather than as a major risk. A related problem in general comprehension of flood frequency concerns the 'return period'. A 100-year flood (i.e. one that will occur on average once a century) is often misunderstood to be an event which will occur regularly every 100 years. This misapprehension affects residents' cognition of flood risk and influences their propensity to take risk-reducing action. In addition, in the USA, the pre-eminence attached to property rights and the strong belief in the freedom of the individual to locate where they choose are often accompanied by a view that individuals should be responsible for the outcome of their own actions. In reality, of course, the costs arising from unplanned development can impact upon wider society through an increased likelihood of flooding and in relief and repair work (Tobin 1982). It is clear therefore that there is a need for public action to mitigate the flood risk in urban areas. Such action can take a number of forms including (a) engineering works as promoted in USA by the Flood Control Act of 1936, (b) forecasting and warning schemes such as that shown in Figure 5.1, and (c) land-use management to reduce the intensity of human occupance of flood hazard zones.

Social hazards

The role of Man as a causal agent is most pronounced in the case of social hazards. These include diverse problems such as noise pollution, outbreaks of fire, nuclear accidents and workplace hazards. Here we

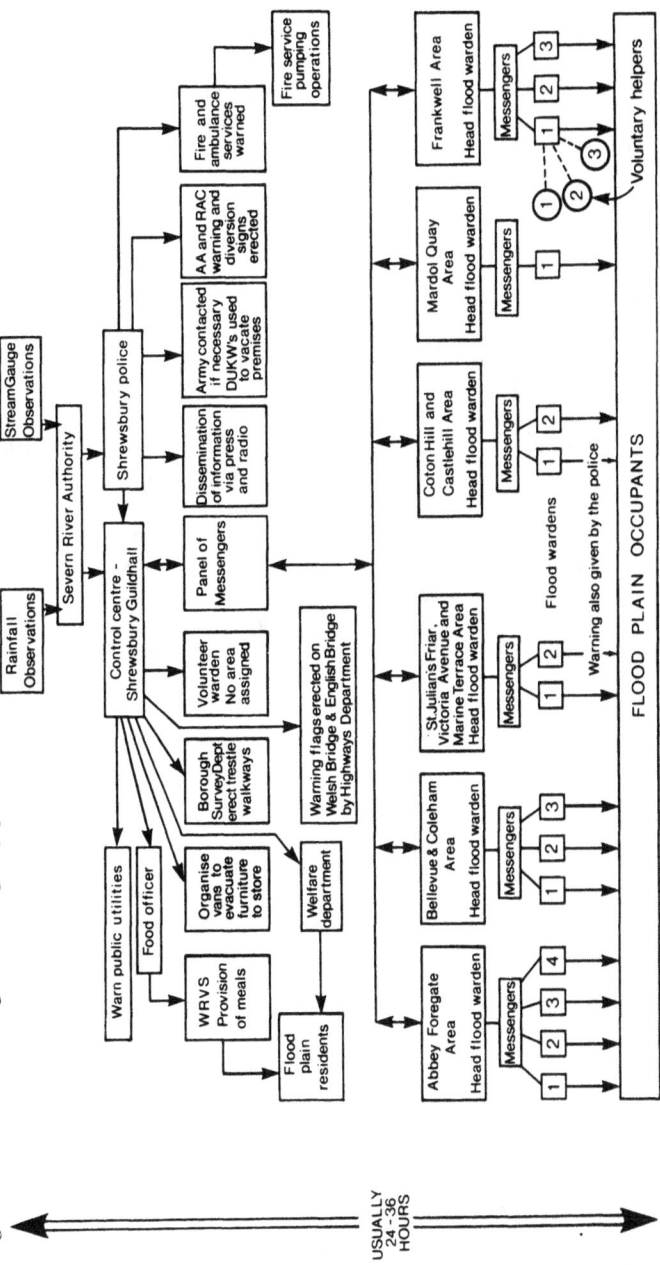

Figure 5.1 Flood warning and emergency plan for Shrewsbury, UK

Source: Harding and Parker 1974: 49

will consider the examples of noise, only recently acknowledged as a major hazard of urban areas, and the potentially catastrophic hazard of a nuclear accident.

Noise

Noise, defined as unwanted sound, is one of the most ubiquitous pollutants in contemporary urban areas yet it is only since the early 1970s that attention hs been focused on noise as an environmental problem. The adverse impacts of noise include (a) annoyance or stress which may contribute to psychological problems such as hypertension and neuroses, (b) physiological effects, e.g. hearing impairment, (c) effects on job performance and (d) a reduction in property values (Finsterbusch 1980). The effect of noise on urban residents is difficult to measure precisely because tolerance levels vary between individuals. At the micro–scale serious noise nuisance can be generated between apartments, offices and other multiple-occupancy venues and, in the case of residential noise, may lead to social conflict between neighbours. Outdoor sources of urban noise fall into four main categories, (a) construction and street repair work, (b) industrial operations, (c) the individual human being, and (d) most serious of all, transportation. The adverse effect of road (Cohen *et al.* 1973), rail (Bronzaft and McCarthy 1975) and air traffic noise (Cohen and Weinstein 1982) on children's achievement scores is well documented. Chicago was one of the first cities to introduce noise zoning but there are difficulties in maintaining and enforcing standards and in preventing the pollutant from crossing into other 'quieter' zones with lower noise limits. Significant alleviation of the road traffic noise nuisance requires a range of measures including technical improvements in vehicles and regulations to enforce their use, restrictions on traffic in certain areas (e.g. hospital zones) and to certain hours of the day, improvements in housing design (e.g. double or triple glazing), and greater attention to noise radiation in highway design (e.g. use of vegetation buffer zones). The problem of airport noise is a function of the location and size of the facility but is an increasing hazard around many cities in the developed world. Residential areas under the flightpath of major city airports such as London Heathrow or New York's J.F.K. have to endure flights every few minutes at peak periods. Resolution of this problem requires a combination of technical improvements to jet engines to reduce noise at source, insulation of dwelling units near flight paths, land-use controls informed by accurate delimitation of noise exposure zones, and geographical research to determine the optimal aircraft flight paths over any urban area.

Nuclear emergency

The risk from exposure to an overdose of radiation as a result of a nuclear power or processing plant accident arouses public concern for several reasons. The first is that although the event is concentrated as a point-source the nature of the emission means that the impact can affect a wide area depending on the amount of pollutant and local climatological conditions. Also, in contrast to other hazards, the effects of a radiological emergency continue for an indeterminate length of time. While flood waters eventually recede science does not yet know the full effects of exposure to radiation. Evidence of cancer-related deaths in communities located close to nuclear installations serves to increase the fear of the unknown in populations at risk. In the USA the National Environmental Policy Act 1969 and the Nuclear Regulatory Commission guidelines have set safety standards for the siting of nuclear power plants. The population centre distance (PCD) defines 'the distance from the reactor to the nearest boundary of a densely populated centre containing more than about 25,000 residents' (Stever 1980: 59).

The functional utility of the concept is unclear however since in practice the PCD is based on a definition of risk which considers only 'credible' accidents (i.e. those for which safety systems are designed). Less probable accidents such as core meltdown are not included within the risk assessment parameters. The demonstrative fallability of technology also serves to underline fear. Evidence of questionable siting decisions (e.g. the Diablo Canyon plant in California is built within three miles of a major offshore earthquake fault) and accidents such as those at Three Mile Island near Harrisburg, Pennsylvania in 1979 and at Chernobyl in the Ukraine in 1986 do little to alleviate concern. As a result few communities voluntarily accept the establishment of a nuclear facility or waste disposal site in their locality.

The nature of the radiological hazard also gives rise to two types of extreme human reaction. At one extreme under-reaction leads the individual either to ignore warnings and continue normal activities or succumb to the 'psychic numbing' effect of warnings and do nothing. At the other extreme the warning of an impending crisis provokes the individual to take protective measures that are both more drastic and sooner than necessary. Ignoring such behaviour on the assumption that people will follow official instructions will result in an under-evaluation of the time and personnel required to evacuate an exposure zone. Evidence from the analysis of public response to the Three Mile Island emergency and from the general field of crisis response planning indicates that in order to devise effective response mechanisms technical projections of the probable hazard area must be complemented by social

93

investigations of likely human behaviour (Johnson and Zeigler 1983). Failure to incorporate this information into emergency plans will undermine their ability to minimize the risk to public health and safety.

Chapter six

Urban liveability

The objective measures of obsolescent and deficient shelter traditionally employed in assessing the quality of different residential environments convey the impression of unequivocal reliability and validity. The concept of urban environmental quality or liveability is more complex, however, being a relative rather than an absolute term where precise meaning depends on the place, time and purpose of the assessment as well as the value system of the assessor. In brief, quality is not an attribute inherent in the environment but is a behaviour-related function of the interaction of environmental characteristics and person characteristics. In order to obtain a full appreciation of environmental quality, it is necessary to employ both objective and subjective measures — in other words we must consider both the city on the ground and the city in the mind.

The residential environment comprising the home and immediate surrounding area is acknowledged to be a major component of overall quality of life. In addition to the direct effects of the objective physical conditions the quality of the residential environment can affect the occupants' self–perception, and in extreme cases physical and mental health. Perceived environmental quality has also been shown to be a significant factor in residential choice decisions. A key factor in understanding the impact of the urban environment on human behaviour and well-being is the psychological concept of stress, defined by Selye (1956) as increased wear and tear in the body as a result of attempts to cope with environmental influences (Figure 6.1). In this the experience or perception of the city is represented as a joint function of the objective environmental conditions (e.g. population density, temperature, pollution levels) and the individual characteristics of the person (e.g. his adaptation level, previous experience, and time in the city). If the perceived environment is outside the individual's optimal range (e.g. if it is overstimulating, contains too many stressors, constrains behaviour or offers insufficient resources) stress is experienced which, in turn, elicits coping. If the attempted coping strategies are successful adaptation and/or habituation occurs though possibly followed by after effects such as fatigue and reduced ability to cope with the next stressor.

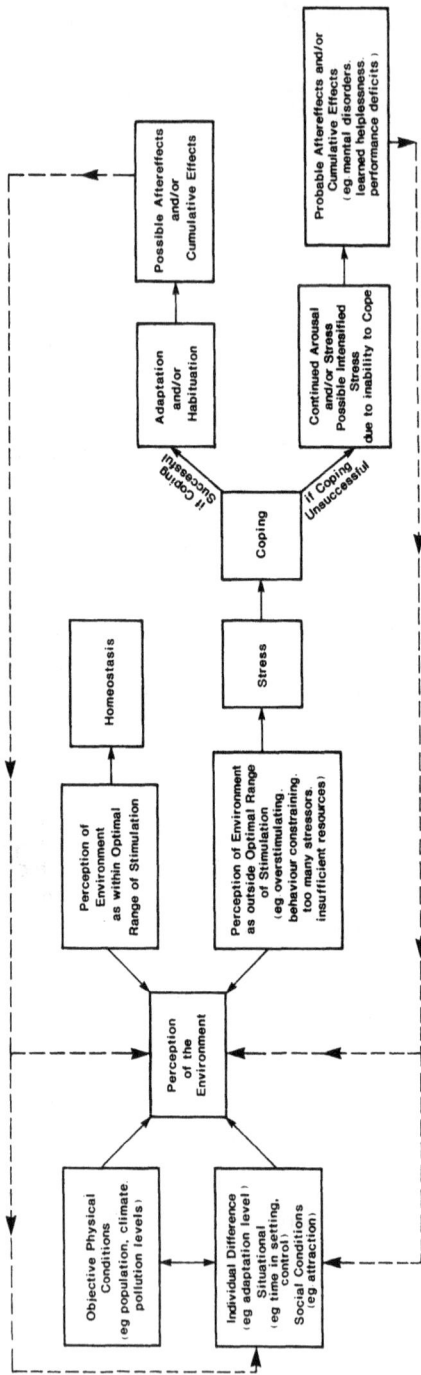

Figure 6.1 The effects of urban life on human behaviour

Boxes (reading through the diagram):

- Objective Physical Conditions (eg population, climate, pollution levels)
- Individual Difference (eg adaptation level) Situational (eg time in setting, control) Social Conditions (eg attraction)
- Perception of the Environment
- Perception of Environment as within Optimal Range of Stimulation
- Perception of Environment as outside Optimal Range of Stimulation (eg overstimulating, behaviour constraining, too many stressors, insufficient resources)
- Homeostasis
- Stress
- Coping
- If Coping Successful
- If Coping Unsuccessful
- Adaptation and/or Habituation
- Continued Arousal and/or Stress. Possible Intensified Stress due to inability to Cope
- Possible Aftereffects and/or Cumulative Effects
- Probable Aftereffects and/or Cumulative Effects (eg mental disorders, learned helplessness, performance deficits)

Source: Bell *et al.* 1976: 285

Positive cumulative after effects would include a degree of learning about how to cope with the next occurrence of undesirable environmental stimulation. If the coping strategies are not successful however stress and/or arousal will continue possibly heightened by the person's awareness that strategies are failing. Possible after effects include exhaustion, learned helplessness, severe performance decrements, illness and mental disorders. Finally, as indicated in Figure 6.1, experiences feed back to influence perception of the environment for future events and also contribute to individual differences which affect future experiences. One of the most widely investigated stress agents is crowding.

Urban crowding

The urban dweller is confronted by high-density conditions in a wide range of everyday settings. Despite the volume of empirical research on the stress impact of crowding the field is still 'preparadigmatic' and the findings inconclusive. According to Dunstan (1979) a major difficulty has been the failure of researchers to derive adequate measures of density and crowding. Density is a physical objective description of people in relation to space and is a necessary but not sufficient condition for crowding. Crowding is a psychological and subjective experience that stems from recognition that one has less space than desired. The factors which determine the extent of crowding are related to the characteristics of (a) the physical environment (e.g. density, site design, temperature, colour, availability of resources, duration of exposure), (b) the social environment (e.g. the nature of the individual's relationship with proximate persons, and the individual's status position in the group), (c) the task environment (e.g. the degree of congruence between the behavioural goal of the individual and the environmental setting), and (d) the individual (e.g. based on sex, age, ethnic or cultural norms as well as personality factors such as self-esteem, personal space preference, and prevailing mood).

Evidence from empirical studies suggests that the effects of density and social structure are so closely related that they can not be discussed as if they had independent effects. Other problems which confront those seeking to employ the concept of crowding in explaining certain urban ills include the fact that most of the evidence is based on aggregate data (e.g. persons per room or crimes per 100,000 population) and is open to the criticism of ecological fallacy. In addition the relationships identified between crowding/density and certain pathologies are correlations only and cannot be taken to indicate that one event is the cause of the other. Furthermore any relationship between a high–density environment and anti–social behaviour can be two-way, with criminals or delinquents seeking out a particular preferred environment.

Despite the difficulty of separating out the density/crowding effect as an independent factor in social malaise there is sufficient evidence that crowding at least intensifies the influence of related environmental stressors. Several authors have proposed ways of reducing the negative effects of crowded settings. Rusbult (1979) identifies two main possibilities. The first is for the planners to affect the physical environment in order to decrease the potential for environment–behaviour incongruence. This may be achieved in three ways. First, the greater importance of primary settings (often-used environments such as home, neighbourhood and workplace) to the individual indicates that the planner should attach greater priority to reducing stress in these zones than in relatively unimportant areas such as shopping streets. Secondly, since perceived control is an important determinant of satisfaction high-density housing schemes should be built with small parks located so that a relatively small number of dwellings may use and defend each facility. Thirdly, since environment--behaviour incongruence can arise from scarcity of resources the planner should seek to ensure the adequate provision of essential facilities. The second main approach to alleviate crowding stress is to facilitate the individual's coping behaviour by creating a flexible physical and social environment. An example of this principle applied to the residential environment is the traditional Japanese home with its moveable partitions.

Another urban stressor is isolation, the polar opposite of crowding, yet there have been relatively few studies of the relationship between this variable and behaviour (Galle and Gove 1983). Stress is also often the result of 'daily hassles' (Lazarus and Cohen 1977). These are minor annoyances which taken individually or as once-occurring events would not tax the city dweller's coping mechanism. In the modern city however these events tend to be multiple, chronic and repetitive. Examples of common daily hassles include the urban commuting journey and the bureaucratic hassle. Work by de Longis *et al.* (1982) found the number and rate of hassles experienced to be a good predictor of an individual's overall health status and perceived energy level. Other forms of urban stressor include physical environmental characteristics such as noise and air pollution, discussed in the previous chapter.

Urban legibility

A particular kind of stress is that associated with orientation and ease of movement in the city. As Ittelson *et al.* (1974: 246) remarked 'ease of movement is as much psychological as physical'. The ability to navigate one's environment is a prerequisite for survival. People have to learn their way around, i.e. they must invest their environment with order and meaning. In so doing they are transformed from 'people carrying maps in their hands to people carrying maps in their heads' (Krupat 1985: 68). Cognitive maps are complex, abstract and selective representations of the environment as people believe it to be. They are not necessarily accurate by objective standards and in fact usually contain erroneous pieces of information. Distortion of sizes, linkages between places, distance and direction are common. There is now ample evidence to show that the perceived spatial relations between places in the city are influenced by (a) the relative attractions of origins and destinations, (b) the kinds and numbers of barriers between places, (c) familiarity with the area and connecting paths, (d) the attractiveness and complexity of the connecting routes, (e) mode of travel, and (f) whether estimates assume 'crow-flight' or consider the number of turns en route.

Apart from Trowbridge's (1913) early ideas on imaginary maps the seminal work on urban orientation was undertaken by Lynch (1960) in his studies of the 'public image' of Boston, Los Angeles, and Jersey City. For each city he produced a mental map based on the perceptions of a selection of residents. Analysis revealed five major elements in the urban image. These are:

1 Paths — channels along which the person moves,
2 Nodes — strategic locations such as a point of route convergence,
3 Districts — medium to large sections of the city recognized as having a common character,
4 Landmarks — physical reference points such as a building or monument, and
5 Edges — boundaries or barriers between areas, e.g. a rail track.

The public image of Boston (which Lynch found to be highly imageable) is shown in Figure 6.2.

Lynch's basic proposition was that the quality of the city image was important to well-being and should be considered in designing or modifying any locality. According to this view a successful landscape should possess the two desirable urban qualities of imageability (the ability of objects to evoke strong emotions in an observer) and legibility (the organization of the elements of a city that allows them to be seen as a coherent whole). A city that is highly legible and imageable would contain individual structures and whole areas that are both distinctive individually and clearly interconnected in a way that the citizens could appreciate. While Lynch's work can be criticized on methodological grounds — e.g. the extremely small sample sizes (sixty in total), and the map drawing method of eliciting cognitive representations — the value of the underlying concept has survived to stimulate a host of related investigations. In addition Lynch's primary concern with the visual component of urban schema has been supplemented by studies of non-visual attributes such as environmental sounds (Porteous and Mastin 1985) and smells (Porteous 1985).

There is now a sufficient body of empirical knowledge on the urban image to suggest a number of principles of relevance for urban design.

Figure 6.2 The image of Boston derived from sketch maps

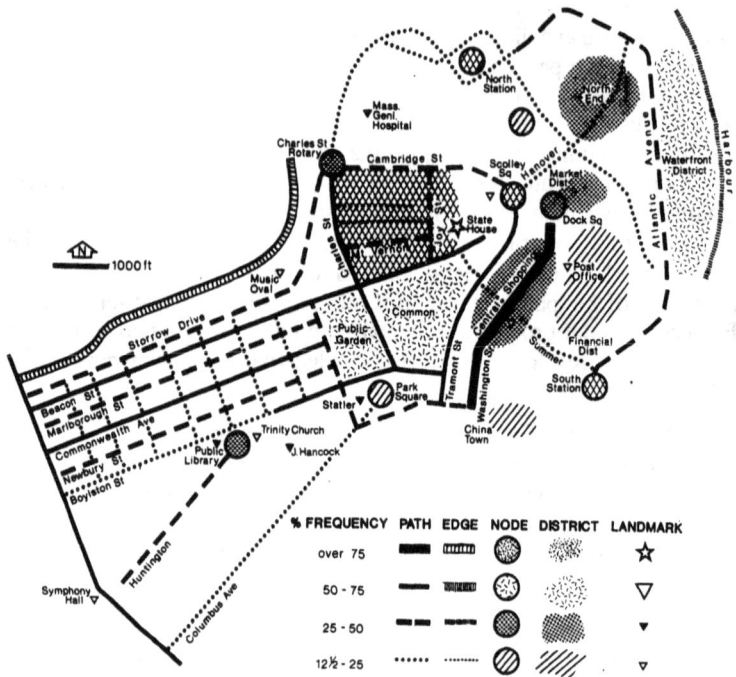

Source: Lynch 1960: 146

1   Perhaps most fundamental is the suggestion by Evans *et al.* (1982), based on a comparison of the towns of Cuidad Guayana (Venezuela) and Orange (California), that the basic principles of urban legibility are not site specific. Building features such as large size, sharp singular contours, complex shape and high use generally enhance imageability and legibility.

2   Settings can be made more legible by placement of landmarks at major route nodes to maximize visibility.

3   Building function contributes to legibility with well-used structures usually highly-memorable. This aspect can be combined with form and location factors to provide a distinctive landmark where needed as, for example, in a homogeneous residential area, or where the street pattern is confusing.

4   Wherever possible highways should be designed so that a functionally efficient network can also provide legible routes and visual satisfaction, as well as avoiding 'turnpike hypnosis' (e.g. through the use of billboard art).

5. Careful attention should be given to the design of individual components of the street scene including paving, lighting, seating and planting elements.
6   Greater attention to how people use public information cues can lead to improved guidance systems for both pedestrians and public transport users.
7   It is essential to avoid an overemphasis on the physical aspects of settings *per se* since this may ignore the symbolic meaning of places and spaces to various people. High-rise buildings, for example, may be viewed as symbols of corporate power, with other symbolic attachments for city hall, historic buildings, or the home area. As Appleyard (1970: 116) commented 'too often city planners and design professionals structure their communities so that they read well at an altitude of 30,000 feet'.
8   Finally, since urban images are influenced by personal characteristics planners must take account of the unique design needs of urban sub-groups including, for example, the elderly, disabled or people with restricted mobility.

The biggest problem is no longer identifying the components of urban imageability and legibility but in translating these into practice. Lynch (1984) in a review of his own work, has admitted that findings have proved difficult to apply to actual public policy; a general comment on academic research being that 'the results are interesting, but hard to put to use' (p. 159). A principal reason for this is that the image of the city is idiosyncratic. Despite the evidence of the generality of certain design features, when one is dealing with a diverse area such as a city it is difficult to establish common problems and solutions. This scale factor and the need to consider the requirements of different population groups suggest that the tehniques may be of greatest value in relation to sub-areas within the city.

Site design and social behaviour

While we can reject the notion of architectural determinism it is equally clear that the built environment can influence the behaviour and well–being of people by, for example, facilitating or discouraging interaction, fostering a sense of identity or alienating people from their surroundings. The general goal of the urban designer and planner is to organize physical space to facilitate certain forms of behaviour and to promote the satisfaction of human needs. According to Zeisel (1981) a behavioural approach to urban design can address six common human needs:

1   security — the need to feel safe in the residential environment,
2   clarity — the need for ease of movement and a legible environment,
3   privacy — the ability to regulate the amount of contact with others,
4   social interaction — the need for sociopetal environments which facilitate desired interaction,

101

5 convenience — the ease of accomplishing tasks at the domestic, neighbourhood and city scales, and
6 identity — the relationship between self and environment encapsulated in the notion of sense of place.

The urban designer, as well as acknowledging the range of needs, must appreciate that not all needs are of equal importance for all social groups at all times. For example, as Rainwater (1966) observed, the home and its surroundings have different meanings for different groups of people. This complexity is summarized in the concept of the user-needs gap. The extent of the potential gap between planners and public was illustrated by Lansing and Marans (1969) and is highlighted in Bolan's (1971) view that 'planners are not doctors; they do not deal with individuals'. The weakness of the links between producers and consumers contributes significantly to the social–behavioural problems encountered in certain residential environments. Particular criticism has been levelled at the negative effects of urban renewal programmes, particularly those carried out in the 1950s and 1960s.

An example of the negative social-psychological effects of such programmes is provided by the clearance of the physically deteriorated ethnic (mainly Italian) working-class West End area of Boston. In the view of the Boston Housing Authority the 48 acre area was a slum for which the best solution was comprehensive clearance and redevelopment with new high-rise apartments and office buildings. The physically-based assessment of the planners contrasted with that of the residents who identified the area as a community with strong local relationships and feelings of solidarity (Gans 1962). The loss of home and neighbourhood disrupted people's lives and led to a grief reaction in many of those displaced. As Fried (1963) reported, the signs of grief ranged from physical symptoms (intestinal disorders, crying bouts, and nausea) and depression, to visits to the sites of their former homes during and after demolition. That the West End was not an isolated example is shown by Reynolds's (1961) survey of housing relocation preferences in forty-one US cities which reported that twelve city blocks was the maximum distance from their old address selected by a majority of all relocated families. It is not possible to identify precisely the extent to which this response was enforced choice (due to the higher rents) or a free decision. What is clear, however, is the failure of urban designers to consult with residents before carrying out the renewal policy.

For many of the former residents of clearance areas, particularly in the UK, replacement accommodation is located in the public sector. While the majority enjoy an improved residential situation a significant minority of tenants live in unsatisfactory conditions. In UK particular concern focuses on the system-built multi-storey tower blocks or decked developments (such as those modelled on the Park Hill estate in Sheffield), in which nearly all of the dwellings are flats and most are above ground level. By conventional standards these schemes provide good accommodation which is structurally sound with the full range of basic amenities, and mostly built to Parker Morris standards. Yet in many cases there is evidence of above average levels of anti-social behaviour and higher than normal rates of suicide and crime. A classic example of the user-needs gap in public housing is provided by the ill-fated Pruitt-Igoe project. Built in 1954 in the inner city of St. Louis the 57 acre development housed 12,000 people in forty three eleven-storey buildings. By 1970 twenty- seven of the buildings were vacant and two years later the entire project was demolished. Among the reasons suggested for the failure of this project were the predominantly black racial composition which made it as much a ghetto as the housing it replaced, the sheer scale of the project, isolation from surrounding neighbourhoods, poor administration and inadequate funding. Design, however, was also a key factor. The physical design of the Pruitt-Igoe development was praised for having no 'wasted space' but socially it proved to be a failure. Among the major design mistakes were (a) the absence of sociopetal semipublic spaces and facilities around which neighbourly relations might develop, (b) the high-rise building made it difficult for parents to supervise children, and (c) the stairwells and elevators provided opportunities for criminal and other anti-social activities (Yancy 1971).

Not all conventional housing projects are such failures. Wilner *et al* (1962) studying a public housing development in Baltimore found that with an architectural design which facilitated interpersonal communication through the provision of common spaces and facilities, neighbouring, visiting, mutual aid and personal satisfaction with life were all higher than for a control group who remained in a slum area. Drawing on this and other work, Newman (1972) developed the concept of defensible space in an attempt to design more humane living environments. Defensible space is seen as 'a model for residential environments which inhibits crime by creating the physical expression of a social fabric that defends itself'. Its goal is to create an environment 'in which latent territoriality and a sense of community in the inhabitants can be translated into responsibility for insuring a safe, productive and well maintained living space' (p.3). To put the theory into effect Newman suggested eight design guidelines:

1   Institutional appearance — the structural materials and architectural design should be compatible with the surrounding neighbourhood to avoid stigmatization of residents.
2   Project size — a density of 50 units per acre is suggested, especially where the development contains many children, to allow sufficient space for recreation.
3   Building height — buildings should not exceed six storeys.

4   Population density — should be limited to a maximum of 200 persons per acre so that residents can distinguish neighbours from strangers.
5   Public social spaces — areas within the project provided to promote social interaction and community feeling.
6   Differentiation of transfer points — symbolic or real barriers should indicate the change in function and accessibility between public and private areas thus promoting greater respect for privacy.
7   Casual surveillance — the high visibility of semi-public areas should deter intruders.
8   Entryways — should be clearly defined and provide for differential access for residents and strangers (e.g. via security devices such as entry phones).

In order to test these ideas Newman compared two adjacent New York housing projects. The Brownsville project built in 1947 has buildings of 3–6 storeys and houses 600 people at 29 per acre. The Van Dyke project was built in 1955 and consists of mainly fourteen-storey buildings which accommodate 76.0 per cent of its population. In terms of total population, density and social characteristics the projects were similar but as Table 6.1 shows the incidence of crime was significantly different. The superior Brownsville design achieves many defensible space objectives. Entrances are visible just off the public street and serve only 9–12 families each. Six families occupy each floor grouped in two sets of three around a common vestibule. An open central stairway and 'skip-stop' lifts facilitate surveillance. By contrast, the Van Dyke project exemplifies the typical high-rise pattern with a large open central space and all entrances on the project's interior, each serving between 112 and 136 families. More recent work by Newman and Franck (1982) in a survey of over 2,500 households in Newark, New Jersey, San Francisco, and St Louis has supported the efficacy of defensible space concepts. Coleman (1984) applied defensible space principles to a study of problem public-housing estates in London and Oxford. Based on an analysis of eighteen design variables she was able to recommend a series of design modifications aimed at reducing the disadvantages of life in such environments.

Critics of Newman's argument have questioned whether the Brownsville and Van Dyke respondents were comparable on all relevant social characteristics, and have pointed out that since territorial behaviour

Table 6.1 Comparison of crime incidents in two New York housing developments

Crime incidents	Van Dyke	Brownsville
Total incidents	1,189	790
Total felonies, misdemeanours, and offences	432	264
Number of robberies	92	24
Number of malicious mischief	52	28

Source: Newman 1972

and cognitions can vary according to social group a single set of design solutions could not have the same effect for all groups. Much of the criticism stems from the seemingly *deterministic* nature of the model. Subsequent statements by Newman (1980) have sought to reduce this impression and emphasize the *probabilistic* basis of the theory. Physical design changes alone are unlikely to create a social fabric that eliminates crime and other unwanted activity but they can encourage and enable people to take an active role in their residential environments. Approaches which employ a combination of defensible space design and social strategies (such as community policing, and locally-based management of problem estates) have the greatest chance of effecting improvement in poor residential environments.

In order to close the user-needs gap and achieve greater involvement of residents in planning and design, Sommer (1972) has proposed a process of user-generated design. This suggests that at the first critical planning stage, referred to as programming, client and designer-planner should make explicit their assumptions and requirements for the project. The resulting detailed programme should specify the anticipated spatial and temporal patterns of living, giving information on detailed questions such as the arrangement of room walls and stairways and materials to be used. Among the methods for obtaining the views of prospective users (e.g. those in a planned redevelopment area) are community meetings, questionnaire surveys and trade-off games. Zeisel *et al.* (1977) have employed this 'user-friendly' approach to design low-rise housing for the elderly. In general designers/planners should offer several alternative project plans for resident review and be prepared to modify designs in the light of user feedback. Clearly no single design solution can incorporate all that is good and avoid all that is negative, nor can it satisfy completely all members of a user group. But 'good planning involves making decisions that are based on systematic knowledge and that maximize the fulfilment of important needs and goals while minimizing the frustration of other needs and goals' (Krupat 1985: 169). The key is to make informed trade-offs to find the solutions whose net outcomes are most positive. With this sort of collaboration in advance of construction the questions, needs, uncertainties and assumptions of all relevant parties can be tested so that the physical product is as responsive to residents' needs a possible. Moreover because the procedure explicitly states how each element of the design is supposed to work it allows for post-occupancy evaluation which can lead to modifications and which can be fed into future design decisions. Whether or not designers and planners accept input from users, another problem is that the end product is normally planned with a high degree of permanency in mind. An alternative known as open-ended design (Rapoport 1977) would seek to reduce the fixed elements of a design to leave a degree of flexibility whereby different users can reorganize the environment to suit their particular needs.

While a new fully developed user-orientated urban residential environment has yet to be seen on the ground, academic researchers have demonstrated how residents' perceptions and preferences can be incorporated into the decisions of those responsible for improving the quality of existing residential environments. Since Peterson's (1967) early attempt to identify the desirability of the visual appearance of residential neighbourhoods numerous increasingly sophisticated efforts have been made to determine the characteristics of a satisfactory residential environment. These have been undertaken both for differing social groups, e.g. the elderly (Rosow 1967), black youths (Ladd 1972) and college students (Hinshaw and Allott 1972); and for different types of area including planned residential areas (Lansing *et al*. 1970), public housing (Pacione 1982a), ethnic areas (Loo 1980), new towns (Zehner 1977) and residential neighbourhoods within large cities (Miller *et al*. 1980) and in the suburbs (Cutter 1982). The fact remains, however, that the subjective approach has yet to attain the level of acceptability achieved by traditional objective measures in the realm of public policy.

Urban sub-areas

Perceived areas exist in every city because their presence is collectively acknowledged by people within and beyond their boundaries and is reinforced by behaviour patterns. Examples of such areas include ethnic enclaves such as Chinatown in San Francisco, racially defined areas such as Watts in Los Angeles, areas defined by lifestyle such as sections of Greenwich village in New York, gang turfs, urban slums, exclusive suburbs, or status areas such as Beacon Hill in Boston. Each of these is primarily a social construction which arises because of shared values and beliefs. An example of how this urban imagery can impose negative impact on people's behaviour and well-being is the way in which some areas become stigmatized with the inhabitants en masse being labelled as troublesome, work-shy or unreliable, thus making it more difficult for them to compete in local housing and job markets, or obtain goods under hire purchase agreements.

Subjective areas in the city are important because they can restrict people's movement and guide behaviour. For example, Milgram (1976) and Milgram *et al*. (1972) have produced 'fear maps' of Paris and New York identifying areas of danger for non-residents. Ley and Cybriwski (1974) have mapped gang areas and stress surfaces in the Monroe district of north Philadelphia and found them to be direct determinants of people's spatial behaviour. The actual travel patterns of residents reflected the stress topography with many preferred routes increasing journey length

by over 50.0 per cent. Planning which ignores this behavioural environment is unlikely to be successful. For example, in the Monroe
neighbourhood planning emphasis in the provision of a new playground
was placed on site design and location. The site selected though
geographically accessible was close to the meeting point of three gang
territories which ensured that the playground became a battlefield from
which children were excluded by fearful parents. In this instance development of a new facility without regard to the meaning of space actually
exacerbated the acute gang problem in the neighbourhood. Another
graphic illustration of the effect of a perceptual barrier on people's
behaviour is the religious divide between Catholic and Protestant communities in West Belfast where trip distance is of secondary importance to
the wish to avoid the territory of the other group (Boal 1969).

These studies provide examples of what Suttles (1972) referred to
as defended neighbourhoods. The wish to establish, maintain or defend
specific bounded areas, known as territoriality, is a basic form of social
organization which involves claiming space by personalizing or marking
it in a way that communicates ownership or control to others. While
boundary markers are normally perceptual or symbolic in some instances
the desire for a separate identity is emphasized physically, as in Oxford
where seven foot high walls topped with revolving spikes once divided
a council estate from a private suburb. This extreme example underlines
the importance of the home area or neighbourhood for urban dwellers,
and it is to this concept that we now turn. From the viewpoint of applied
urban analysis two central questions are (a) the utility of the planned
neighbourhood unit concept and (b) the continued relevance of local
neighbourhood areas in the modern city.

The planned neighbourhood

The roots of neighbourhood planning can be traced to the ideas of urban
reformers like Lever, Cadbury and Howard but it was not until after
the First World War that the widespread creation of new residential areas
provided the opportunity to apply neighbourhood planning principles.
Though devised by Howard the neighbourhood unit was given definition and popularized by Perry (1929). From its inception the concept
had the strong social objective of encouraging community formation
through physical planning. Reducing the distance between residential
units, shared driveways, minimum use of fencing, and strategic location of communal facilities were among the strategies employed to promote contact and allow people to meet in the course of their routine activities. Perry laid down six principles for neighbourhood planning:

1 The neighbourhood unit should be of a size to support one primary

school, and of a density that ensured children would have a maximum walk of 0.25 miles to school.

2   The neighbourhood should have clear boundaries formed by arterial roads which would serve the dual function of deflecting traffic from the centre and allowing residents and strangers to visualize it as a distinct entity.

3   There should be a system of small parks and recreation spaces occupying about 10.0 per cent of the area.

4   The school and other community buildings should be grouped at the centre.

5   The shopping district(s) should be on the periphery to enable shops to be supplied via the arterial road system without infringing residential areas.

6   Streets should be proportionate to their traffice load and should discourage through-traffic but facilitate internal circulation.

According to Perry these principles would ensure that the neighbourhood would stand out geographically as a disinct physical entity and the residents would develop a community identity. This combination of social idealism and physical planning proved popular and in Britain the neighbourhood unit design was advocated for new housing estates in the inter-war period (although the location of shops and open space, and the number of schools differed from Perry's formula). The commitment to neighbourhood planning reached its highest level in the period just after the Second World War being applied both to new urban estates and in the early New Towns. The Reith Report (Ministry of Town and Country Planning 1946) supported the use of the neighbourhood unit principle for the New Towns and added the notion of social balance such that each neighbourhood would reflect the average demographic, social and employment structure, and so avoid the single class council estates of the inter-war period. The inevitable failure of the social balance objective in local planning did not undermine the more general belief in the ability of physical planning to influence social interaction and promote community ties. Thus although the formal neighbourhood unit was eventually abandoned, neighbourhood planning continued in the public sector housing estates of the mid-1960s as well as in new private residential developments which grew on the edge of most British towns during the 1970s.

Urban neighbourhoods

The importance and continued relevance of the urban neighbourhood has been emphasized by many researchers (Warren 1978) and questioned by others (Webber 1963), and despite attempts to synthesize the debate analysts are still confronted with contradictory assessments of the importance of the urban neighbourhood. One view contends that communal ties have become attenuated in contemporary industrial bureaucratic societies. This perspective underlay much of the theoretical writing of the Chicago school of urban studies. The opposite view maintains that neighbourhood communities have persisted in industrial bureaucratic social systems as important sources of support and sociability. Much of the evidence for this argument rests on the empirical demonstration of the continued vitality of urban primary ties.

Table 6.2 Proportion of extra-domiciliary activities undertaken within the local area

Activity	Pacione (1980) (n = 760)	Royal Commission (1969) (n = 2199)	Foley (1950) (n = 400)	Ross (1962) (n = 250)	Foley (1952) (n = 446)	Hunter (1975) (n = 154)
Daily shopping	51.9	47.0*	69.0	80.0	76.3**	48.0**
Durable shopping	11.8	—	5.0	7.0	—	—
School trips	45.9	61.0	68.0	—	—	—
Church visits	36.5	66.0	77.0	36.0	61.5	51.2
Employment	15.3	33.0†	18.0	22.0	17.0	11.4
Organization or club membership	77.9	58.0	—	—	—	—
Entertainment	20.7	55.5‡	58.0	22.0	44.5	9.1
Walks	23.9	41.0§	—	—	—	—
Health visits	27.8	—	30.0	—	46.7	19.3
Visiting friends	27.0	—	—	—	—	—
Visiting relatives	6.2	—	—	—	—	—
Other outings	21.2	56.0§§	10.0	—	25.6††	47.9
$\bar{x}$	30.5	52.2	41.9	33.4	45.3	31.2

* Weekly household shopping.
† Since some also usually travel outside the home area in the course of their work, only 14.0 per cent of all electors may be said to be employed entirely within their home area.
‡ Visit to public house or bingo hall.
§ Public park or garden.
§§ Visit to public tennis court.
** Grocery shoping or small purchases.
†† Banking.

Comparison of the findings from a range of studies carried out in Britain and North America over the period 1950–80 revealed that on average between one-third and one-half of household trips were undertaken within the local area (Table 6.2). For individual activities (such as daily shopping, schooling, church attendance and club membership) the majority of trips were made within the neighbourhood (Pacione 1984). In view of the lack of community attachment and mobility of urban dwellers described by the 'community without propinquity' thesis it is perhaps surprising to find such a high proportion of activities confined to what are very small local parts of the metropolis. Overall the levels of neighbourhood cohesion uncovered supported the view that while a majority of middle-class urbanites may have social networks which are not neighbourhood-centred, for a significant number of activities and for certain groups of people including the elderly, children, lower class and housewives, the neighbourhood remains an important territorial entity. Further evidence of 'neighbourhoods that work' is provided by Schoenberg and Rozenbaum (1980).

The humane city

While the ancient Greeks thought that the good or liveable city was one in which all the free men could participate in face to face government, in modern times criteria have more usually emphasized economic factors such as job opportunities, good housing, schools and shopping facilities, efficient transport systems, and sound urban finance (Zimmerman 1982). Several writers including Lynch (1981), Newman (1972), Rapoport (1977) and Ittelson *et al.* (1974) have sought to leaven this economic viewpoint by consideration of social or 'human' concerns. These have emphasized the need to ease orientation and movement in the city, to reduce the stresses caused by pollution, crowding, poor housing and stimulus overload, and to design a built environment which is responsive to the varying needs of residents. Clearly, in order to attain the goal of a liveable city a wide range of social, economic and physical factors must be satisfied. Not all of these fall within the power of planners and designers to regulate. The city is not a closed system but is linked to regional, national and international systems which impinge upon the quality of urban life. However, those urban components which can be manipulated positively must not be overlooked and in order to do this successfully it is necessary for planners to acknowledge the subjectivity of the objective environment.

Chapter seven

Neighbourhood change

The nature of the residential environment, defined by the characteristics of home and neighbourhood, and the ways in which public and private initiatives affect the process of neighbourhood change are key determinants of the overall life quality of urban dwellers.

Within any large city individual neighbourhoods exist in different conditions or life-cycle stages. Several authors have attempted to portray a long-term neighbourhood development cycle by identifying successive land-use stages. Downs (1981) posits a five-stage neighbourhood change model comprising —

Stage 1: Stable and viable. These are healthy neighbourhoods, either new and thriving or old and stable, in which property values are rising.
Stage 2: Minor decline. These are generally older areas with a level of public services and social status below these typical of stage 1 areas. Minor physical deficiencies are evident in housi.ᵣ units, density is higher than when the neighbourhood was first develop. J, property values are stable or increasing slightly and demographically the neighbourhood is characterized by younger families with relatively few resources.
Stage 3: Clear decline. The housing sector is dominated by rented accommodation often marked by poor tenant–landlord relations due to high absentee ownership. The area generally has occupants of lower socio-economic status. Minor physical deficiencies are widespread and many structures have been converted to higher-density uses than those for which they were designed. Overall confidence in the area's future is weak and there may be some abandoned housing.
Stage 4: Heavily deteriorated. Most housing requires major repair. Properties are marketable only to the lowest socio-economic groups and subsistence level households are numerous. The profitability of rental units is poor and cash-flows are low or even negative leading to widespread abandonment. This has social and environmental consequences for the neighbourhood and financial (tax loss) implications for the city.

111

Stage 5:   Unhealthy and non-viable. These neighbourhoods are at a terminal point marked by wholesale abandonment. Expectations about the area's future are nil and residents are those with lowest social status and income in the region.

Table 7.1 Factors underlying neighbourhood decline and revitalization

Revitalization factors	Decline factors
High-income households	Low-income households
New buildings with good design or old buildings with good design or historic interest	Old buildings with poor design and no historic interest
Distant from very low-income neighborhoods	Close to very low-income neighborhoods or to those shifting to low-income occupancy
In a city gaining (or not losing) population	In a city rapidly losing population
High owner occupancy	Low owner occupancy
Small rental units with owners living on premises	Large rental apartments with absentee owners
Close to strong institutions or desirable amenities, such as a university, a lakefront, or downtown	Far from strong institutions and desirable amenities
Strong, active community organizations	No strong community organization
Low vacancy rates in homes and rental apartments	High vacancy rates in homes and rental apartments
Low turnover and transiency among residents	High turnover and transiency among residents
Little vehicle traffic, especially trucks, on residential streets	Heavy vehicle traffic, especially trucks, on residential streets
Low crime and vandalism	High crime and vandalism

Source: A. Downs 1981: 66

Neighbourhoods can change in either direction along this continuum. Some specific factors which can increase an area's susceptibility to decline or revitalization are suggested in Table 7.1. Problems can arise in the process of change whether the neighbourhod is experiencing an improvement or decline in status. Since the late 1960s, in some cities, the process of gentrification and the related question of displacement have emerged as major issues.

Gentrification

The terms gentrification (London), brownstoning (New York) and white-painting (Toronto) refer to a process operating in the private housing market whereby working-class and derelict property is rehabilitated by higher income groups often with the consequent displacement of many original residents (Smith and Williams 1986). Four major consequences of the gentrification process are (1) a significant rise in the price of both renovated and unrenovated property in the area, (2) a reduction in net occupancy rate and density as individual households replace multiple occupation, (3) an alteration in socio-economic structure and (4) the progressive transfer of housing from rental to the owner occupied sector, with, in some North American cities, an ethnic transition from black to white. As a consequence, the process of gentrification can involve a high degree of social conflict.

Gentrification commonly involves migration by people already living within the inner city and as such is not a 'back to the city' movement in the sense that suburbanites are returning to the inner areas. Gentrification must also be distinguished from both the intensification of existing high-status areas and the process of neighbourhood revitalization involving 'incumbent upgrading' where no spatial mobility is involved in an area's social transformation. While gentrification is not a feature of all western cities, its appearance in cities throughout the developed world including London (Hamnett and Williams 1980), Paris (Bentham and Moseley 1980), Washington (Gale 1979), Vancouver (Ley 1981) and Adelaide (Badcock and Urlich-Cloher 1981) confirms that this is not an isolated process but one which is linked to wider social and economic trends in capitalist society.

All of the main agents of change identified in the urban development process are involved to varying degrees in the effectuation of gentrification, each pursuing a particular set of objectives. Government involvement is both direct and indirect. Central government policies to promote home ownership including taxation policy (e.g. relief on mortgage interest repayments) and grants for home improvement can facilitate gentrification. In North America, more direct influence may be exerted by local governments who stand to benefit from the replacement of low-income groups with their attendant demands for social and welfare programmes by middle-class consumers whose incomes boosts the local economy and whose investments enrich the tax base. Among strategies employed by local governments in the USA are (a) advertising certain neighbourhoods judged to have gentrification potentia., (b) providing tax abatements for rehabilitation (e.g. the J-51 programme in New York City), (c) using community development funds to rehabilitate and improve public services in selected neighbourhoods, (d) employing code enforcement to make owners rehabilitate or sell their property, (e) designating 'historic' neighbourhoods, (f) reducing public service provision in some neighbourhoods to encourage decline prior to facilitating reinvestment, and (f) re-zoning a mixed-use district or failing to enforce existing zoning statutes to facilitate gentrification. For gentrification to occur such enabling strategies by government have to be accompanied by financial

Table 7.2 Neighbourhood, city and metropolitan factors underlying revitalization

Neighbourhood level			
Demand side		Supply side	
Factor	Operation	Factor	Operation
Proximity to amenity such as lakefront, oceanfront, park or downtown	Enhances long-term value	Single-family housing	Simpler to rehabilitate than multifamily housing; fewer management problems
Good public transportation	Enhances convenience, especially for households with more than one worker	Housing with interesting architectural features such as high ceilings, fireplaces, carved woodwork	Attractive to young households, which are most likely to rehabilitate
Access to high-quality public or private schools	Enhances attractiveness to households with school-aged children	Brick housing	Easier to rehabilitate than frame housing, easier to care for, lasts longer
No nearby public housing with school-aged children who would dominate the public schools	Enhances attractiveness to households with school-aged children and incomes high enough to support renovation	Multifamily housing suitable for condominium ownership	Owner-occupied property better maintained and residency more stable than rented property
Perceived in community as safe	Enhances attractiveness as place to live	Financial institution willing to provide mortgages and home-ownership loans	Makes ownership and rehabilitation easier
Proximity to revitalized neighbourhoods	Creates expectation that revitalization will work here as well	Commitment by local government to upgrade infrastructure and public services	Reassures private investors of long-term value of homes
		Strong neighbourhood organization dominated by home owners	Creates pressure on local government to enforce housing codes and improve public services
		Housing and other structures in relatively good condition	Encourages private investment by owners and lenders

City and metropolitan level

Demand side		Supply side	
Factor	*Operation*	*Factor*	*Operation*
Strong downtown business district with growing employment	Creates demand for housing close to downtown jobs	Long commuting times to downtown business district	Make living near downtown more desirable
Rising real incomes	Increase household's ability to rehabilitate housing	Strong restrictions on suburban development	Limit suburban housing and jobs, enhancing city housing and jobs
Formation of many small, childless households	Increases households that need less space, are oriented to urban amenities, and do not need public schools	Rapid increases in prices of suburban housing	Make city housing more attractive
Rapid in-migration of nonpoor households	Increases demand for good-quality housing	Loose housing market	Enables poor households displaced by revitalization to find adequate housing, possibly reducing resistance to revitalization
No in-migration of poor households	Permits older neighbourhoods to stabilize	Rents not controlled	Encourages property maintenance and investment in new rental units
		Easy condominium conversion	Increases owner occupancy

Source: A. Downs 1981: 75-6

and property agencies becoming interested in the redevelopment potential of a neighbourhood. Landlord developers and real estate agents have an important part to play in guiding potential gentrifiers to a neighbourhood, buying property and speculating, and displacing residents (e.g. by raising rents). Property interests, in turn, require the co-operation of financial institutions able to lend capital for investment in the built environment. When all of these agents come together in a particular spatial context gentrification can occur. Potential locations are generally characterized by substandard but structurally sound housing 'with potential' clustered to allow a contagion effect to occur, often with a unique spatial amenity such as a view, proximity to or with good transport links to the CBD, and the presence of local commercial activities (shops, restaurants) attractive to gentrifiers. In short, a satisfactory theory of the gentrification phenomenon must involve both supply-side and demand-oriented explanations (see e.g. Table 7.2).

The classic example of gentrification occurs in a residential area which is initially middle-class. Typically the original residents move out from the central city as they establish families and their incomes rise, to be replaced by households of successively lower income. Eventually, the cost of maintenance and reinvestment in the housing exceeds the financial ability of occupants and the area undergoes significant deterioration. The result is further immigration of low-income households, overcrowding, subdivision of large houses into rental units to provide a rent income acceptable to landlords and the eventual transition from owner-occupation to rented tenure. Landlords may decide to act as 'free-riders' and take no steps to invest in the maintenance or rehabilitation of their property (possibly in response to declining real profits due to inflation and/or rent controls, and the presence of alternative investment opportunities). If so, the process of deterioration accelerates possibly leading to abandonment and destruction (including 'torching' for insurance purposes). As Beauregard (1986: 48) observes, 'the housing stock in this area is now inexpensive'.

As well as this general model of gentrification the process can occur in working-class areas or even in areas of mixed industrial, residential and commercial land uses. In the first case, neighbourhoods may consist of housing which has been well-maintained by successive working-class occupants. The fact that, relative to other parts of the city, the housing may be inexpensive can attract gentrifiers. The second and less common cause of residential change refers to 'loft conversions' i.e. the creation of inexpensive housing from mixed-use districts, as has occurred in areas of disused industrial and waterfront premises in older cities such as New York and Philadelphia (Zukin 1982). In addition to these manifestations of gentrification produced by individual households large-scale developers and speculators can also purchase multi-family housing and convert an area into luxury condominiums and co-operative apartments. One can also identify a gentrification process in which local government takes the initiative through a major urban renewal project.

Reaction to gentrification has varied from its being characterized as a driving force for revitalization of the declining inner-city (Sumka 1983) to its vilification as an agent for the displacement of the working class (Hartman *et al*. 1981). There is little firm evidence on the net contribution to a city. Clearly deteriorated areas have been upgraded and historic neighbourhoods preserved but for many population groups the social impact has been negative. In addition little is known about the net impact of revitalization on the financial situation of a city. Certainly middle- and upper-income newcomers pay more in real estate taxes (rates) and, in USA, other local taxes, stimulate business activity and require less welfare services. But they also demand other costly services as, for example, in Philadelphia's Queen Village where residents requested more police protection, better garbage collection, an improved school curriculum, cobblestone streets, buried electrical wires and new landscaping. There is a need for a detailed cost-benefit analysis of gentrification. On the basis of the available evidence it is clear that while the upgrading of selected areas of the inner city is occurring the process is locality-specific and does not represent a general resuscitation of the inner city (e.g. between 1968 and 1979 only 0.5 per cent of the twenty million housing units in US cities were affected by rehabilitation). Revitalization must be viewed more accurately as the continuing redistribution and reconcentration of selected households within the city — a dynamic consistent with and not counter to the prevailing central city deconcentration trend.

Displacement

The problem of displacement of former residents is a major social consequence of both public clearance and rehabilitation programmes, and 'free market' gentrification. The displacement of working-class families reflects the weak position of the poor in society in general and the housing market in particular. Paradoxically, whereas they were once *concentrated* in the inner city because of their limited purchasing power they are now being *displaced* from gentrifying inner areas for the same reason. As Ley (1981) points out, the market which has failed the disadvantaged in the industrial inner-city through under-investment is penalizing the same group in the post-industrial city through over-investment. Displacement due to the superheating of a local housing market by gentrification can occur in four ways —

1 the eviction of low-income tenants from buildings scheduled for rehabilitation as upper-income residences.

117

2 the involuntary departure of long-term families or elderly residents on fixed or limited incomes becomes of their inability to pay sharply escalating property taxes.

3 the inability of newly married children of existing residents to afford housing within the area they have traditionally regarded as their community.

4 reluctant migration of residents from an area because of the loss of friends or supportive social, religious or economic institutions.

The 1981 Department of Housing and Urban Development report to the US Congress noted that in 1979 2.4 million Americans were displaced by private activity alone (i.e. this figure does not include the various forms of public displacement such as local housing code enforcement, construction of roads and public facilities, and urban renewal projects). Abandonment is also a major cause of displacement. Between 1970 and 1981, 341,000 housing units were abandoned in New York City. It should be noted however that as a result of chain displacement (the removal of households occupying the unit prior to the last resident being removed) and moves due to displacement pressure (e.g. from street crime or a fire hazard from adjacent property) more households were displaced than in indicated by the number of abandoned units. The spatial concentration of abandonment-created displacement is also illustrated in New York where the Bronx with 17.5 per cent of the city's households in 1970 and 41.0 per cent of the total demolished buildings over the period 1970–1981. (By contrast the borough of Queens with 24.0 per cent of the city's households had only 3.6 per cent of the demolished buildings). Taken together, in New York City abandonment and gentrification currently displace between 100,000 and 250,000 persons per year (Marcuse 1986) with, as elsewhere, particular hardship impacting upon ethnic minority groups, the elderly and low–income households.

While gentrification is a recently identified phenomenon the contrary process of urban decline has long been part of capitalist urban development. When the processes of neighbourhood decline reach an advanced stage the result is the slum, an area characterized by an impoverished social and physical environment. While most official definitions of slums emphasize the visible physical characteristics of the area the basic concern is to improve the welfare of the inhabitants and, increasingly, this requires government action.

Apart from the building of new towns on green field sites, the three principal approaches to the problem of slum housing are filtering, clearance and rehabilitation, the importance of each strategy varying between societies and through time.

Filtering

While clearance and rehabilitation involve some form of public intervention to improve housing conditions filtering requires no direct government involvement. The raising of housing standards is entrusted to the interplay of market forces whereby the provision of improved accommodation for the lower-income members of the community is effected through construction of new properties for upper- and middle-income groups. In principle a chain of sales is initiated by the insertion of new housing at the top end of the market. Properties vacated by those moving to the new housing filter down the social scale and enable individual households to filter up the housing scale, leaving the worst housing vacant and ready for demolition. Empirical research has questioned the ability of the filtering mechanism to work towards the elimination of slums. A major weakness is that the filtering process at best works slowly and many of the vacancy chains are broken before the poor benefit to a significant degree. Filtering also assumes that the poor are mobile physically and economically whereas the unemployed and under-employed are often unable to move out of the slum dwellings because they cannot afford to devote more of their income to rent. Continued migration of lower-income and, especially in USA, ethnic minority groups into the urban housing system also increases demand for the relatively small number of units vacated and can thus maintain price and rent levels beyond the means of many households. A final criticism of filtering is that unmitigated the process will lead to the permanent concentration of poorer households in the worst housing and such distributional consequences are unacceptable in many countries. The concept of filtering has played an important part in the formulation of housing policy in USA. Until the early 1930s Britain also relied almost entirely on the filtering process for improving the housing conditions of the working classes. Not until the Housing Act of 1930 (Greenwood Act) and the Housing (Financial Provisions) act of 1933 did the British government officially acknowledge that the housing problems of the lower-income groups were unlikely to be resolved through private house building.

Clearance

Britain emerged from the Second World War victorious but with 450,000 dwellings destroyed or made uninhabitable and a further three million damaged to a lesser extent. As a result for almost twenty-five years there was general political agreement on the need for high volumes of housing construction in order to eliminate shortages, to remove the slums, and to provide for a growing population. From 1945 to 1954 the dominant objective of the Labour government was to increase the supply of dwellings and slum clearance was held in abeyance. During this period local authorities dominated housing construction (Figure 7.1). When the Conservatives came to power in 1954 the objective of high output remained but the mechanism altered with a reduction in council-house building and an expansion of the private sector. Nationally local authority house completions fell from 229,305 in 1953 to 105,529 by 1961. The Housing (Rent and Repairs) Act of 1954 also reactivated the programme of slum clearance in order to tackle the 140,000 houses that remained from pre-war schemes and the hundreds of thousands that had since deteriorated due to neglect. Local authorities were to concentrate on the slum clearance fraction leaving the private sector to provide general needs housing (Table 7.3). Another peak period of housing production characterized the Labour government years 1964–68 when public housing was expanded to a situation of broad parity with the private sector. After 1968 council house completions decreased to reach a low of 88,000 in 1973 (Figure 7.1). The slum clearance programme accelerated from a 1955 level of 24,000 demolitions or closures to 57,500 in 1959 then remained at around 60,000 per year throughout the 1960s. Along with the decline in council house building towards the end of the 1960s the

Figure 7.1 Housebuilding and clearance in England and Wales, 1920–80

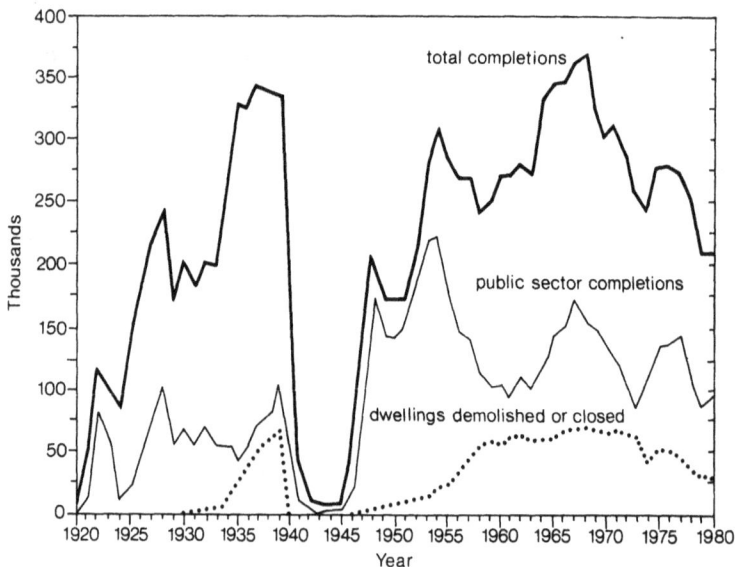

Source: Gibson and Langstaff 1982: 25

120

rate of slum clearance began to fall, partly due to the high cost of redevelopment and the monetary crisis of the late 1960s, and between 1973 and 1979 the clearance rate fell by fifty per cent from 64,000 to 33,000, the lowest annual total since 1955. Criticism of the urban redevelopment machinery has focused on (a) the immediate impact of the clearance process, and (b) the longer term social implications for residents and communities.

While there can be little doubt that the clearance and redevelopment programmes have provided a superior housing and residential environment for many families the timing of the process, the effect on existing environments and the stress imposed on residents have all been criticized. Slum clearance can be a complex and lengthy process and the delay and uncertainty which often surrounds a programme casts a pall of planning blight over a neighbourhood and exacerbates the disruptive effect. In Britain it generally took two years for a compulsory purchase order to be confirmed and another two years for most of the residents to be rehoused. In the period prior to confirmation of the order repair and maintenance work practically ceased, and by the time residents are eventually rehoused 'their homes and the state of the surrounding streets are naturally far worse than when the public health inspector represented the homes as unfit two years or more previously' (Gee 1974: 6). Delays caused by national cutbacks in housebuilding or failure at the local level to tie demolition to completion of new dwellings intensify the strain on residents. In Liverpool, for example, during the late 1960s and early 1970s the rate of clearance outpaced the capacity to rebuild in demolished areas. The resultant expansion of vacant land was particularly marked where sites were set aside for non-residential purposes such as public open space, community centres or schools for which finance was in short supply, or for private industrial or commercial development for which demand was low. Often the policy decision to clear an area can be made 5–10 years before a CPO is issued and although most authorities kept detailed clearance programmes confidential the probability of an area being affected was advertised by the reduction of public service investment and the council buying property and leaving it unoccupied. Empty houses attract the attention of anti-social activities including squatters, flytippers, vandals and vermin. Such physical conditions can have a demoralizing psychological effect on the remaining residents of an area. The extended nature of the redevelopment process can also result in disruption of friendships and neighbouring patterns leaving individuals isolated. Feelings of insecurity arising from the physical and social break-up of a community, loss of friends and relatives and the disappearance of familiar features in the environment are compounded by the uncertainty over the future caused by a lack of communication between redevelopment authorities and residents. Genuine public participation to provide residents with accurate and timely information about the future of their homes was commonly absent. Similar adverse consequences of the renewal process have been recorded in several US studies (Finsterbusch 1980).

Long-term effects on displaced residents principally involve the increased cost of replacement housing and the quality of the new accommodation. In a survey of clearance programmes in forty-one American cities Anderson (1964) found that 60.0 per cent of displaced households relocated in other slums, and a general conclusion of US clearance activity is that most households move to neighbourhoods similar to those from which they have been moved, usually on the fringe of the clearance area and often scheduled for clearance in the near future. As Hartman (1964: 278) concluded for many households relocation means 'no more than keeping one step ahead of the bulldozer'. In many US urban neighbourhoods racial 'tipping' occurred as displaced black families moved en masse into formerly white communities. This phenomenon aggravated racial tensions and conflicts and contributed to the racial unrest in US cities in the 1950s and 1960s. The low proportion of displaced households relocated in public housing in most US cities (10.0 per cent) is in marked contrast to the UK where between 80.0 and 90.0 per cent of slum dwellers find accommodation in council housing.

Evidence from both USA and UK clearly establishes that clearance programmes have resulted in increased housing costs for those affected, largely without any direct consideration of the ability or desire of households to absorb these costs. In USA the residents of clearance areas are typically among the poorest and least powerful members of society with most clearance zones located in ethnic neighbourhoods. In such instances racial discrimination can compound the difficulty of relocatees' obtaining decent affordable housing. The evidence for racial discrimination in the allocation of housing in USA is unequivocal (Weink *et al.* 1979). The practice has been furthered by the activities of property developers, estate agents and lending institutions as well as local government segregation ordinances, restrictive covenants on building occupancy and, more recently, exclusionary zoning laws. Since the 1968 Civil Rights Act fair housing legislation has attempted to make discrimination on the grounds of race, colour, religion or national origin illegal in connection with the sale rental or financing of housing and land offered for residential use. The enaction and enforcement of a law are separate issues however and housing market discrimination on racial grounds continues. For the victims this means adverse effects on rents, house prices and access to job opportunities in addition to the more obvious physical segregation of ethnic groups. In general, black Americans typically pay between 5.0 and 20.0 per cent more than white households for the same housing package, and are less likely to be home-owners and therefore to receive the capital gains ensuing from that tenure status. In UK, of those relocatees who do not move into council housing, some decline the move because of the increased rent and travel costs which can cause financial difficulty, while others prefer to remain in private-rented accommodation within a familiar locality.

Rehabilitation

The Housing Act of 1969 signalled the end of the period of high levels of construction and marked a shift away from clearance towards rehabilitation and improvement of existing dwellings as the main tool of urban renewal. Implementation of an improvement policy depends upon the combined initiatives of local government, private owners and housing associations.

As Table 7.3 shows, the 1969 Housing Act extended the system of housing improvement grants and introduced the General Improvement Area within which environmental improvements could be carried out by local authorities financed by the exchequer. As Figure 7.2 shows this had an immediate effect on the uptake of grants. In numerical terms the take-up of 3,324,000 grants between 1949 and 79 (with over 1,900,000 since the 1969 Act), represented a considerable achievement of the rehabilitation policy. However several criticisms are possible:

1 Although the absence of basic amenities was most serious in the pre-1919 stock the proportion of grants taken up by these dwellings was less than that for inter-war houses. Similarly, owner-occupied housing accounted for 70 per cent of grant approvals in 1973 despite the fact that private-rented property was most in need of improvement. In social terms the effects of the improvement boom were largely regressive, with the better-housed and better-off sections of the community deriving most benefit (Gibson and Langstaff 1982). In London the majority of improvement grants were to landlords and property developers (the proportion varying between 40.0 and 70.0 per cent in different boroughs), and in parts of west London the take-up of grants led directly to gentrification and displacement of working-class residents. Since properties with vacant possession are worth considerably more to a landlord than their value with sitting tenants (e.g. the ratio of 2.5 in west London in 1984 translated into a difference of more than £100,000) the incentive to displace tenants and rehabilitate to increase value even further led at times to harassment by neglect until tenants had little option but to vacate. Some property developers also took advantage of the liberalized conditions for improvement grants and

Table 7.3 Principal housing legislation in the UK, 1945–1986

Act of Parliament		Government in power
1946	Housing (Financial & Miscellaneous Provisions) Act. Raised level of subsidies and rate fund contributions.	
		Labour
1949	Housing Act. Removed statutory restriction which limited public housing to 'the working classes'. Introduced improvement grants.	
1952	Housing Act. Raised subsidies.	
1954	Housing Repairs and Rents Act. Restarted slum clearance and encouraged private-sector improvements. Introduced '12 point standard' for improvement.	
		Conservative
1956	Housing Subsidies Act. Reduced subsidies for general-needs housing. Rate fund contributions made optional. Subsidy structure encouraged high-rise building.	
1957	Housing Act. Major consolidating Act.	
1957	Rent Act. A measure to begin decontrol of rents at next change of tenancy.	
1958	Housing (Financial Provisions) Act. Consolidating Act for financial matters.	
1959	House Purchase and Housing Act Extended improvement grant system. Encouraged local authority mortgage lending.	Conservative
1961	Housing Act. Reintroduced subsidy for general-needs housing, but at two rates.	
1964	Housing Act. Extended improvement grants. Established the Housing Corporation.	
1965	Rent Act. Introduced 'Fair Rents'.	
1967	Housing Subsidies Act. Introduced a new subsidy system, more general to local authorities.	
		Labour
1968	Rent Act. A consolidating Act.	
1969	Housing Act. Raised level of improvement grants and introduced 'general improvement areas'.	

1971	Housing Act. Increased rate of improvement grants in assisted areas.	
1972	Housing Finance Act. Introduced fair rents for council tenants and replaced all existing subsidies with a new deficit subsidy system. Housing revenue accounts now permitted to generate a surplus. Introduced a mandatory rent-rebate scheme.	Conservative
1974	Housing Act. Introduced Housing Action Areas and expanded the role of the Housing Corporation.	
1974	Rent Act. Gave security of tenure to tenants in furnished dwellings.	
1975	Housing Rents and Subsidies Act. Fair rents abandoned. Rebate scheme retained. New interim subsidy arrangements to replace 1972 Act provisions.	Labour
1977	Housing (Homeless Persons) Act. Placed a duty on local housing authorities to provide accommodation for homeless households in certain priority-needs groups.	
1980	Housing Act. Introduced: (i) statutory right to buy for council tenants (and some housing association tenants) with generous discounts. (ii) a 'tenants' charter'. (iii) new deficit subsidy system. (iv) new provisions for review for fair rents. (v) new tenures known as shorthold and assured tenancies.	
1980	Local Government and Planning Land Act. Changes to local government finance.	
1982	Social Security and Housing Benefit Act. Established housing benefit system.	
1984	Housing and Building Control Act. Extended and tightened 'right to buy'.	
1984	Housing Defects Act. Obligations placed on local authorities in respect of sold defective dwellings.	Conservative
1985	Housing Act. Consolidating.	
1985	Housing Associations Act. Consolidating.	
1986	Building Societies Act. Enabled building societies to own and invest in housing directly.	
1986	Housing and Planning Act. Extended 'right to buy' discounts (but Lords' amendment excluded dwellings suitable for the elderly). Facilitated block sales of estates.	
1986	Social Security Act. Modifications to the Housing Benefit Scheme.	

Source: Malpass and Murie 1987

made huge profits from the grant-aided conversion of large multi-occupied houses into small self-contained flats which were sold or let to higher-income groups attracted to selected areas.

2   The General Improvement Areas had only a limited impact. Approximately one-third of GIA declarations between 1969 and 1973 were in council-owned areas (mainly inter-war estates) with most of the remainder in largely privately-owned areas of by-law housing. While council owner-ship of housing and land ensured systematic improve-ment on a block contract basis the private sector GIAs made a dis-appointingly small contribution to housing improvement with only 18 per cent of houses in need of improvement actually improved by 1973. Reasons for this failure include the fact that (a) even limited improvements took several years to implement due to inefficiencies in local authority management, (b) more significant environmental improve-ment required more exchequer funding, and (c) even in completed GIAs the improved environment had only a marginal impact on grant take-up which was affected by more fundamental economic factors.

3   In contrast to the gentrifying areas of London the provisions of the 1969 Act had little impact in areas where there was no middle-class demand for conversion. In many northern industrial towns local authority intervention was minimal and few GIAs were declared. Most of these areas continued to house low-income tenants often in multiple-occupancy properties. In short, the less attractive areas continued to decline.

Revision of the improvement policy in the Housing Act 1974 led to (a) the introduction of Housing Action Areas to tackle small areas (up to 300 houses) of the worst housing conditions within a 5–7 year timespan leaving GIAs to deal with better areas, and (b) a greater role for Housing Associations to combat the abuses of the system by some private landlords. The effect of the new legislation on the number of improve-ment grants taken up is indicated in Figure 7.2. Renovation grants fell from the 1973 peak of 361,000 to 127,000 in 1975 before rising slightly to 136,000 by 1979. Within these totals grants to private owners slumped from 238,000 to 66,000. The encouragement given to the Housing Association movement was reflected in the fact that by 1979 grant approvals were, at 19,000, four times the 1973 level.

Though initially concentrated in London, Housing Association activity has subsequently spread to most British cities and although the total con-tribution is small (2.0 per cent of stock) the local impact can be signifi-cant and this key element of the voluntary housing sector has been encouraged by governments as a partial substitute for the declining private-rented sector. Housing Associations have been particularly

Figure 7.2 Renovation grants approved in England and Wales, 1949–80

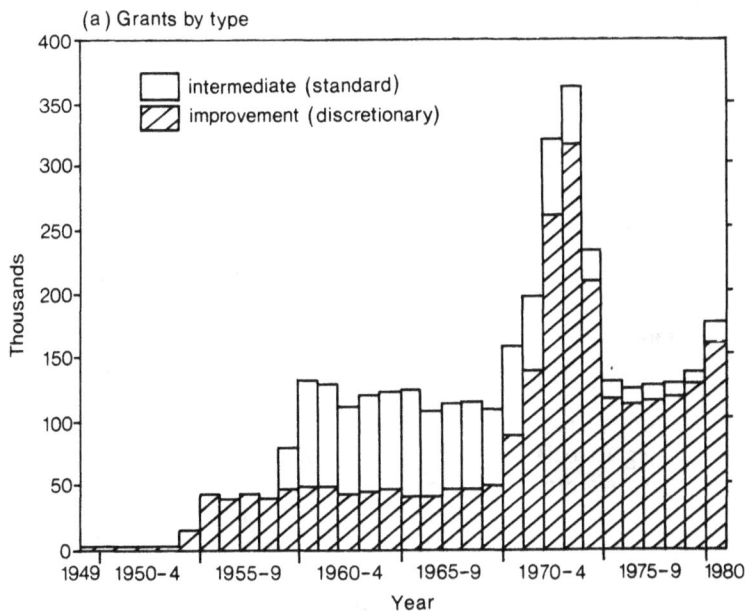

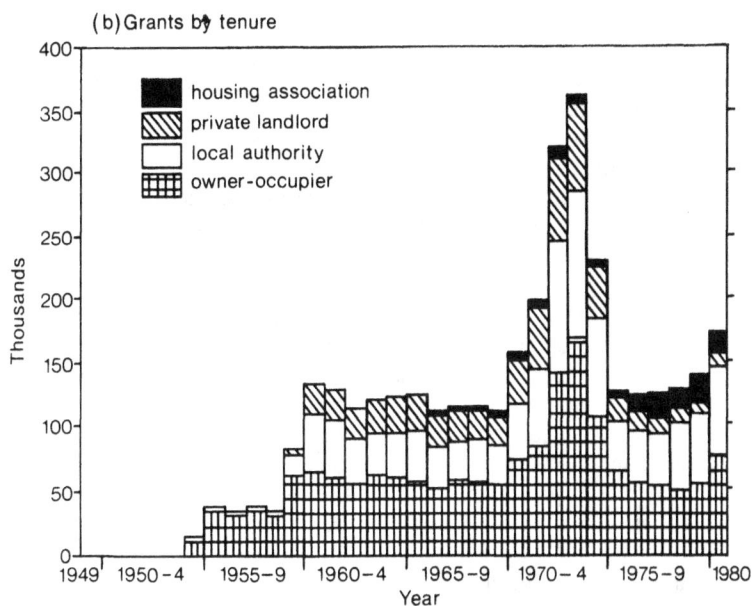

(a) Grants by type

intermediate (standard)
improvement (discretionary)

(b) Grants by tenure

housing association
private landlord
local authority
owner-occupier

effective in providing housing for special needs including the elderly, single people, lone parent families and the unemployed as well as minority groups such as discharged mental patients. Their impact on housing supply is especially noteworthy in areas where council house building has been cut and in parts of the inner-city where private-rented opportunities have been decimated.

Housing Associations are also active agents of urban renewal, working at a smaller scale than local authorities and often involving rehabilitation of individual properties. On the debit side Housing Associations, particularly the smaller ones, have been criticized on the grounds that (a) rents are often higher than council rents for similar accommodation despite receiving subsidies from local authorities and the Housing Corporation (established in 1974 to oversee Housing Association activity), (b) much improvement or conversion work carried out in the 1970s was inferior to council housing due to the non-application of Parker-Morris standards, (c) selection of tenants is largely in the hands of Housing Association managers providing scope for discrimination, (d) tenants were not protected by the Rent Acts, (e) there has been inefficient use of resources due to high turnover of staff and diseconomies of small-scale operations, and (f) although receiving public funds Housing Associations are neither accountable to central government nor to their local community, their development programme being controlled by the Housing Corporation. Nevertheless Housing Associations enjoy a degree of support from all the main political parties in the UK. This indicates a continuing role for them in providing accommodation for minority groups and households not wishing or unable to qualify for a council house or mortgage.

In USA urban renewal was a central component of national urban policy from the enactment of the 1949 Housing Act to the 1974 Housing and Community Development Act which terminated the programme and established the community development block grant as the principal avenue for federal assistance to cities. The original programme of slum clearance and redevelopment (1949–67) was not designed to aid the slum dweller directly but to effect a change in land use. It represented a mix of public and private initiatives. The federal government defined the outlines of the programme, approved local projects submitted for consideration and provided the bulk of the financing. Local government selected projects and their locations, directed the process of acquisition and clearance (using eminent domain if necessary), and then made the land available to private developers. The task of new development lay with the private real estate market with profit as a central motivating force. The scale of profit involved is demonstrated by the renewal project undertaken south of Washington Square in New York. The city purchased the land for $41 million and resold it to private interests for $20 million.

Two-thirds of the $21 million difference (the write-down) was received in the form of a federal grant to the city, the other third being borne by the city. In effect public funds 'subsidised the purchase of prime land by private entrepreneurs, with the federal government paying the lion's share of the subsidy' (Bellush and Housknecht 1967: 12).' Understandably, throughout the 1950s private developers co-operated enthusiastically with the urban renewal programme. By the end of 1964, 970 different redevelopment projects had been approved throughout the USA accounting for a total of 36,400 acres of inner city land. The inability of local governments to direct the development process was a major limitation on the programme's effectiveness in providing replacement housing for those displaced. In many instances the main reason for renewal was to facilitate expansion of non-residential facilities, to remove an aesthetic or social eyesore, or to construct luxury housing projects. The West End renewal project in Boston, for example, cleared 20 acres of working-class private housing and replaced it with 2,400 new dwellings designed almost entirely for middle- to upper-income occupancy, with only a 150 unit elderly project directly aided by federal subsidy (Gans 1962).

From 1967 to 1974 the objectives of the US urban renewal programme were stated more precisely by the Department of Housing and Urban Development as (1) the conservation and expansion of the housing supply for low- and moderate-income families, (2) the development of centres of employment for the jobless, the underemployed, and lower income persons, and (3) projects serving areas of 'physical decay, high tensions, and great social need' (US Congressional Research Service 1973). Effectively, this shifted emphasis from wholesale clearance towards rehabilitation and spot clearance, as in the UK. While the 1974 Act officially ended urban renewal as a federal programme cities were expected to devote most of their grant allocation to continuing urban renewal type activities such as land acquisition, slum clearance, demolition, housing rehabilitation and neighbourhood redevelopment. The Act stated that a city's activities should principally benefit low- and moderate-income groups and ensure citizen participation but the Department of Housing and Urban development had no powers to withhold funds from non-conforming cities. Section 8 of the 1974 Act introduced a housing allowance programme to aid lower-income households. Instead of making payments directly to needy tenants the programme consisted of long-term contracts between the Department of Housing and Urban Development and private developers, landlords or public housing agencies designating specific apartments for Section 8 subsidies. Approved apartments could be existing units or units to be constructed or rehabilitated. Rental payments for tenants were on a par with those for public housing amounting to between 15.0 and 25.0 per cent of their total income.

Housing owners received from Section 8 funds the difference between the tenant's contribution and a pre-determined 'fair market' rent based on prevailing private rents in the locality. Overall as Fox (1985: 215) observed, 'It was an ingenious combination of subsidies for deserving families with incentives for private owners and developers.'

One of the major reasons behind the switch from clearance to rehabilitation was the criticism of household displacement and community disruption associated with the former strategy. It is argued that under rehabilitation 'families are not forced to move away from their accustomed surroundings and are not faced with more difficult and costly journeys to work, shop and school: the community is maintained and the pattern of life remains unchanged' (D. Kirby 1979: 50). While this may be generally true it is unusual for the community to remain intact even after rehabilitation. The rehabilitation process often involves a reduction in the number of housing units. In addition, subsequent rent increases can force people to vacate refurbished homes. In an extreme example in one London borough rents for furnished accommodation rose from an average of £5.70 (at 1972 prices) before improvement to £22.39 after. Another difficulty has been that where the property has been refurbished specifically for occupation by lower income groups criticism has fallen on the quality of accommodation provided. Limitations imposed by the built form of older housing (e.g. back-to-backs or Glasgow tenements) and failure to regularly increase the cost limits for grants has resulted in an erosion of standards with some schemes regarded by residents as second-class houses in second-class environments. One of the main arguments in favour of rehabilitation is that it is quicker and cheaper than redevelopment. Doubts exist, however, over whether the process is significantly speedier. A decade after the introduction of GIAs few had been completed, and the National Community Development Project (1975) concluded that 'improvement policy has often proved slower than redevelopment' (p. 12). In crude unit-cost terms evidence from the USA has suggested that rehabilitation is cheaper than redevelopment. However, as D. Kirby (1979: 52) points out, 'although it is cheaper rehabilitation need not be more economic'. Generally the factors influencing rehabilitation and redevelopment are so varied that it is impossible to state categorically that one policy is more or less economic than the other. The merits of individual projects have to be analysed independently.

Chapter eight

Housing issues

The availability of shelter and equality of access to housing are basic social goals, fulfilment of which is directly affected by government policies relating to tenure structure and the role of public housing, housing finance and the distribution of housing benefits, and the particular needs of disadvantaged social groups. These questions form the focus of the present chapter.

Trends in housing tenure

A major transformation has been effected in the tenure balance of housing in the UK over the course of the present century. In 1913, 90.0 per cent of Britain's households rented their accommodation privately, 2.0 per cent rented from local authorities and the remainder were owner-occupiers. By 1981 the position had been almost totally reversed with only 13,0 per cent of households still renting privately compared to 56.0 per cent who were owner-occupiers and 31.0 per cent council tenants. The greater part of this transformation has taken place in the post-war period. These tenural changes are interrelated.

The decline of private-rented housing has been attributed to a number of factors. These include:

1   The private-rented sector includes a high proportion of the oldest and poorest dwellings, most built before 1919. Slum clearance programmes have demolished hundreds of thousands of homes, with demand being directed to the council or owner-occupied sectors.

2   Government policies to deal with overcrowding (e.g. the Housing Acts of 1961, 1964 and 1969), increased controls over multi-occupation and consequently reduced the number of private tenants.

3   As we have seen, rehabilitation aided by improvement grants has often been followed by tenant displacement and the sale of property to owner-occupation, particularly in gentrifying neighbourhoods.

4   The comparatively poor rate of return from investment in private-rented housing was apparent by the turn of the century. With the extension of the principle of limited liability in the late nineteenth century, the development of the stock exchange and building societies, the expansion of government and municipal stock, and increased overseas investment opportunities, capital flowed out of private-rented property. During the twentieth century increased public intervention (e.g. rent controls) further reduced the attraction of housing investment, while the increasing costs of repair and maintenance eroded profits.

5   Although there was a certain amount of building for private rental in the inter-war period the bulk of private construction during the building boom of the 1930s (prior to widespread planning controls) was for owner-occupation.

6   In contrast to subsidies provided to council tenants and tax allowances for mortgage holders it is only since 1973 that private tenants have received rent allowances. Landlords, however, were unable to set a 'depreciation allowance' against taxation and this encouraged them to sell for owner-occupation. This trend was even apparent during the period 1957–65 when rents were de-controlled.

The diminution of private-rented housing, the traditional source of shelter for those denied access to the owner-occupied sector, eventually led to direct government intervention (Balchin 1985). The growth of municipal housing however cannot be attributed to a single cause. Other important motivating factors were the failure of nineteenth-century philanthropic housing associations to demonstrate that it was possible to provide decent dwellings at a rent affordable by the low-paid, increased working-class militancy over housing conditions vividly displayed in the Glasgow rent strikes of 1915, the shortage of housing in the post-First World War era, and a gradual shift away from the dominant Victorian ideology of self-help and the pervading belief in the efficiency of the market mechanism. Taken in combination those factors led the state to pass the 1919 Housing Act (Addision Act) which offered subsidies to local authorities to make up losses incurred in providing homes over and above those borne by a one-penny rate (Merrett 1979). The Wheatley Act 1924 gave a major boost to council-house building with over 500,000 houses stemming from this legislation but for the great majority of working class accommodation was still to be found in the private-rented sector. The poorest of the working class still lived in overcrowded slum conditions.

Acknowledgement of this led to the enactment of the Greenwood Act 1930 which requested local authorities to prepare five-year slum clearance programmes. The bulk of council-house building has occurred since the Second World War. For most of this period there was tacit agreement across the political spectrum on the need for a council housebuilding programme. Following the return of a Conservative government in 1979 a major ideological gap opened with the government's conceptualization of council housing as a welfare service assisting those households unable to afford other types of housing differing radically from the Labour Party's belief that the public sector should supply housing for general needs (i.e. should satisfy the demand from all households who wish to rent rather than buy). As we shall see later, prosecution of the government's philosophy has led to a residualization of the council stock. By 1981 the number of public sector housing starts had fallen to 32,000, the lowest level since the first Labour Housing Act of 1923.

An important component of Conservative housing policy introduced in the Housing Act of 1980, is the right of council tenants to buy their homes. The case for council house sales rests on:

1 The rising costs of council housing and the growing gap between cost rents and the 'fair rents' charged required increasing government subsidies. Some proponents argued that if long-standing (over 30 years) tenants were given their houses and others sold at favourable terms the savings on subsidies and revenue raised could lead either to a reduction in taxation or allow funds to be diverted into other areas.

2 By the late 1970s it was possible to argue that over the long term it was of more economic benefit for tenants to own rather than rent their council house. Kilroy (1982) demonstrated that over 35 years the net outgoings (at 1982 prices) of an average tenant who bought his £14,000 home (at a 40.0 per cent discount) would be £12,000 less than one who continued to rent. The purchaser would also have a well-constructed appreciating asset which they can pass on to their children.

3 In addition to the financial advantages owner-occupation offers a feeling of independence, freedom over the care and condition of the property and greater locational mobility.

Critics of council house sales refute these arguments on the grounds that:

1 The 'cost of council-housing subsidies' case is often based on extreme examples (such as inner London) and ignores the fact that local authorities are able to distribute these costs over the whole of their stock by using the rent surpluses from older houses to keep down rents on newer houses built when capital costs and interest rates were high. The argument that selling houses can contribute to a major cut in public expenditure has also been attacked by several authors who have questioned the financial calculations employed (Kilroy 1980). They point out, for example, that

proponents have included supplementary benefits in the cost of council housing yet this would still have to be paid to low-income householders if they converted to owner-occupation. Omitting this income-support cost would have meant that in 1977-8 the cost of council house subsidy (at £1,100 million) would have been broadly equal to the tax relief given to owner-mortgagers.

2   Normally only higher-income tenants could afford to buy even with a discount and even some of these might face financial difficulty if (a) they reach retirement age before they have paid off their mortgage (over 50 per cent of cases) or (b) mortgages were based on contributions from the incomes of several family members (over 20 per cent of cases).

3   It is mainly the better sited higher quality dwellings that are sold off leaving families on lower-incomes with a reduced chance of improving their housing position through a transfer within the local authority system. In addition the sale of older rent-surplus yielding housing in attractive locations would reduce the possibility of cross-fertilization and thereby necessitate higher rents for disadvantaged tenants in inner-city locations.

Possibly the biggest indictment of the right to buy policy is that it was being implemented at a time of the lowest level of council housebuilding for half a century, resulting in a net loss of 80,000 units in 1981. The re-election of a conservative government in 1983 was followed by the Housing and Building Control Act 1984 which introduced further increases in discount available (up to a maximum of 60 per cent) and a reduction in the eligibility period (from 3 to 2 years), and by the Housing Defects Act 1984 which provided 90.0 per cent repair grants to remedy defects not apparent at the time of purchase. Such policies have contributed to the residualization of council housing (Balchin 1985). Residualization is apparent in three ways. First, since 1979 when the tenure accounted for 6,840,000 dwellings or 32.1 per cent of the UK housing stock there has been both an absolute and relative decline in the contribution made by council housing. Secondly the quality of the council stock has been declining with increased incidence of design and structural faults and difficult to let dwellings. Compared to the inter-war and immediate post-war periods when council housing was a privileg-ed tenure it has become less popular. Thirdly, since the early 1970s the social composition of council tenants has altered with a relative decline in the proportion of intermediate non-manual and skilled manual workers and an increase in personal service and semi- or unskilled manual workers. In addition an increased proportion of council tenants (lone-parent families, the elderly, sick and disabled and the unemployed) are dependent upon supplementary benefits. It is, of course, important to realize that these are general characteristics and that in practice the degree of residualization varies across the country. Also these symptoms are not in themselves causal factors. The residualization of council housing is the result of broader economic and social processes including the deskilling of labour as a consequence of deindustrialization and technological innovation, high unemployment, the withdrawal of private landlords from the low-rent market, and increased demand for owner-occupation among the more affluent, as well as recent government policy.

The restricted role envisaged for council housing by the political Right in Britain finds an echo in the history of USA attempts to enact a programme of public housing (Meehan 1977). Essentially public housing in the USA, like many other social programmes, is a product of the New Deal era as enunciated in the Housing Acts of 1937 and 1949. Two basic methods of supplying housing to low-income families have been used. The first employed a public agency to develop, own and manage housing. By the end of 1974, 67.0 per cent of the total public housing supply (860,000 units) have been developed in this way. Another 230,000 units (turnkey housing) was produced by private interests and sold to a public agency, usually a local housing authority. The second main approach authorized by the Housing Act 1965 was the leasing of privately owned facilities and by the end of 1974, 169,000 units accounted for 14.0 per cent of the total public stock.

A fundamental reason for the failure of the US public housing initiative was that it did not have widespread political support being alien to the dominant market philosophy. Even the initial rationale behind the programme was multifaceted being seen as a way of simultaneously reducing the high levels of unemployment in the 1930s and assisting the housing industry, as well as a means of eliminating slums and increasing the supply of cheap decent housing to the poor. Weak federal control over development costs and housing quality inevitably led to major difficulties. In particular local housing authorities received no operating subsidy from federal government, their sole source of income being rental payments. As costs rose minimum and average rents increased steadily. Prior to the 1974 Housing and Urban Development Act, which introduced a degree of control, rent payments equivalent to half a tenant's gross income were common.

The 1974 Act also foreshadowed a major switch of emphasis away from conventional public housing towards the use of leased housing. Signs of increased privatization of public housing had emerged during the 1960s with the 1965 Housing Act authorization of turnkey housing, the sale of public housing to tenants and the contracting out of management services to private firms. By the mid 1970s construction of public housing projects had fallen significantly and some of the most deteriorated schemes, such as Pruitt-Igoe in St Louis were demolished. In its 1983

135

housing legislation Congress authorized 100,000 units of low-income housing, less than half of the annual level for the 1970s.

The residualization of public housing, as defined earlier, is almost complete in USA with the sector catering for a dependent population characterized by low-income, unemployment, reliance on public assistance, high concentration of the very old, very young and minority groups often occupying a deteriorating physical environment. Structural forces encapsulated in the post-war suburbanization of population and industry, and an unenthusiastic government attitude towards public provision of housing have combined to ensure the low status of public housing in the US city.

Access to council housing

Apart from a duty to rehouse homeless persons, those living in unsatisfactory conditions and priority groups (such as a family with children, a pregnant woman, or an elderly person), local authorities in Britain have almost complete autonomy over the allocation of council housing. With the diminution in supply of private-rented accommodation since the Second World War and the more recent reductions in the council housing stock the power of local authorities to determine the residential situation of large numbers of city dwellers is profound. In such circumstances the criteria upon which local authority allocation procedures are based assume central importance. This has been underlined by recent research which indicates that ethnic minorities, atypical families (notably single parents) and lower socio-economic status groups tend to occupy less satisfactory accommodation either in terms of dwelling type, location or both.

Clearly, the extent to which this may stem from council allocation practices is a question of considerable moral, legal and operational significance (Henderson and Karn 1986).

Several factors influence the pattern of council house allocation including:

1   Restrictions on eligibility — these include residential qualifications and rules debarring owner-occupiers from council housing.
2   Grading of applicants — until recently most housing authorities employed grading procedures to categorize applicants according to their suitability for different quality accommodation (Gray 1976).
3   Waiting time — even where points schemes based on an applicant's 'need' are in operation the length of waiting time can be of crucial importance in determining the quality of housing allocated. Long-term applicants with less acute need can obtain housing in preferred locations while economically and socially disadvantaged households receive the least attractive units.

4 Refusal of offers — although only a small minority of authorities apply penalties for refusal of a housing offer, there is evidence that applicants *believe* there is some upper limit to the number of refusals permitted. Clapham and Kintrea (1986) in Glasgow found that there was an increasing tendency for offers to be refused as incomes rise and that later offers tended to be of higher quality than earlier ones.

5 Informal allocation procedures — these arise from the operational objectives of allocation personnel. For central housing department staff there is pressure to maximize the number of successful offers. For staff in area offices the chief goal is avoiding management and neighbourhood problems. These objectives, in conjunction with informal stereotyping of applicants in terms of their suitability for different areas and dwelling types, can determine the housing offers made to applicants.

6 Expressed preference — this view contends that ethnic minority groups prefer to live in proximity to other members of the group both for positive (cultural retention) and negative (fear of discrimination) reasons. Others have suggested that poor people actually prefer the less demanding lifestyle on a run-down estate. The importance of a related factor, that of differential rent-paying ability, has been reduced since the introduction of a uniform housing benefit scheme has offset spatial variations in rent levels.

In general, the major cause of differential allocation centres on the ability of households to wait for good quality accommodation (the desperation factor) and the strategies employed by allocation staff in pursuing their aims of filling vacancies and housing as many applicants as possible (English 1987). The desperation level of an individual household is seen in (a) their constrained choice, i.e. an expression of preference for an area or type of dwelling which is constrained by the expected length of waiting time, and (b) their ability to refuse offers in the expectation of obtaining something better. Council allocation staff seeking to maximize the likelihood of an offer being accepted tend to match popular vacancies with 'discerning' applicants (indicated by previous refusals) and less popular areas with the more desperate. This approach may be reinforced by judgemental views about the just desserts for 'respectable' or 'disreputable' households. Such practices may be facilitated and legitimized by a formal grading system for applicants although the existence of a *de facto* grading makes this unnecessary for practical purposes.

Resolution of the problem of differential allocation is far from simple, not least because the major causal factor appears to be the informal operational practices of staff seeking to maximize the efficiency of council allocation procedures. A strategy of improvement of the council stock to eliminate the wide differences in quality between areas is currently not feasible given constraints on housing finance. The continuing sale of council houses will further reduce the stock of better quality accommodation and it seems likely that in most cities the chief price of a popular council house will remain a relatively long period on the waiting list.

Housing finance

In the UK, because of the central involvement of government in the production and distribution of housing, particular attention has been devoted to the area of housing finance dealing with *housing subsidies*. During the 1970s this dimension of housing finance emerged as a major component of the political debate due to (a) the effects of inflation and rising interest rates on the cost of council housing subsidies, and in particular (b) the spiralling cost of tax relief as a result of the unprecedented rise in house prices in 1972–73, increases in the mortgage rate, and the growing number of mortgages. In the period 1967–68 to 1976–77 total relief to mortgagers rose by 146.0 per cent in real terms while public sector subsidies rose by 107.0 per cent.

As well as the increasing cost of subsidies concern was also expressed over the inequitable distribution of financial benefit between council tenants and owner-occupiers. For example, whereas mortgage tax relief increased from £865 million in 1975–76 to £1,925 million in 1982–83 direct exchequer subsidies have fallen in recent years from £1,809 million in 1979–80 to £592 million in 1982–83. In total, 'the average mortgager received 78.0 per cent more than the average council tenant in 1982–83' (Balchin 1985: 239). All governments, however, have shied away from tackling the politically explosive question of the reform of housing finance.

The major criticisms of the existing system are:
1   The inequity of the system is well documented (Goss and Lansley 1981). Basically, while mortgage interest relief increases automatically in relation to rate of tax and the size of the mortgage, since the Housing Finance Act 1972 which introduced fair rents in the public sector, council house rent rebates (housing benefit since 1983) have been based on assessed need. During periods of inflation when owner-occupiers benefit from increased mortgage tax relief and a declining debt in real terms council tenants normally face rising rents. In 1982 income-based subsidies replaced less than half the income lost by council house tenants through higher rents (Roistacher 1984).

2   Mortgage tax relief artificially stimulates demand and so inflates house prices. It also contributes to the residualization of council housing by 'creaming-off' the relatively well-endowed working class.

3   The post-war flow of finance into housing demand rather than into housing supply (i.e. into exchange of existing housing rather than construction of new units) represents an inefficient allocation of resources. Kilroy (1980) has shown how in the UK 90.0 per cent of net personal savings flow into housing, life insurance and pension funds, three areas which receive the most favourable tax treatment (the corresponding figure for USA being 60.0 per cent). This effectively reduces the capital available for more productive investment such as industrial regeneration. In terms of the circuits of capital concept mortgage interest relief ensures that surplus value is transferred from industrial capital (in the form of wages) to interest-bearing capital — i.e. from the primary circuit of capital to the secondary circuit, to the detriment of the former.

4   Mortgage tax relief represents a leakage from the tax system which has to be made good by other means such as VAT.

Suggestions for reform range from radical calls for the abolition of tax relief on mortgage interest to approaches which involve the retention of mortgage tax relief and the introduction of tax on imputed rent income. Supporters of reform point out that the savings to the exchequer could be diverted to housebuilding or renovation, could lead to reduced income tax, and insure that house prices increased only in line with other investments and so not draw off a disproportionate amount of funds.

Alternative strategies

The continued existence of a 'housing problem' testifies to the partial achievements of past policy and suggests the value of considering some alternative strategies. Between the policy extremes of municipalization and social ownership on one hand and private-sector initiative and self-help on the other lie a range of possible approaches.

Those who argue for the decommodification of housing support the principle of social ownership (i.e. the take-over of private rented housing) as a means of promoting greater equality in housing consumption by allocating housing according to need, and as a way of improving the condition and maintaining the supply of rented accommodation. The advantages of social ownership include the fact that it (a) brings empty private dwellings into use, diversifies the council stock and so provides low-income households with greater choice, (b) caters for minority groups and those in urgent need as well as satisfying general housing needs, (c) affords security of tenure and protects tenants from unscrupulous private landlords, and (d) reserves capital gains arising from property appreciation for the community good. In operation social ownership could involve a variety of publicly responsible bodies including (a) local authorities, the municipalizing agents who would become responsible for the total housing situation in their area, (b) housing associations and co-operatives which would manage dwellings acquired by local authorities, and (c) possibly a Social Housing Authority set up by central government to promote municipalization and offer advice to lower-tier agencies on the policy and practice of social ownership.

To achieve its aims the socialization of housing would have to be accompanied by sensitive management practices which took real account of the differing needs and preferences of different sections of the community. Although social ownership is more complex than municipalization alone it offers the promise of greater tenant participation and local democracy, and the increased choice would make the system superior to the previous private-rented sector and, in some cases, preferable to traditional council housing. Pursuit of such a radical approach to the housing problem is clearly dependent on the political climate. While municipalization and social ownership are central elements in the Labour Party's housing policy they are an anathema to Conservative philosophy.

Less politically contentious are the various voluntary housing initiatives. While the Housing Associations are the most prominent, other strategies include co-ownership, cost-rent, and self-build societies. All of these, however, are of minor importance in terms of the housing inventory and do not contribute to the wellbeing of lower-income groups. Initiatives specifically intended to promote low-cost home ownership include:

1 The option mortgage scheme introduced in 1968 whereby the option mortgager is charged a lower rate of interest on his loan (since he would not qualify for a basic tax allowance), the difference between the option rate and the prevailing mortgage rate being paid by the government to the institution or local authority providing the loan.

2 Local authority direct mortgage lending, mainly for tenants wishing to buy their council house. Related to this is the Building Society Local Authority Support Scheme intended to promote the purchase of older properties by, for example, first-time buyers, council tenants moving out of the sector or those on the council house waiting list. The local authority is able to refer suitable applicants to building societies who have allocated funds for the scheme as requested by the Department of the Environment.

3 Equity sharing in which the occupier owns part of the equity in the house and rents the rest from the local authority.

4 Local authority building for sale.

5 Homesteading, i.e. the sale of improved council dwellings on concessionary terms.

6 Sale of land to private developers for the provision of 'cost-price' starter homes.

7   Local authority improvement of older houses which are modernized then offered for sale.

8   Use of local authority guarantee powers which enable local authorities to guarantee building society mortgages to persuade them to lend on properties normally outwith their scope.

While this list represents a considerable investment of policy innovation and ingenuity in an attempt to extend 'down-market home ownership' the collective impact on the housing market and on the needs of special groups has been less than hoped for (Booth and Crook 1986).

The notion of improvement through self-help, private investment and limited government intervention is particularly strong in USA and has underlain recent approaches to the urban housing problem. Of major importance has been the Neighbourhood Housing Services programme. An NHS programme is a partnership between residents, local government and private financial institutions in revitalizing a neighbourhood. Its primary aims are concerned with the rehabilitation of housing, improvement of the environment, and with fostering self-help and owner-occupation. An inter-agency (Department of Housing and Urban Development and the Federal Home Loans Bank Board) central organization, the Neighbourhood Reinvestment Corporation, has the task of assisting cities to establish NHS programmes. The Neighbourhood Reinvestment Corporation provides advice on staff training and selection and helps set up a revolving loan fund for the NHS programme by using seed money and attracting other sources such as the local authority Community Development Block Grant funds, charitable foundations, and private financial institutions. The involvement of local lending institutions is critical to the success of neighbourhood improvement and is engendered by a combination of carrot (funds devoted to improvement schemes are exempt from tax) and stick (legislation which requires disclosure of local lending practices). This fund provides individually tailored loans to those who cannot meet normal commercial credit requirements. Once the NHS programme is established the NRC withdraws leaving a local self-supporting operation, and will only intervene if difficulties become apparent in their annual audit of NHS finances. The criteria for selecting a neighbourhood for a NHS programme are:

(a)   housing must be basically sound but showing 'warning signs' of lack of maintenance and deterioration.

(b)   mortgages and home loans must be difficult to obtain in the area.

(c)   at least 50.0 per cent of the dwellings must be owner-occupied.

(d)   the area must have distinct boundaries and be large enough to stimulate the imagination of potential participants but small enough to allow for early visible success. On average NHS areas have about 4,900 dwellings, 2,300 buildings and 12,500 people.

141

(e)   the medium income of the residents must average 80.0 per cent of that of the city.

It is clear, therefore, that NHS programmes would not be applied to areas which had declined too far or in which there was no tradition of owner-occupation. The selection of areas with a good chance of success is considered necessary to maintain the credibility of the programme and ensure the participation of the private sector. This means that the degree to which NHS assists low-income households depends largely on the size of the revolving fund available to high-risk applicants. Application of the NHS idea to Britain would seem to have the greatest chance of success in similar environments such as GIAs or some HAAs. The economic ethos of the scheme, however, implies a readiness to 'write–off' those areas with little hope of regeneration and this may be less generally acceptable in UK.

An alternative approach to an NHS programme is to employ local or community development corporations in upgrading housing in an area. These are non-profit organizations working in partnership with the local government and the private sector and accountable to the residents of the neighbourhood. Following the Neighbourhood Self Development Act 1978 aid has been targetted on low-income areas and community development organizations have been most active in the older larger cities such as Baltimore, New York and Chicago where they help to fill a gap left by public housing authorities. Two problems must be overcome before community development organizations can assume a greater role in developing assisted housing. First, the reduction in federal funding for subsidized housing have made it more difficult to provide units within reach of low-income households.

A major challenge for community development organizations is to accomplish the financial engineering to restrict repayments to appropriate levels. This may be approached through, for example, property tax abatements, reduced code requirements or graduated payment mortgages. Secondly, community development organizations require technical assistance and seed money to hire and train staff, possibly on the lines of the technical assistance model operating in Massachussetts (Peltz 1982).

A third strategy employed in USA is the concept of urban homesteading which developed in response to the growing problem of property abandonment. It was envisaged that 'sweat equity' (people's self–help efforts) would reduce the amount of cash the homesteader would have to contribute to the scheme. In practice, however, the amount and skilled nature of work involved has required the use of contractors and the provision of technical advice as well as financial assistance. The properties considered for homesteading have to be in a repairable condition and in areas with the possibility of upgrading. Although initially viewed as a means of providing low-income homes the high costs of rehabilitation and the skills required militate against this. A further problem is that the selection of homesteaders depends on the ability to pay rather than their housing needs with the result that in some neighbourhoods gentrification has taken place in contradiction to the original spirit of the idea.

Interestingly, the homesteading concept has recently been applied on a small scale in the peripheral council estates in a number of British cities. In many of these areas inadequate housing is combined with low incomes, limited access to jobs and opportunities and high incidence of social pathologies. The resulting multiple deprivation serves to emphasize that the housing crisis is but one aspect of a multi-faceted socio-economic problem whose common denominator is the personal, social and financial poverty of residents.

Chapter nine

Urban retailing

A wide range of economic and social forces have combined to influence the nature of the urban retailing system in the post-war period. The major factors on the demand side have included,

1 Changes in residential location: the single most important factor has been the widespread suburbanization of population. Despite signs of growth in some inner-city areas related to gentrification and the arrival of immigrant groups, the overall metropolitan population trend has been one of decentralization. In general it has been the younger, richer and more mobile elements of society that have migrated to the suburbs to create new large sources of demand in areas where few shopping facilities had existed previously. An older poorer and less mobile population has been left behind in the inner city where their lower levels of purchasing power have been insufficient to support the surfeit of shopping facilities that remain. These changes have been most pronounced in the US city where the earlier pattern of retailing has been altered by the growth of new suburban and outlying centres and the decline of central shopping areas. In Britain by contrast strict planning controls have restrained the process of retail decentralization and where it has proceeded it has been mainly associated with convenience trades.

2 The growth of female employment: the fact that women now account for a significantly higher proportion of the total workforce than they did a quarter of a century ago has had two major implications for consumer behaviour — first, through the increased purchasing power created by additions to household incomes and secondly, through the time constraints imposed on shopping, particularly for women engaged in full-time work. The result has been an increase in bulk buying, especially for food, and a reduction in the frequency of shopping trips. This trend has been facilitated by the increased ownership of refrigerators and freezers. There has also been a rise in the proportion of shopping trips originating (and for lunchtime trips, ending) at the workplace.

3   The increase in purchasing power: until the mid 1970s most sections of society had experienced an increase in purchasing power during the post-war period. Coupled with the growth in population numbers the rise in general consumption stimulated the expansion of durable goods and comparison goods trade sectors. Levels of purchasing power fluctuate with the condition of the national economy however and some types of business have been more able to withstand downturns in retail expenditure. In both food and non-food trades the larger companies have retained economic health by increasing their market share at the expense of traditional outlets. This was achieved by offering lower prices and attracting customers from further afield. While the benefits of cheaper shopping are available to the majority of consumers there remain large numbers of low-income households, particularly the elderly on limited pensions, single-parent householders and the unemployed, who lack the ability to buy in bulk or to travel to superstores and hypermarkets.

4   Increased mobility: the growth in car ownership and car-borne shopping has been another factor in the trend towards bulk buying and the shift from daily to less frequent shopping. This has occurred most in the affluent suburbs, particularly in relation to the redevelopment of new district shopping centres, superstores and hypermarkets.

Changing attitudes and expectations: there has been a general demand for more convenience and comfort in shopping which newer rather than older centres can more readily satisfy. Other factors which have affected the nature of retailing include (a) the linking of service stations with superstores and the development of convenience outlets within service stations, (b) television advertising which has generated growth in mail order trade, and (c) technical innovations such as credit cards and EPOS (electronic point of sale) equipment in stores which have increased efficiency.

On the supply side the most significant developments have been:

1   Structural changes in retailing: since 1950 major changes have occurred in the organization and operation of the retail system. Most far reaching has been the expansion of the multiple retailers' share of turnover which has occurred largely at the expense of independent shopkeepers (Table 9.1). The independent food retailers increasingly have had to make use of voluntary buying groups (such as Mace or Spar) or cash and carry warehouses in order to withstand competition from multiple traders. Declining profit margins on food retailing and, in Britain, the abolition of resale price maintenance in 1964 have also altered operational tactics in the retail trades. Self-service outlets have mushroomed and the need to achieve economies of scale has promoted the development of larger units.

Table 9.1 Retail sales by organization type in the UK

	1961 (%)	1966 (%)	1971 (%)	1976 (%)	1978 (%)	1980 (%)
Multiples	28.2	33.0	36.4	40.1	42.2	42.8
Independents	53.9	49.9	48.1	43.0	41.0	40.7
Co-operative Societies	9.5	7.7	5.8	6.2	6.0	5.8
Department stores (incl. Co-ops)	5.9	5.7	5.8	6.0	5.8	5.7
Mail order	2.5	3.7	3.9	4.7	5.0	5.0

Taken together these trends have reduced the total number of establishments. In Britain between 1961 and 1971 the number of shops fell from 542,301 to 504,781 with a further reduction to 354,131 by 1980. In North America the greatest decline in small independent shops occurred in the 1950s in response to the spread of supermarkets and suburban shopping centres. The total number of establishments in USA fell from 537,000 in 1948 to 319,000 in 1963, while over the same period the number of supermarkets increased from 2,313 to 14,518.

2   The introduction of new shops: the general trend towards large self–service outlets resulted in the transfer of the supermarket to Western Europe during the 1960s. Extension of the concept culminated in the development of superstores and hypermarkets. In Britain, in contrast to most of Western Europe, the growth of these stores was restrained by planning controls which have sought to mitigate the adverse affects of these innovations on the existing system. Pressure for retail decentralization has been maintained however and by the 1980s also emanated from retail warehouses operated by multiple groups. Even in Europe, the rapid expansion of superstores and hypermarkets and their burgeoning size (up to 250,000 sq. ft.) has led to the introduction of restrictive legislation in some countries including France where, in 1981, there were 433 of these outlets accounting for one-fifth of food sales and 10.0 per cent of non-food sales. Similar trends can be identified in North America with the development of junior department stores (the equivalent of European superstores) and giant superstores (hypermarkets).

3   The development of new shopping centres: while the origins of the modern purpose-built shopping centre can be traced back to the beginning of the century the concept developed most rapidly during the post-war period. The free-standing car-oriented suburban shopping centre was pioneered in North America where a variety of types now exist. The number of new shopping centres in USA rose from 100 in 1950 to 22,750 in 1981 when they accounted for 42.0 per cent of total retail sales. Several

hundred of these developments are regional shopping centres while a smaller number are super-regional centres.

The competitive impact of these large planned shopping centres on the central shopping area of US cities is well documented. The most serious repercussions have been felt within the largest metropolitan areas. In cities such as Detroit the central area has lost the bulk of its external market to the newer outlying centres and has become increasingly dependent on an internal captive market comprising mainly the poor, elderly, and coloured ethnic groups. Other possible sources of support for some central cities include the office workforce, visiting tourists and businessmen, and the growing number of higher-income residents. In cities such as Denver and Seattle the general decline in central area retail sales has been offset as a result of these groups. In other cities, however, the presence of differing consumer groups in the central city has resulted in a segregation of the shopping area into two distinct zones, comprising a growth area of new specialized shops catering mainly to fashion demands, and a deteriorating area comprising older remnants of the retail trade.

In contrast to the USA, developments in Britain in the early post-war years were largely associated with city centre reconstruction and the implementation of the precinct scheme, particularly in conjunction with the building of new towns. The consistent refusal of British planners to permit the widespread development of free-standing out of town shopping centres is based on a concern that these would undermine the existing retail hierarchy and lead to the same kind of decline in status of the central shopping area that has occurred in many USA cities (Robertson 1983). It is argued that planning regulations are necessary to protect the large amount of public capital invested in post-war redevelopment schemes and to mitigate the competitive impact on the smaller retailers who serve local consumer groups. As a consequence, American influence on British cities is primarily seen in the introduction of enclosed shopping malls, the first of which was the Arndale centre in Leeds, built in 1962. Since then more than 150 similar centres have been developed. The majority have been town centre schemes but a large number also serve as district shopping centres in outlying residential areas. The sole British example of an 'out of town' shopping development akin to these in North America is the Brent Cross centre in north-west London (Newby and Shepherd 1979).

4 New technology: the potential impact of new technology on retailing is considerable but the rate at which innovations, such as electronic point of sale (EPOS) terminals, electronic funds transfer, and teleshopping, will be adopted is unclear. Electronic point of sale terminals linked with in-store mini computers offer several advantages for the efficiency of the

retail operation. These include (a) speeding the sale of goods through a checkout (and checking the work speed of operators), (b) calling up information from the computer when a bar-coded good is sold and providing a descriptive receipt to customers, and (c) monitoring stock control and automatically ordering replacement goods. An on-line system for electronic funds transfer would have an EPOS terminal linked through a central computer in the store to the store's bank and from there to the whole clearing bank system. This would allow a retailer to check the funds available in a customer's account and then if sufficient to carry out a direct debit. An off-line alternative could be based on the credit card concept with customers carrying an electronic money card which is charged up by their bank and 'spent' in shops having the necessary equipment to read and debit the card. Because of the capital costs involved the benefits of this new technology are most likely to accrue to large retailers further accentuating their competitive advantage.

The effects of outlying shopping developments

The impact of hypermarkets and superstores and purpose-built shopping centres in outlying locations has been a dominant issue of retail planning in UK for the last two decades. The impact of these developments can be assessed in three ways.

1 Economic considerations

(a) For the retailer the development costs of establishing a large store in an outlying location are usually less than for a town centre site. These savings may be passed to consumers in the form of cheaper prices and a more attractive shopping environment. Disadvantages for the public in general relate to the possibly higher cost of providing service infrastructure, a lower yield from rates, and perhaps a reduction in value of alternative sites in the urban area.

(b) Large stores can act as small growth points in areas of economic decline. It is known that they can make a significant contribution to local employment creating several hundred jobs on opening. What is less clear is the extent of employment contraction amongst smaller stores through competition and whether there is a net gain in jobs in the long term.

(c) The retailers most adversely affected by hypermarkets and superstores are the smaller branches of multiples engaged in convenience goods trade. Since these, mainly supermarkets, often serve as the anchor tenants of neighbourhood and smaller district shopping centres their demise can have a delayed ripple effect on other small independent shops. There are generally few adverse effects on durable goods outlets or specialist goods trade, especially those located in larger district shopping centres or town centres.

148

2   Environmental considerations

(a)   While it is easier for the retailer to acquire sites of a suitable size and shape in outlying areas developments can contribute to urban sprawl. A particularly sensitive issue in UK has been the potentially adverse effect of a new shopping centre in the green belt. It is possible however that the facility could occupy a derelict site and contribute to an upgrading of the peri-urban landscape.

(b)   The visual impact of hypermarkets and superstores is a negative externality which developers and local authorities have not addressed adequately. Equally any development which threatened prime agricultural land or a site of historical importance would be open to question.

(c)   The growth in traffic along local roads may create problems of congestion and audible nuisance as well as being a safety hazard.

3   Social considerations

The principal social objection to large outlying stores is that their provision will contribute to increased social and spatial polarization in standards of shopping facilities with most of the benefits of new developments accruing to a car-oriented middle class. Lower income groups who have the most to gain from the lower prices offered in superstores and hypermarkets are frequently those who benefit least because of their inability to reach the new facilities.

The impact of town centre shopping schemes

No other country in Western Europe has sought to contain the process of decentralization to the same degree as in Britain. Consequently much of the post-war pressure for growth has been re-directed into town centre developments. The policy of concentration instead of decentralization was fostered by two specific influences, (a) the evolution of town centre plans emphasizing redevelopment and segregation of land uses in the first half of the post-war era, and (b) a series of ad hoc policy directives, largely issued through Development Control Policy Notes from central government indicating how local authorities should respond to the pressure for new suburban retailing developments.

The procedure for the preparation of town centre plans was established by the 1947 Town and Country Planning Act which gave local authorities power to obtain land through compulsory purchase and to designate comprehensive development areas. Initially redevelopment was stimulated by the need to renew war damaged areas in towns such as Coventry, Hull and Plymouth (core replacement schemes). The formulation of town centre redevelopment plans accelerated from the mid 1950s however largely due to four factors. These were (1) the abolition, in 1954, of the war-time system of licences on new buildings, (2) the increasing amount of private finance that became available and a marked shift in investment from residential to commercial property, (3) rising personal incomes and their reflection in a growing demand for new retail floorspace, and (4) the growth in vehicular traffic which was causing localized congestion (Bennison and Davies 1980). The major design concept in this new retail development was the precinct. This was applied successfully in Coventry, in several of the new towns, and many of the neighbourhood shopping centres built by the larger local authorities.

By the mid 1960s however there was a marked change in the nature of shopping provisions envisaged in the development plans as private developers pressed for the introduction of new enclosed centres, similar to those that had been built in suburban areas of North America. The initial desire of private developers in Britain to build the new centres in out of town locations was resisted through the development control process by local authorities concerned about the potentially damaging competitive effect on existing resources, not least those built or due to be built under central area redevelopment plans. Only where a suburban shopping development provided the basis for a new district centre in an area of substantial population growth did local authorities relax their opposition. This position was encouraged by Development Control Policy Note 13 which required that all applications for new developments over 50,000 sq. ft. be sent to the Department of the Environment for scrutiny. Generally, as we have seen, most applications for outlying schemes that went to public enquiries were refused by the inspectors. The effect of this opposition was to force private developers to introduce most of the new covered shopping centres into existing central areas. Many of the larger of these developments were joint ventures between a local authority and a property development company. The authority maintained overall control of the scheme especially in terms of its locational relationship to the existing retail system and its integration with other elements in the overall redevelopment programme. Detailed design aspects and particularly the layout of shops were left to the property developer. The main objective of such core replacement schemes is to replace structurally and functionally obsolete retail property in prime locations with new retail space designed for contemporary retail techniques. The redevelopment of the central shopping area in Clydebank provides a detailed example of one such development (Pacione 1980a). Large core replacement shopping centres have existed in European cities for several decades B. Smith 1977) and since the 1970s have also become a feature of many American cities (Urban Land Institute 1980).

In UK during the second half of the 1970s a combination of factors resulted in a reduction in central area shopping schemes. These included

(a) a shift of attention from the central area to the problems of the inner city and peripheral estates, (b) a decline in the birth rate with its implication for future spending, (c) rampant inflation, (d) the growing importance of a conservation ethic and (e) the fact that much of the necessary retail modernization redevelopment had been accomplished. At the same time a revision to Development Control Policy Note 13 indicated a more flexible attitude towards future suburban shopping proposals. This was reflected in the increased number of superstores and hypermarkets granted planning permission (Lewis 1985). The major forms of impact arising from a town centre shopping scheme are summarized in Table 9.2.

Methods of impact assessment

As we have seen the impact of any new retail development is multi-faceted involving environmental, social and economic considerations. By far the greatest attention however both from local planners and the business community, has focused on the actual and potential trading repercussions of a development. Despite numerous empirical studies and public enquiries there is no single commonly-agreed approach. Techniques employed range between the extremes of sophisticated mathematical models to rule of thumb assessments. Examples of the latter include assumptions that one new 10,000m^2 hypermarket leads to the closure of sixty small shops, or that supermarkets in towns where a hypermarket develops may expect a 30.0 per cent fall in sales volume. Davies (1984) identifies four main approaches,

1   Survey methods

Most detailed studies of the trading effects of hypermarkets, superstores and new shopping centres have employed surveys. The most common technique has been to carry out consumer questionnaire surveys before and after development of a new retail facility in order to identify changes in consumer behaviour and expenditure patterns. A second approach is to conduct the survey only after the store or centre has been opened and ask people to recall earlier patterns of behaviour. A third approach involves surveying retailers in the vicinity of a new development. A combination of these survey techniques was employed to study the impact of an inner city retail redevelopment in Glasgow (Pacione 1982b).

2   Costing procedures

Limited use has been made of techniques such as cost–benefit analysis and the planning balance sheet to assess the economic case for a new retail development largely because of the limitations imposed by the quality of data that is required. Guy (1980) has indicated how a matrix presentation akin to the planning balance sheet may

Table 9.2 The impact of town centre shopping schemes in Britain

Economic		Environmental		Social	
Positive	Negative	Positive	Negative	Positive	Negative
Adds new stock	Reduces old stock	Modernizes outworn areas	Changes traditional shopping	Allows for efficient shopping	May favour car-borne shoppers
Accommodates larger modern stores	Discriminates against small independents	Reduces land use conflicts	Creates new points of congestion	Provides new shopping opportunities	May limit choice to stereotypes
Increases rates and revenues	Increases monopoly powers	Scope for new design standards	Intrusive effects on older townscapes	Provides more safety	Creates new stress factors from crowds
Creates new employment	Changes structure of employment	Provides weather protection	Creates artificial atmosphere	Provides more comfort and amenities	Attracts delinquents and vandals
Improves trade on adjacent streets	Reduces trade on peripheral streets	Leads to upgrading of some streets	Causes blight on other streets	Concentrates shopping in one area	Breaks up old shopping linkages
Enhances status of central area	Effects status of surrounding centres	Integrates new transport	Causes pressure on existing infra-structures	Potentially greater social interaction	Becomes dead area at night

Source: Bennison and Davies 1980: 38

be employed to evaluate the costs and benefits incurred in alternative superstore location policies.

3 Modelling techniques

Spatial interaction models were employed widely during the first half of the 1970s to forecast the potential sales impact of new retail developments. The popularity of these techniques has declined, however, partly because of the Department of the Environment's (1977) revised Development Control Policy Note which reported on conflicting evidence submitted at planning appeals by local authorities and developers using the same models. The degree of latitude available to researchers, particularly during the calibration of the models, was considered to over-complicate the impact argument and undermine the model's practical utility in planning enquiries. Nevertheless interaction models remain one of the main tools used by developers and researchers in estimating retail store trade areas.

4 Area-based calculations

Prior to the introduction of spatial interaction models most local authorities employed a 'step-by-step' approach to forecast the economic effect of a new shopping facility. Details of the method are provided by National Economic Development Office (1970). A modified form of this traditional approach was applied to assess the potential impact of new hypermarket and superstore developments in Gloucestershire (Breheny *et al.* 1981). The process involves six steps:

(a) determine future levels of available expenditure per capita.
(b) apply the expenditure estimates to estimated population in each zone (obtained from planning information on residential development) to find the total available expenditure in each isochrone.
(c) assess the likely turnover of the new store (by analogy with comparable stores already operating).
(d) calculate the proportion of the store's turnover that is likely to be accounted for by consumers in each isochrone (based on surveys undertaken of the origins of customers patronizing similar stores).
(e) link step (a) and (d), i.e. relate the proportion of store turnover from each isochrone to the estimated total expenditure in each isochrone.
(f) determine where the expenditure that is expected to be captured by the new store would have gone if the store was not built (based on an examination of existing patterns of consumer behaviour and possibly use of spatial interaction models).

An example of the procedure is shown in Figure 9.1. Despite not inconsiderable data requirements the approach has the benefits

Figure 9.1 Calculating the impact of a proposed hypermarket in Gloucestershire

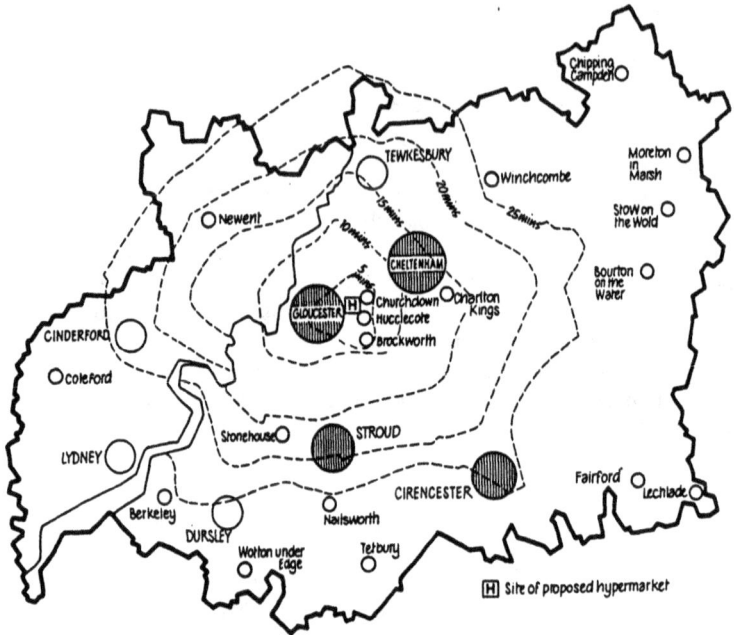

Step 1. Expenditure rates
Convenience goods 0.0% = £148
Comparison goods 2.0% = £170
Total at 1981 = £318

Step 2. Isochrone expenditure

	Isochrones (minutes)		
(in £000s)	0-10	10-20	15-25
Convenience goods	24,420	11,100	21,460
Comparison goods	28,050	12,750	24,650
Total	52,470	23,850	46,110

Step 3. Store turnover
(Lower estimate)
Convenience goods = £5.32 m
Comparison goods = £2.28 m
Total = £7.60 m

Step 4. Isochrone contribution

Isochrones (minutes)		
0-10	10-20	15-25
45%	20%	25%

Step 5. Isochrone impact

	Isochrones (minutes)		
	0-10	10-20	15-25
Convenience goods	9.75%	9.59%	6.20%
Comparison goods	3.64%	3.57%	2.30%
For all goods	6.49%	6.37%	4.10%

Step 6. Centre impact

	Convenience goods	Comparison [goods]	Total [goods]
Gloucester	13.9%	4.7%	7.6%
Cheltenham	10.2%	3.0%	4.9%
Stroud	6.9%	2.4%	4.4%
Cirencester	5.3%	1.0%	2.7%
Tewkesbury	6.7%	1.9%	4.5%
Suburbs	19.0%	–	–

(Repeated for upper estimate of store turnover)

Source: adapted from Breheny *et al.* 1981: 462

of avoiding undue complexity, making its assumptions explicit, and has the virtue of practicability.

The role of small shops

There has been a significant decline in the number of and share of total sales commanded by small retail outlets. The number of single-outlet retailers in Britain fell by 41.5 per cent between 1971 and 1980 from 338,210 to 197,884 and, as Table 9.1 indicates, the share of sales accounted for by independent retailers has fallen consistently since 1961. Among the independents the greatest numerical decline has been experienced by single-outlet grocery and general food traders. Most of the causes of their decline are a function of their size. These include (1) a limited amount of selling space which restricts the range of goods available and inconveniences customers, (2) restricted storage space which leads to higher transport costs through more frequent visits to wholesalers and an inability to buy large quantities of goods at discount prices, (3) disproportionately high overhead costs in terms of the amount of capital tied up in rents, repairs of ageing premises and bank loans for stock. Administrative burdens, such as completing VAT returns, are also more time-consuming for the individual small businessman than for chain companies. This is compounded by the general lack of training and expertise amongst independent retailers. These inherent problems of scale are exacerbated by external factors. First, urban redevelopment programmes have led to the loss of small shops either directly through clearance or indirectly because of planning blight. Second, development control policies encouraging the concentration of retailing activity in central areas have intensified competition for the most accessible sites and meant that multiples have relegated small shops to secondary positions with a lower trade potential. Third, traffic management schemes, such as parking restrictions along main roads, closure of many side streets joining arterials, and one-way systems, have depleted the trading base of many small shops particularly in inner city areas.

The weak competitive position of small shops has led to some calls for government assistance. The case has been argued on two grounds. The first is that small shops can make an important contribution to local employment creation. Second, closure of small shops or even a decline in quality of service can cause problems for certain groups of consumers dependent on local shopping facilities. There are three main ways in which government assistance could be provided:

1 Financial provisions: most common in Britain is the rent and rates relief given to many small shops occupying premises owned by a local authority. This has the advantage of allowing aid to be targetted to

155

particular shops of importance to local communities. Grants and loans to assist expansion or modernization of premises is a second possible form of financial assistance. This policy is more common in Europe than in the UK (Ekhaugen *et al.* 1980). A third possible strategy is to provide guaranteed minimum levels of income to selected small shops in the same way that basic salaries are paid to sub-post office operators by the Post Office (Dawson and Kirby 1979).

2   Removal of restrictive legislation: initiatives such as the reduction of VAT, corporate taxes and national insurance contributions would have to be applied as a form of positive discrimination in favour of small shops if they were to produce a significant advantage. Disquiet could be anticipated from other retailers. In terms of planning controls and building regulations there may be scope for improving the choice of sites and allowing shops greater locational freedom. This less restrictive form of development policy could be applied to 'designated shopping areas' in the city.

3   Special advisory and support services: the business skills of small shopkeepers could be improved by the provision of more formal educational and training programmes. In Italy and the Netherlands a certificate of proficiency in retailing from a vocational training course is a prerequisite to obtaining a licence to establish a new small business.

Although problems related to size have been a major handicap for the small shopkeeper in the UK the small scale of operation can, in some circumstances, be an advantage. This is the case in the USA where, in recent years, there has been a re-emergence of the convenience store albeit a modern larger (up to 5,000 sq. ft.) version of the traditional 'ma and pa' corner store. This new convenience store has a more diversified merchandizing mix, occupies sites with ample parking and often adjacent to supermarkets, and operates an 'open all hours' trading policy (Kirby 1976). These have arisen in response to the increasing size and dispersed distribution of supermarkets, which has resulted in gaps in the suburban market into which these convenience stores can fit to provide customers with opportunities to 'top-up' on the bulk weekly shopping expedition. Such stores are also becoming common in Western Europe, particularly in those countries such as France and West Germany where large-scale retailing is well established.

Disadvantaged consumers

The increasing size and decentralized location of new large stores, disinvestment in smaller supermarkets by the major food retail multiples who dominate the grocery market, and the decline in number of small independent shops have all contributed to the formation of a class of disadvantaged consumers. These include the poor, elderly and mobility-deprived residents of poorly served inner city areas and peripheral housing estates.

Several measures of differential level of access to shopping facilities are available. Guy (1983) employed a model of the form

$$Ai \cdot \Sigma \ Sj \ exp \ \left\{ -\tfrac{1}{2} \left\{ \frac{Dij}{d*} \right\}^2 \right\}$$

where: Ai = a measure of access to shopping opportunities for home i.

Sj = the size of store j (in 000s of square feet).

dij = the straight line distance from i to opportunity j.

d* = the point of inflection at a pre-determined distance from the home.

The value of d* is arbitrary and should reflect the distance at which access to shops becomes inconvenient. This distance will vary among sub-groups of the population. Guy (1983) suggested it should be set between the normal walking distance (0.6km) and the distance conveniently overcome by using public transport (1.5km). Islington Borough Council (1980) in London adopted a plan to ensure that local shops should be available to all residents within 400m of home. This distance represents a ten-minute walk each way for an elderly person or parent with a toddler. On this basis fifty local centres were identified where the local authority will seek to protect existing shopping facilities. Areas falling outside a 400m radius from these centres are designated 'shopping deficiency areas' where new investment or an upgrading of present resources is encouraged. Cullen and Spear (1985) employed a similar approach to identify over- and under-serviced areas for food stores in Albuquerque, New Mexico.

Translating planning proposals into concrete facilities requires the co-operation of retailers and, to date, while many have voiced concern over the limited access of low-income groups to new superstores (Lewis 1985) few have been prepared to direct developments to deprived areas in the absence of government financial assistance. It is necessary, therefore, to consider alternative ways in which relatively housebound consumers can be assisted in satisfying their shopping requirements. One possibility is the use of telecommunications and micro-computer facilities to link individual homes or community focal points to a large store or shopping centre some distance away. One such scheme is the Gateshead shopping and information service. This has two main objectives (Davies 1985). The first is to improve the choice of shopping opportunities

157

available to disadvantaged consumers and to afford them access to stores which offer goods at cheaper prices. The second is to improve the access of the relatively housebound to a variety of sources of information on local events, welfare, entertainments, transport timetables and other social services. In contrast to most of the teleshopping schemes in North America, the Gateshead SIS is operated as a joint venture between the public and private sectors, is aimed at providing a food and convenience-goods shopping service rather than non-food items, and most significantly is oriented to disadvantaged rather than to affluent consumers. While there is considerable potential for extension of such schemes realistically, in the short term, the majority of residents of inner city and deprived council estates will continue to rely on conventional retail outlets for their basic shopping needs. Analysing the shopping behaviour and problems of the immobile and underprivileged is, therefore, an ongoing issue of key importance for applied urban researchers.

Chapter ten

Urban transportation

The transport system affects urban quality of life in many positive ways. It aids the creation of wealth by enabling people to reach their workplace, moving raw materials and distributing finished products. It affords access to shopping, health, education, leisure and other welfare facilities both by enabling individuals to travel and by conveying facilities to people. The provision and use of a transport system can also have negative effects on quality of life by causing injury and premature death, by displacing people from their homes, businesses and land, by encouraging location patterns which accentuate class inequalities in the degree of access to activities and facilities, by degrading the environment, by the fatigue and frustration associated with some forms of travel, and by feelings of infringement of personal freedom associated with the enforcement of transport regulations. These negative effects often bear disproportionately on particular individuals and groups in society. Nevertheless, urban society as a whole accepts the negative effects because it values the positive ones so highly.

Thomson (1977) identified seven interrelated components of the urban transport problem which confront municipal authorities throughout the world (Figure 10.1). Particular attention has been devoted to the problems of traffic movement and congestion, public transport, and the environmental and socio-economic impact of transport systems.

1 Traffic movement

The primary purpose of urban transport is to provide mobility for people and goods within a city but the efficiency with which this is achieved can be severely reduced by congestion. The major cause of traffic congestion in cities is the automobile. In the USA between 1945 and 1977 total vehicle numbers rose by 336.0 per cent from 29.5 million vehicles to 128.6 million. By the mid 1970s one-third (22,843,000) of US households had more than one car. The growth rate of car ownership is currently twice that of the number of households. Similarly, in

Figure 10.1 Dimensions of the urban transport problem

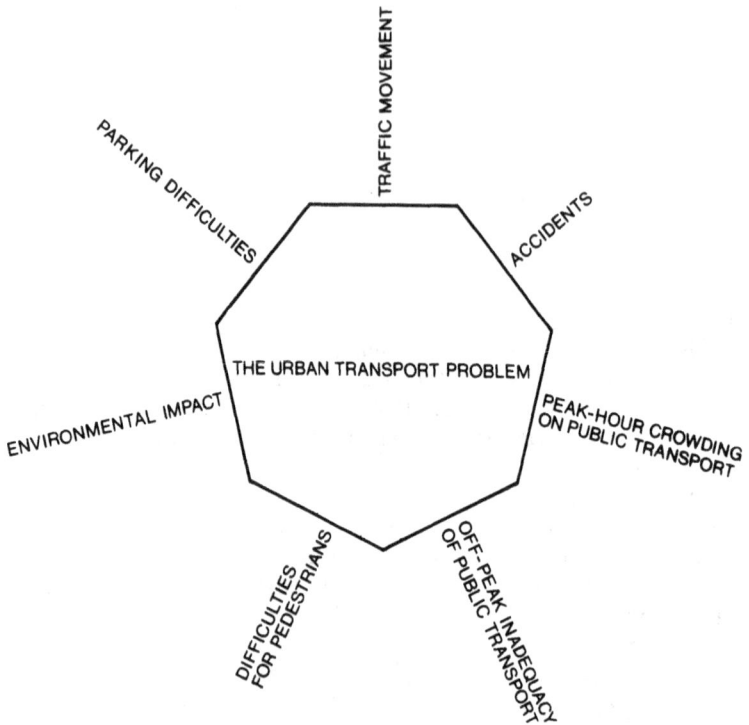

TRAFFIC MOVEMENT

PARKING DIFFICULTIES

ACCIDENTS

THE URBAN TRANSPORT PROBLEM

ENVIRONMENTAL IMPACT

PEAK-HOUR CROWDING ON PUBLIC TRANSPORT

DIFFICULTIES FOR PEDESTRIANS

OFF-PEAK INADEQUACY OF PUBLIC TRANSPORT

Source: Thomson 1977: 20

UK between 1948 and 1978 the number of registered private cars and vans rose from 1.4 million to 14.4 million. It is the concentration of travel flows at certain times during the day that leads to congestion and the principal reason for the typical double-peak distribution of daily trips is the journey to and from work. Different parts of the city may experience peaking and congestion at different times of the day depending on the mix of traffic.

Three general approaches to the relief of traffic congestion have been employed

(1) during the 1950s and 1960s the 'supply-fix' approach emphasized the provision of new infrastructure to increase the capacity of the road system to meet demand. The manifestation of this policy were massive road-building and road-improvement programmes and investment in

160

public mass transit systems. The emphasis was firmly on the supply side and transport policy was effectively a *vehicle–orientated* policy. Large increases in highway capacity in many cities tended to exacerbate the problems of traffic congestion and environmental degradation in accordance with Down's (1978) law — i.e. on urban commuter expressways peak hour traffic congestion rises to meet maximum capacity. In addition, the increased mobility of car owners stimulated the development of low-density urban areas with unstructured travel demands resulting in substantial reductions in the role and effectiveness of public transport.

(2)   During the late 1960s and early 1970s the character and emphasis of urban transport policy shifted. The policy objective became accessibility rather than simply mobility. Greater emphasis was placed on the exploitation of existing facilities, on minimizing the environmental impacts of the automobile, and on the equity with which all sections of the urban population were served by transport. The shift to *people-oriented* non-capital intensive policy options was stimulated by reductions in the growth rate of many large urban areas, lower levels of national economic growth, the rise of a popular movement opposed to the environmental and social costs of major highway projects, and the energy crisis initiated by the Arab oil embargo of 1973. The resultant transport system management (TSM) strategies have sought to manipulate demand (e.g. by promoting car pooling or by synchronizing traffic lights to speed flow) and make more efficient use of existing highway capacity.

(3)   The third approach is by means of 'non–transportation initiatives'. These include staggering work hours and designing cities to reduce the need for travel by limiting distances between home and the other activity.

Currently, the emphasis in transport policy is on the second and third of these strategies. Reaction against continued large-scale provision of highway infrastructure has resulted in literally hundreds of techniques for better use of existing transport facilities. These include channelization of traffic especially at intersections (e.g. segregation of left- and right-turning flows, and bus-only lanes), computer controlled traffic signals, more traffic-light controlled junctions and mini-roundabouts to increase the flow that can be handled by a single intersection, one-way streets to reduce conflicting traffic movements at junctions, limitations on street parking (e.g. clearways) to increase the carrying capacity of traffic routes, and reversible traffic lanes in which priority changes with time of day. All of these management techniques can be easily implemented at relatively low cost and involve minor physical alterations. More radical strategies include road pricing, auto-restraint policies, and encouragement of ride-sharing.

Road pricing: While in many countries road travellers pay to use inter-city motorways tolls for travel within urban areas have not been widely adopted. The extent of traffic congestion in Singapore and Hong Kong has stimulated the authorities to experiment with road pricing. In Hong Kong the burgeoning car population and limited space led to the introduction of a set of traffic limitation strategies in 1982. These included doubling car registration fees, tripling annual licence fees and substantially raising the tax on petrol. In addition a sophisticated electronic road pricing system was instituted. Using special plates fitted to the bottom of each automobile and control points distributed throughout the most congested parts of the city the movement of vehicles can be electronically metered and owners subsequently presented with a bill. By moving the locations of the control points planners can experiment with ways to alter trip flows and maximize traffic flow in the system (Young 1985). The pricing system adopted in Singapore is less technologically sophisticated and less flexible for experimentation but has had a significant impact on traffic flows (Wang and Tan 1981). The package of constraints employed in the central area includes the prohibition of all large vehicles with three or more axles during peak hours, increased parking fees, a revision of parking regulations to discourage commuter traffic but facilitate short-term business and commercial trips, and the Area Licensing Scheme. The latter, initiated in 1975, designates the centre of the city as a restricted travel zone. Between 7.30 a.m. and 10.15 a.m. only specially licensed vehicles are permitted into the zone. Licences are sold according to a sliding scale which ensures that company-owned vehicles pay the highest rates. Carpool vehicles (defined as those carrying four or more persons) are exempt. Table 10.1 indicates the effect of the Singapore A.L.S. on the modal-split choice for work trips.

Tabel 10.1 Changes in modal split for work trips in the restricted zone, Singapore

Mode	inbound home-to-work trips (%)		outbound work-to-home trips (%)	
	Before ALS	After ALS	Before ALS	After ALS
Bus	33	46	36	48
Car	56	46	53	43
car driver	32	20	35	23
car pool	8	19	5	12
car passenger	16	7	13	8
Motorcycle	7	7	7	6
Others	4	2	4	3

Source: Wang and Tan 1981: 235

Advocates of road pricing favour it as an example of using market forces to achieve policy ends. Rather than mandating modification of travel directly road pricing encourages it through monetary disincentives. Objections to road pricing have centred upon equity, political and practical issues. The last of these is the least serious constraint. The Smeed report concluded that the practical difficulties of implementing a system of road pricing can be overcome without excessive cost (Ministry of Transport 1964). One of the strongest arguments against is that because it is based on the price mechanism road pricing could discriminate against lower-income car owners. Most significant however has been the political opposition by the 'motoring lobby' and the general recognition by governments that the social benefits of road pricing would most likely be offset by the political costs.

Auto-restraint: Road pricing is, in effect, one kind of auto-restraint policy in that one of its goals is to promote the use of public transport by making car travel more difficult. Other restraint policies include banning on-street car parking and provision of additional downtown parking areas. The ultimate form of auto-restraint is to ban cars from a section of the city. The conversion of some city streets into pedestrian malls is now a common feature of most large cities. Vehicular traffic is also excluded from residential areas in most new towns while historic European cities like Vienna and Goteborg have limited traffic penetration in the interests of enhancing the liveability of the city centre.

Ride-sharing: Three quarters of the 84.0 per cent of the American labour force that travel to work by car are solo drivers. Nationally the average private vehicle in USA transports only 1.15 persons on its trip to the workplace. One way of increasing highway capacity is for transport planners to implement programmes to encourage ride-sharing through car- and van-pooling schemes. Research suggests that to maximize the possibility of adoption such schemes should be targeted at particular populations. Many people are not amenable to giving up the freedom of solo driving or are constrained from participating by other daily activity patterns such as collecting children or shopping. It appears that the most effective programmes are those arranged through employers. Evidence from Phoenix suggests that employees favour van-pools over car-pools because their private cars need not be used, they need not drive rush-hour conditions, the arrangements are made for them, and they have an opportunity to socialize with colleagues (Plane 1986). Assisting employers to set up van-pooling as an employee benefit is thus often more cost-effective than media campaigns aimed at the general public. While there is considerable scope for the introduction of ride-sharing strategies no single policy is sufficient to promote the optimum use of the urban road system. What is required is a package

163

of self-reinforcing strategies that are integrated into the overall planning process for the metropolitan area. This means considering both transport and non-transport options.

Non-transport strategies seek to capitalize on the relationship between transportation, daily activity patterns and the aggregate land use structure of the city. The problem of the commuting peak might be alleviated by promoting alternative work schedules such as those in Table 10.2 which spread the journey to work period or reduce the number of work days per week. Advances in telecommunications technology can also reduce the need for some trips during the business day and in some cases allow employees to work from home or from regional suburban 'work stations'. The principle of flexible working hours has been applied most widely in West Germany where more than half of the labour force is permitted to work non-standard hours. The potential benefits for urban traffic movement are considerable. For example, Jovanis (1981) in a study of the San Francisco–Oakland Bay bridge traffic corridor found that even small increases in the number of flexi-time workers can have substantial impacts in alleviating peak-period congestion. To date, however, urban transportation planning agencies have devoted only limited effort to promoting such strategies. A final non-transportation perspective centres on the belief that the fundamental design of many urban areas is ill-suited to the demands of the automobile age and that more sensitive forms of comprehensive land use planning which promote a better integration of residential and non-residential land uses represent the most effective means of facilitating movement within cities.

Table 10.2 Types of alternative work schedules

1. *Flexible work hours ('Flex–time')*. Employee chooses his or her own schedule, with some constraints. Employee may be free to vary the schedule daily, vary the lunch breaks, or 'bank' hours from one day to the next or one pay period to the next. Typically all employees are required to be at work five days per week during designated 'core' periods (usually 9:30 a.m. to 3:30 p.m.).
2. *Staggered work hours.* Employee works a five-day week, but starting and ending times are spread over a wider time period than usual. Individual employee schedules are assigned by management; employees do not choose them.
3. *Four-day (or compressed) work week.* Employee works the same total number of hours as in a typical five-day workweek, but reports to work only four times per week. The four days may be the same each week, or the extra day off may rotate from week to week.
4. *Job-sharing/part-time work.* Employee works less than the standard 40-hour workweek, either by working fewer than five 8-hour days, or by working less than 8 hours per day. Job-sharing means that two or more people share the same office space and work responsibilities.

Source: Plane 1986

2 Environmental impact

A range of techniques are available for measuring the environmental impact of transportation developments. Two of the most commonly employed are cost–benefit analysis and the environmental impact statement. It was the particular difficulty of incorporating non-monetary valuations into the economic framework of cost–benefit analysis that led to the search for alternative methods of assessing environmental impacts. One of the most important developments stemmed from the passage of the US National Environmental Policy Act in 1969. This required a written environmental impact statement (EIS) for all major federal development projects. The effect on urban transportation was (a) to slow the development of new projects, (b) to involve the public in the decision-making process to a greater degree, (c) to increase public awareness and preservation of local communities and natural environments, and (d) to utilize existing transportation infrastructure more efficiently (Cohn and McVay 1982). The drafting of an EIS is now an important early

Table 10.3 Steps in drafting an environmental impact statement for a proposed transport project

---

I. Purpose and need for the proposed project
   A. How is project linked to total system?
   B. What future capacities are needed in system?
   C. What are the current and future demands?
   D. What legislative authority will direct the project?
   E. What are the economic and social effects?
   F. What are the intermodal relationships of the project?
   G. Will there be overall safety improvements?
II. Alternative projects proposed
   A. No-build, status quo option
   B. Transportation systems management option (TSM)
   C. Small-scale improvement alternative
   D. Medium-scale improvement alternative
   E. Large-scale improvement alternative
III. Affected environment and consequences
   A. Existing social, economic, and physical setting
   B. Expected social and economic impacts
   C. Expected relocation impacts and mitigation
   D. Expected land use impacts and mitigation
   E. Expected noise and air quality impacts and mitigation
   F. Expected energy and conservation impacts and mitigation
   G. Stream, river, and floodplain impacts and mitigation
   H. Wetlands and water quality impacts and mitigation
   I. Threatened or endangered species impacts and mitigation
   J. Prime and unique agricultural lands impacts and mitigation
   K. Expected visual impact

Source: Stutz 1986: 353

step in most significant urban transportation projects in USA. The major stages in the EIS process are shown in Table 10.3. In brief, the first step is to state the purpose and need for the proposed transportation project. The reasonable alternatives are set out in step two. In the third stage a designation of the existing social, economic and natural environmental setting of the areas affected by all of the alternative proposals is presented. Finally, the probable environmental consequences of the alternatives and the measures needed to mitigate adverse effects are set out. In USA the EIS has become an integral element in the Department of Transportation decision-making process. The procedure has ensured a more thorough and scientific assessment of project alternatives, enlarged the range of values considered in reaching decisions, and contributed to public participation in transport planning.

3 Social impact

The negative social impacts of urban transportation include those related to the construction of highways to accommodate the automobile, and to the operation of the public transport system.

The first of these impacts is illustrated in USA where the suburbanization of primarily middle- and upper-income whites whose work locations remained in the central city meant that between 1957 and 1968 a total of 335,000 housing units were destroyed to facilitate highway construction. In the great majority of cases displaced households were from the lower economic and social strata. An extreme example of community disruption and household displacement as a result of highway construction is the routing of Interstate 40 through the black area of Nashville Tennessee. This destroyed the heart of the black business community, removed 650 homes and 27 apartment buildings and cut between the campuses of three major black educational institutions (Seley 1970). While the Nashville I-40 is an extreme case practically every major US city experienced similar impacts during the highway construction era. The ongoing legacies of air and noise pollution and the effect of these hazards on physical and mental health also represent negative impacts which are inequitably distributed among social classes.

There is little doubt that the modern city offers unparalleled mobility for most residents. However the nature of the automobile-dominated transportation system, particularly in US cities, also discriminates against the car-less. One-fifth of families living in metropolitan areas and nearly a third of central city households have no car. In addition to the poor, the mobility-deprived include the elderly who cannot or choose not to drive, the handicapped, the young, and housewives who do not have access to a car for much of the day.

In the UK 'special needs groups' cover about 10.0 per cent of the adult population, the figure rising to 30.0 per cent if the unemployed are included (Benwell 1985). Catering for these transport-disadvantaged groups is one of the major goals of public transport. Indeed equity considerations have been cited by some policy analysts as the most compelling justification for subsidizing mass transit systems (Altshuler 1969). In view of this it might be expected that low-income households have been the main beneficiaries of the fifteen-fold growth in public transport subsidies in the USA between 1970 and 1980. In fact, in many ways 'transit systems have been constructed, operated and financed such that precisely this mobility-disadvantaged group, which most needs transit service, has been implicitly discriminated against' (Pucher 1982: 315). The inequitable social impact of public transport provision is seen in (a) the quality and quantity of services provided, and (b) the financing of the system.

(a)   In the USA the issue of differential levels of service has been raised particularly in connection with Title VI of the Civil Rights Act of 1964 which explicitly prohibits discrimination against minority groups in a federally funded project. Since two-thirds of poor transit riders in US urban areas are black or Hispanic any failure of transit operators to provide an equal quality of service in poorer inner-city areas may, in effect, represent a violation of the Act. The most common complaints are that (1) insufficient service is provided within ghetto areas or from ghetto areas to suburban job sites, and (2) the transit service provided to low-income and minority users is less dependable, more crowded, slower and generally inferior to comparable services provided to non-minority middle- and upper-income riders. In the case of Hartford Connecticut such allegations were upheld by the US Department of Transportation, and the transit authority was compelled to allocate new buses to minority central city areas and to establish a reverse commuting service to suburban job locations.

(b)   The second type of negative social impact in public transport involves inequities in the financing of transit services which place an unfair portion of the burden of paying transit costs upon low-income and minority users who can least afford them. Three main sources of such inequities are (1)   more intensive subsidization of transit modes and routes patronized by relatively affluent travellers. As Pucher (1981) has shown, in the USA during the 1970s commuter rail and rail rapid transit services received significantly greater operating and capital subsidies per passenger than bus systems. Since the lower income and minority groups are more dependent on bus travel this represented a distribution of subsidy which was inversely related to need (2)   implicit cross-subsidies *within* each transit mode from relatively low-income, short-distance, off-peak riders to relatively affluent long-

167

distance peak hour riders. The inverse correlation between per mile fare and trip distance common in urban fare structures favours longer distance travellers who are effectively subsidized by those making shorter trips. Also it has generally been found that the costs of providing peak-hour transportation are much greater than the corresponding costs of off-peak travel with, once again, the latter subsidizing the former. There are also differences in subsidy according to the method of fare payment with some transit systems offering discounts on monthly passes, which tend to be used more frequently by affluent transit riders than by low-income riders. The fact that some authorities also offer larger discounts to riders making long trips exacerbates the inequities of discount passes, and (3) the third source refers to regressive tax financing of state and local transit subsidies. Although the total tax burden of transit subsidies is progressively financed, at the state and local level, it is regressive with lower-income households paying a greater part of their income towards transit taxes than high-income households. The degree of regressivity is greatest in those cities, such as Phoenix, that rely entirely on local sales and property taxes to finance transit. The extent to which federal tax progressivity can offset the regressivity in state and local financing ultimately depends upon the willingness of federal government to provide transit subsidies.

While the presence of these inequalities is undeniable it is less certain that these are intentional impacts. In most cases they are more likely to be the unintended side-effects of an authority pursuing goals such as maximizing transit ridership or reducing automobile use. Nevertheless the effects are real and need to be addressed by any responsible transport policy. Possible strategies to offset inequities include increased fares on commuter rail services, the provision of discount transit passes for the poor, similar to the concessionary fare available to pensioners in Britain, and the introduction of user-side subsidies targeted to the needy in the same way as food stamps or supplementary benefit payments.

4 The problem of public transport

Increasing levels of car ownership and the suburbanization of population have contributed to a decline in use of public transport in cities throughout the industrialized world. Declining fare revenues and increasing costs have produced a situation in which few metropolitan mass transit systems now operate without subsidies.

Public transport is used most in large metropolitan areas, with the worktrips to the CBD accounting for the majority of weekday transit trips in most cities. In 1980 60.0 per cent of CBD–bound work trips in New York were made by mass transit. Comparable figures for

Boston, Chicago, and San Francisco–Oakland were 59.0 per cent, 74.0 per cent and 52.0 per cent respectively. In smaller cities, and for most other non-work trips, however, public transport cannot compete with the private car. Generally mass transit has come to be regarded as a social service rather than a commercial enterprise. This, however, does not remove the pressure to improve the performance of public transport systems. Fielding (1986) has suggested seven performance indicators which may be used to compare the efficiency and effectiveness of a transit agency, and in the USA in 1982 legislation mandated that triennial audits be conducted for all transit agencies receiving federal subsidies. Other possible cost-reduction strategies include the use of part-time labour to cover periods of peak demand, linking wages to productivity, differential pricing of routes to reflect their cost, computer scheduling of routes and timings, and operational planning and monitoring to ensure a good fit between the transit service and its market. This last strategy acknowledges that the urban transportation market is highly fragmented and requires a variety of types of service rather than a single area-wide system. Small community-based systems which have lower overhead costs and can adjust more rapidly to changing patterns of demand may be able to provide service more efficiently and economically than a single large public agency. The possibility of variety in the provision of public transit also underlies the suggestion for alternative forms of transport which can provide a more flexible and cheaper mode of service during off-peak periods when standard buses run with surplus capacity. These 'paratransit' options include dial-a-ride, subscription bus and jitneys or privately-operated mini-buses. In the UK opportunities for these kinds of unconventional transport service were enhanced by the de-regulation of public transport services (Button and Gillingwater 1986).

Another problem in US cities is that the downtown orientation of transit operators has largely ignored the market potential of new concentrations of employment in the industrial parks, shopping malls and office centres which have grown up in the post-war years. Multi-dimensional transit systems which enable travellers to move conveniently between many locations throughout the metropolitan area could attract a larger proportion of travellers. In Toronto, for example, 70.0 per cent of public transit trips do not cross the central area indicating the success of the system in attracting non-downtown travel.

Other technological strategies to overcome the cost disadvantages of traditional mass transit systems have examined the potential of new metropolitan railways, light rail transit, mono rails, automated systems such as the VAL opened in Lille in 1982, and guided busways. Particular attention has been given to light rail transit. Proponents argue that it is less expensive to build than a metro-line, costs no more to operate than a conventional bus system and offers a superior service. It has also been

suggested that a new light rail line has the capacity to stimulate revitalization of central city areas. The evidence from studies of projects in Buffalo
(Berechman and Paaswell 1983), San Diego, Calgary and Edmonton
(Gomez-Ibanez 1985) suggests that the positive impacts of a light rail
rapid transit on the CBD are not in themselves sufficient to generate
revitalization. Complementary private and public sector programmes to
enhance the attractiveness of the area are necessary to capitalize on the
accessibility benefits of the LRRT system.

Transportation and urban structure

There is a symbiotic relationship between city structure and transport
policy. Thomson (1977) has identified five general urban transport
strategies based on the degree of car ownership to be accommodated
in the city (Figure 10.2). The archetypes range from a model (A) which
facilitates full car ownership to one based on traffic limitation (E). In
the intermediate structures (models B and C) public and private transport
are in conflict. Clearly, no city fits any single strategy exactly. Rather,
these archetypes provide guidance on the appropriate package of transport
options for different forms of city.

Figure 10.2 The relationship between transport strategies and urban form

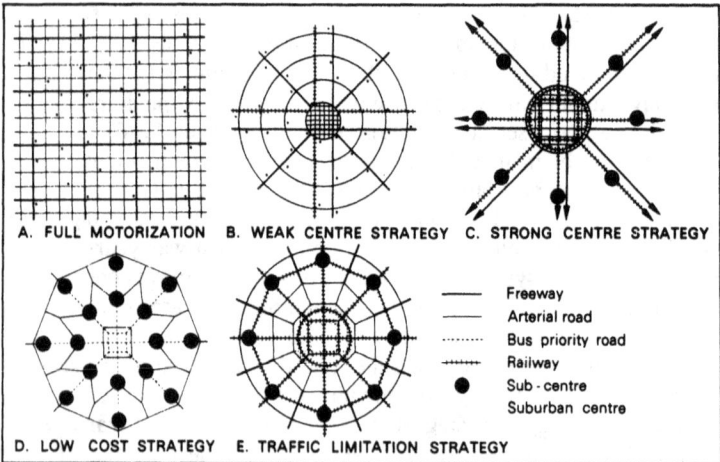

A. FULL MOTORIZATION   B. WEAK CENTRE STRATEGY   C. STRONG CENTRE STRATEGY

D. LOW COST STRATEGY   E. TRAFFIC LIMITATION STRATEGY

- Freeway
- Arterial road
- Bus priority road
- Railway
- Sub-centre
- Suburban centre

Source: Thomson 1977

Conclusion

In this book we have sought to illuminate the interrelated complexity of contemporary urban social, economic and environmental problems, and to illustrate the ways in which an applied or problem-oriented analytical approach can provide the basis for planning remedial action. We have ranged widely over the academic terrain identifying problems and assessing strategies in an international and interdisciplinary context.

That the modern metropolitan environment is linked to regional, national and international political-economic systems is acknowledged to be a significant structural influence in the analysis and resolution of urban problems. Yet, despite constraints exerted from beyond the city, the importance of local circumstances must be underlined. As Harvey (1984: 6) remarked, we need to marry consideration of the global processes restructuring social, economic and political reality with an understanding of 'the specifics of what is happening to individuals, groups, classes and communities at particular places at certain times'. It is worth reiterating the dictum that applied urban analysts must think globally and act locally.

In practice, applied urban analysts will be confronted with a wide range of possible solutions to urban problems, and the power of critical evaluation will be at a premium. In order to achieve the goal of a humane city strategies must be judged not only on the basis of technical and financial criteria but on socially informed assessments of citizens' preferences and priorities. It is axiomatic that if poor selection of approaches and poor utilization of research results are to be avoided the applied urban analyst must have recourse to a varied methodological toolkit which includes both 'objective' and 'subjective' techniques.

The diversity of disciplinary interest represented in research activity in applied urban analysis is at once a source of strength and of weakness. While, on the one hand, applied urban analysis has benefited from the growth of research output, on the other the field has lacked a clear focus with the result that findings produced by researchers attached to different disciplines have been scattered throughout the academic literature. The identification of a number of general principles underlying the practice of applied urban analysis would clearly be of value as a first step in drawing together the disparate disciplinary strands. Accordingly we conclude our discussion by presenting a set of ten broad guidelines for applied urban analysis.

Principles of applied urban analysis

1   Applied urban analysis is an empirical discipline with clear links to planning and a focus on real world problems. Despite its emphasis on problem-solving, applied urban analysis does not operate in a theoretical vacuum. At the macro-level social theory necessarily provides the benchmark against which problems, such as urban deprivation, are identified while at the micro-level theory provides the guidance for investigating substantive relationships embodied in a problem. Expressed in a realist framework, theory is essential to ensure that the issues or problems investigated are rational abstractions from the whole and not chaotic conceptions.

2   Both holistic modes of explanation which accord absolute supremacy to structural constraints and voluntarism which explains social life in terms of the independent actions of individuals are rejected in favour of a middle ground realist position in which Man and society are related in a dialectic manner. Acceptance of the realist philosophy requires that empirical analyses are carried out within the context of the overall theoretical framework.

3   The concept of value-free research is an illusion. Whether consciously or unconsciously, values affect the choice of research topic, mode of analysis and conclusions drawn. While research can be presented in an objective and politically neutral manner the researcher cannot guarantee the use to which his work will be put. The fact that knowledge *may* be employed in a socially-regressive manner, however, does not undermine the validity of applied urban research.

4   While the concept of the urban is of limited importance in the construction of social theory the notion of the urban place as a distinctive object of analysis remains valid despite the convergence of urban and rural lifestyles in modern society. Towns and cities are meaningful entities and, on the basis of unique physical properties, provide clearly defined areas for analysis. Applied urban analysis is concerned with both general societal problems magnified in the city by the concentration of population, and specific problems of the city which arise as a consequence of the particular physical environment.

5   The value of a spatial perspective in the examination of contemporary

urban problems is emphasized. This does not view space as a causal entity in its own right but as a partner with social processes in the reproduction of society. The importance of the spatial dimension lies not at the level of general social theory but is related to the uniqueness of individual places. Space is of central importance for applied urban analysis since the problem-oriented perspective requires consideration of specific situations. This view is supported by the fact that post-war government policy to alleviate urban problems has consistently adopted an explicitly spatial perspective.

6 The importance of undertaking investigations at the most appropriate level is emphasized. Structural forces constrain but do not predetermine local manifestations of general societal processes. What is required is a pluralistic hierarchical approach with relevant social theory providing the explanatory framework at the level of production, middle-range theory of the operation of institutions and interest groups (the level of distribution) and local (consumption) level analysis of the particular socio-spatial outcomes of structural processes. Within this context the practice of applied urban analysis focuses primarily on analysis at the distribution and consumption levels.

7 While each of the major paradigms in contemporary social science is conceived as a philosophical entity which, in epistemological and ontological terms, cannot logically be disaggregated, some of the methodologies (such as quantitative techniques) are not necessarily tied to a particular paradigm. Appropriate techniques taken from different approaches can be employed in resolving particular problems.

8 The limitations of statistical inference, as developed in the positivist era, for the analysis of urban problems is acknowledged. While the utility of other appropriate quantitative techniques is reaffirmed, the use of objective data and techniques must be complemented by use of qualitative data and analytical methods.

9 Knowledge of the various forces inherent in the capitalist mode of production and underlying social phenomena is crucial for an understanding of the evolution of urban problems. The role of the state, both central and local, is of particular importance for applied urban analysis. To operate successfully as problem analyst and policy advocate the applied urban researcher must combine investigation at the local scale with an appreciation of the organizational and functional linkages between local and national government. The central state in pursuit of its particular objectives sets the structural parameters within which local authorities operate. Knowledge of how the central–local state power relationship operates in practice is essential for the effective implementation of applied urban analysis.

10   Finally, the complexity of the real world and the fact that urban patterns, processes and problems cut across many of the traditional academic boundaries emphasize that while each of the social sciences can make an individual contribution to urban analysis a full understanding of urban phenomena must be sought outside the confines of a single discipline.

References

Alcock, P. (1986) Poverty, welfare and the local state, in P. Lawless and C. Raban *The Contemporary British City* London: Harper and Row, 107-23.

Alexander, I. (1973) City centre redevelopment *Progress in Planning* **3**, 1-269.

Alfors, J. *et al.* (1973) Urban geology — master plan for California *California Division of Mines and Geology Bulletin* **198**: 112.

Alinsky, S. (1969) *Reveille For Radicals* New York: Vintage Books.

Alterman, R. (1982) Planning for public participation *Environment and Planning B* **9**, 295-313.

Altshuler, A. (1969) Transit subsidies *Journal of the American Institute of Planners* **35**, 84-9.

Anderiesen, G. (1981) Tanks in the streets *International Journal of Urban and Regional Research* **5**, 83-95.

Anderson, D. (1972) Towards the equalization of municipal services *Journal of Urban Law* **50**, 177-97.

Anderson, M. (1964) *The Federal Bulldozer* Cambridge MA: M.I.T. Press.

Appleyard, D. (1970) Styles and methods of structuring a city *Environment and Behaviour* **2**, 100-17.

Arnstein, S. (1969) A ladder of citizen participation *Journal of the American Institute of Planners* **35**, 216-24.

Austin, D. (1972) Residential participation *Public Administration Review* **32**, 409-20.

Badcock, B. and Urlich-Cloher, P. (1981) Neighbourhood change in inner Adelaide 1966-76 *Urban Studies* **18**, 41-55.

Bailey, S. (1982) Central city decline and the provision of education services *Urban Studies* **19**, 263-79.

Baker, E. and Patton, D. (1974) Attitudes towards hurricane hazard on the gulf coast, in G.F. White *Natural Hazards* New York: Oxford University Press, 30-6.

Balchin, P. (1985) *Housing Policy* London: Croom Helm.

Baldock, P. (1982) The Sheffield rent strike of 1967-8, in P. Henderson *et al. Successes and Struggles on Council Estates* London: Association of Community Workers, 118-31.

References

Baran, P. and Sweezy, P. (1966) *Monopoly Capital* New York: Monthly Review Press.

Barke, M. (1977) Social deprivation in West Newcastle, in B. Fullerton *North Eastern Studies* Department of Geography University of Newcastle upon Tyne, 19–26.

Barlow, I. (1981) *Spatial Dimensions of Urban Government* Chichester: Wiley.

Barnes, J. (1979) *Who Should Know What?* Harmondsworth: Penguin.

Beauregard, R. (1986) The chaos and compexity of gentrification, in N. Smith and P. Williams *Gentrification of the City* London: Allen and Unwin, 35–55.

Beer, S. (1973) The modernisation of American federalism *Publius* **3**, 49–93.

Bellush, J. and Housknecht, M. (1967) *Urban Renewal: People, Politics and Planning* New York: Doubleday.

Bennison, D. and Davies, R. (1980) The impact of town centre shopping schemes in Britain *Progress in Planning* **14**, 1–104.

Bentham, G. and Moseley, M. (1980) Socio-economic change and disparities within the Paris agglomeration *Regional Studies* **14**, 55–70.

Benwell, M. (1985) Access and mobility, in A. Harrison and J. Gretton *Transport U.K. 1985* London: Policy Journals, 85–94.

Berechman, J. and Paaswell, R. (1983) Rail rapid transit investment and CBD revitalisation *Urban Studies* **20**, 471–86.

Berry, D. and Plaut, T. (1978) Retaining agricultural activities under urban pressures *Policy Sciences Journal* **9**, 153–78.

Best, R. (1978) Myth and reality in the growth of urban land, in A. Rogers *Urban Growth, Farmland Losses and Planning* London: Institute of British Geographers, 2–15.

Best, R. (1981) *Land Use and Living Space* London: Methuen.

Beveridge, W. (1942) *Social Insurance and Allied Services* Cmnd 6404 London: HMSO.

Blaut, J. (1983) Assimilation versus ghettoization *Antipode* **15**, 35–41.

Bloch, P. (1984) *Equality of Distribution of Police Services* Washington DC: The Urban Institute.

Bluestone, B. and Harrison, B. (1980) *Capital and Communities* Washington DC: The Progressive Alliance.

Boal, F. (1969) Territoriality on the Shankill–Falls divide, Belfast *Irish Geography* **6**, 30–50.

Bolan, R. (1971) The social relations of the planner *Journal of the American Institute of Planners* **37**, 386–96.

Booth, P. and Crook, T. (1986) *Low Cost Home Ownership* Aldershot: Gower.

Bowlby, S. (1979) Accessibility, mobility and shopping provisions in B. Goodall and A. Kirby *Resources and Planning* Oxford: Pergamon, 293–324.

Bradley, J. *et al.* (1978) Distance decay and dental decay *Regional Studies* **12**, 529–40.

Bradshaw, J. (1974) The concept of social need *Ekistics* **37**, 184–7.

Breheny, M. *et al.* (1981) A practical approach to the assessment of hypermarket impact *Regional Studies* 15, 459–74.

Breitbart, M. and Peet, R. (1974) A critique of advocacy planning, in D. Lay *Community Participation and the Spatial Order of the City* Vancouver: Tantalus, 97–107.

Bronzaft, A. and McCarthy, D. (1975) The effects of elevated train noise on reading ability *Environment and Behaviour* 7, 517–27.

Bruton, M. and Gore, A. (1980) *Vacant Urban Land in Cardiff* Cardiff: U.W.I.S.T.

Busteed, M. (1975) *Geography and Voting Behaviour* Oxford: Oxford University Press.

Button, K. and Gillingwater, D. (1986) *Future Transport Policy* London: Croom Helm.

Burrows, J. (1978) Vacant urban land *The Planner* 64, 7–9.

Cadman, D. (1979) Private capital and the inner city *Estates Gazette* 249, 1257–60.

Camina, M. (1975) Public participation — an Australian dimension *The Planner* 61, 232–35.

Case, F. and Gale J. (1984) A public utility approach to land use *Policy Studies Journal* 12, 491–8.

Castells, M. (1978a) Urban social movements and the struggle for democracy *International Journal of Urban and Regional Research* 2, 133–46.

Castells, M. (1978b) *City, Class and Power* London: Macmillan.

Castells, M. (1983b) Crisis, planning and the quality of life *Environment and Planning D* 1, 3–21.

Catalano, A. (1983) *A Review of Enterprise Zones* London: Centre for Environmental Studies.

Central Statistical Office (1986) *Social Trends* London: H.M.S.O.

Civic Trust (1977) *Urban Wasteland* London: Civic Trust.

Clapham, D. and Kintrea, K. (1986) Rationing, choice and constraint: the allocation of public housing in Glasgow *Journal of Social Policy* 15, 51–67.

Clark, T. (1981) Race, class and suburban housing discrimination *Urban Geography* 2, 327–38.

Clark, T. (1982) Federal initiatives promoting the dispersal of low-income housing in suburbs *Professional Geographer* 34, 136–46.

Clark, T. (1984) Suburban economic integration, in D.T. Herbert and R.J. Johnston *Geography and the Urban Environment* vol. 6 Chichester: Wiley 213–44.

Cloward, R. and Ohlin, L. (1960) *Delinquency and Opportunity* Glencoe Ill: Free Press.

Cochrane, A. (1986) Local employment initiatives, in P. Lawless and C. Raban *The Contemporary British City* London: Harper and Row, 144–62.

Cockburn, A. and Ridgeway, J. (1979) The city the bankers are killing *New Statesman* 9 February, 178–81.

Cohen, S. *et al.* (1973) Aircraft noise, auditory discrimination and reading ability in children *Journal of Experimental Social Psychology* **9**, 407–22.

Cohen, S. and Weinstein, N. (1982) Non auditory effects of noise on behaviour and health, in G. Evans *Environmental Stress* Cambridge: C.U.P.

Cohn, L. and McVay, G. (1982) *Environmental Analysis of Transportation Systems* New York: Wiley.

Coit, K. (1978) Local action not citizen participation, in W. Tabb and L. Sawers *Marxism and the Metropolis* New York: Oxford University Press, 247–311.

Cole, K. and Gattrell, A. (1986) Public libraries in Salford *Environment and Planning A* **18**, 253–68.

Coleman, A. (1978) Agricultural land losses, in A. Rogers *Urban Growth, Farmland Losses and Planning* London: Institute of British Geographers, 16–36.

Coleman, A. (1984) Design influences in blocks of flats *Geographical Journal* **150**, 351–62.

Community Development Project (1974) *Inter-Project Report 1973* CDP Information and Intelligence Unit London: H.M.S.O.

Community Development Project (1975) *Coventry Final Report Part 1 Coventry and Hillfields* London: H.M.S.O.

Community Development Project (1977) *Gilding the Ghetto* CDP Inter-Project Editorial Team London: H.M.S.O.

Cox, K. (1979) *Location and Public Problems* Oxford: Blackwell.

Cullen, B. and Spear, L. (1985) Retail coverage and market equilibrium *Proceedings of the Applied Geography Conferences* **8**, 1–15.

Cullingworth, J. (1982) *Town and Country Planning in Britain* London: Allen and Unwin.

Culver, L. (1982) The politics of suburban distress *Journal of Urban Affairs* **4**, 1–18.

Cutter, S. (1982) Residential satisfaction and the suburban homeowner *Urban Geography* **3**, 315–27.

Damerall, R. (1968) *Triumph in a White Suburb* New York: Morrow.

Danson, M. *et al.* (1980) The inner city employment problem in Great Britain, 1952–76 *Urban Studies* **17**, 193–210.

Davidoff, P. (1965) Advocacy and pluralism in planning *Journal of the American Institute of Planners* **31**, 331–8.

Davidoff, P. and Davidoff, L. (1971) Opening the suburbs *Syracuse Law Review* **22**, 509–36.

Davidson, R. (1976) Social deprivation: an analysis of intercensal change *Transactions of the Institute of British Geographers* **1**, 108–17.

Davies, R.L. (1984) *Retail and Commercial Planning* London: Croom Helm.

Davies, R.L. (1985) The Gateshead shopping and information service *Environment and Planning B* **12**, 209–20.

Davies, W. (1973) Buffalo Creek dam disaster *Civil Engineering* **43**, 69–72.

Dawson, J. and Kirby, D. (1979) *Small Scale Retailing in the United Kingdom* Farnborough: Saxon House.

Dear, M. and Clark, G. (1981) Dimensions of local state autonomy *Environment and Planning A* **13**, 1277–94.

Dear, M. and Taylor, S. (1982) *Not On Our Street* London: Pion.

Dear, M. and Wolch, J. (1987) *Landscapes of Despair* Cambridge: Polity Press.

Department of the Environment (1977a) *Inner Area Studies: Liverpool, Birmingham and Lambeth* London: H.M.S.O.

Department of the Environment (1977) Policy for the inner cities *Cmnd 6845* London: HMSO.

Department of the Environment (1977c) *Change or Decay: Final Report of the Liverpool Inner Area Study* London: HMSO.

De Longis, A. *et al.* (1982) Relationship of daily hassles, uplifts and major events to health status *Health Psychology* **1**, 119–36.

Docklands Joint Committee (1976) *A Strategy For Docklands* London: L.D.J.C.

Douglas, I. (1983) *The Urban Environment* London: Arnold.

Downs, A. (1978) The law of peak-hour expressway congestion *Traffic Quarterly* **19**, 622.

Downs, A. (1981) *Neighbourhoods and Urban Development* Washington DC: Brookings Institute.

Dunleavy, P. (1980) *Urban Political Analysis* London: Macmillan.

Dunstan, J. (1979) The effect of crowding on behaviour *Urban Studies* **16**, 299–307.

Earney, F. and Knowles, B. (1974) Urban snow hazard: Marquette, Michigan in G.F. White *Natural Hazards* New York: Oxford University Press, 167–74.

Edel, M. (1981) Capitalism, accumulation and the explanation of urban phenomenon, in M. Dear and A. Scott *Urbanization and Urban Planning in Capitalist Society* London: Methuen, 19–44.

Edwards, J. and Batley, R. (1978) *The Politics of Positive Discrimination* London: Heinemann.

Ekhaugen, K. *et al.* (1980) State support to small stores *Journal of Consumer Policy* **4**, 195–211.

Elias, P. and Keogh, G. (1982) Industrial decline and unemployment in the inner city areas of Great Britain *Urban Studies* **19**, 1–15.

Elsom, D. (1983) Pollution in M. Pacione *Progress in Urban Geography* London: Croom Helm, 251–77.

English, J. (1987) Access to public sector housing, in M. Pacione *Social Geography: Progress and Prospect* London: Croom Helm, 62–89.

Evans, A. (1980) Poverty and the conurbations in G. Cameron *The Future of the British Conurbations* London: Longman, 189–207.

Evans, G. *et al.* (1982) Cognitive maps and urban form *Journal of the American Planning Association* **48**, 232–44.

Fagence, M. (1977) *Citizen Participation in Planning* Oxford: Pergamon.

Farley, R. *et al.* (1978) Chocolate city vanilla suburbs *Social Science Research* **7**, 319–44.

Feagin, J. (1982) Urban real estate speculation in the United States *International Journal of Urban and Regional Research* **6**, 35–59.

Fielding, G. (1986) Transit in American cities, in S. Hansen *The Geography of Urban Transportation* New York: Guildford Press, 229–46.

Finsterbusch, K. (1980) *Understanding Social Impacts* London: Sage.

Fleming, R. *et al.* (1979) Landslide hazards and their reduction *Journal of the American Planning Association* **45**, 428–39.

Fried, M. (1963) Grieving for a lost home, in L. Duhl *The Urban Condition* New York: Simon and Schuster, 151–71.

Friedland, R. (1982) *Power and Crisis in the City* London: Macmillan.

Ford, L. and Griffin, E. (1979) The ghettoization of paradise *Geographical Review* **69**, 140–58.

Foreman, R. (1971) *Black Ghettos, White Ghettos and Slums* Englewood Cliffs N.J.: Prentice Hall.

Fosler, R. and Berger, R. (1982) *Public–Private Partnership in American Cities* Lexington MA: Lexington Books.

Fox, K. (1985) *Metropolitan America* London: Macmillan.

Frazier, J. (1982) *Applied Geography: Selected Pespectives* Englewood Cliffs N.J.: Prentice Hall.

Gale, D. (1979) Middle class resettlement in older urban neighbourhoods *Journal of the American Planning Association* **45**, 293–304.

Gale, S. and Moore, E. (1975) *The Manipulated City* Chicago: Maaroufa Press.

Galle, O. and Gove, W. (1983) Overcrowding, isolation and human behaviour in M. Baldassare *Cities and Urban Living* New York: Columbia University Press, 215–1.

Gans, H.J. (1962) *The Urban Villagers* New York: Free Press.

Gee, D. (1974) *Slum Clearance* London: Shelter.

Gibson, M. and Langstaff, M. (1982) *An Introduction to Urban Renewal* London: Hutchinson.

Gomez–Ibanez, J. (1985) A dark side to light rail *Journal of the American Planning Association* **51**, 337–51.

Goodchild, R. and Munton, R. (1985) *Development and the Landowner* London: Allen and Unwin.

Goss, S and Lansley (1981) *What Price Housing?* London: S.H.A.C.

Gottdeiner, M. (1985) *The Social Production of Urban Space* Austin: University of Texas Press.

Gray, F. (1976) Selection and allocation in council housing *Transactions of the Institute of British Geographers* **1**, 34–46.

Gutstein, D. (1975) *Vancouver Limited* Toronto: James Lorimer.

Guy, C. (1980) *Retail Location and Retail Planning in Britain* Farnborough: Gower.

Guy, C. (1983) The assessment of access to local shopping opportunities *Environment and Planning B* **10**, 219–38.

Hall, P. *et al.* (1973) *The Containment of Urban England* 2 volumes London: Allen and Unwin.

Hambleton, R. (1978) *Policy Planning and Local Government* London: Hutchinson.

Hamnett, C. (1979) Area–based explanations: a critical appraisal, in D.T.

Herbert and D.Smith *Social Problems and the City* Oxford: Oxford University Press, 244–60.

Hamnett, C. and Williams, P. (1980) Social change in London *The London Journal* **6**, 51–66.

Harding, D. and Parker, D. (1974) Flood hazard at Shrewsbury in the U.K. in G.F. White *Natural Hazards*, New York: Oxford University Press, 43–52.

Hart, D. (1980) Urban economic development *Occasional Paper* No. 2. School of Planning Studies, University of Reading.

Hart, J. (1976) Urban encroachment on rural areas *Geographical Review* **66**, 1–17.

Hartman, C. (1964) The housing of relocated families *Journal of the American Institute of Planners* **30**, 266–86.

Hartman, C. *et al.* (1981) *Displacement: How to Fight It* Berkeley: National Housing Law Project.

Harvey, D. (1971) Social processes, spatial form and the redistribution of real income in an urban system, in M. Chisholm *Regional Forecasting* London: Butterworth, 267–300.

Harvey, D. (1973) *Social Justice and the City* London: Arnold.

Harvey, D. (1975b) The political economy of urbanization in advanced capitalist societies, in G. Gappert and H. Rose *The Social Economy of Cities* Beverly Hills: Sage, 119–62.

Harvey, D. (1981) The urban process under capitalism, in M. Dear and A. Scott *Urbanization and Urban Planning in Capitalist Society* London: Methuen, 91–121.

Harvey, D. (1984) On the history and present condition of geography *Professional Geographer* **46**, 1–11.

Harvey, D. (1985) *The Urbanization of Capital* Oxford: Blackwell.

Hasluck, C. (1987) *Urban Unemployment* London: Longman.

Hatch, R. (1968) Some thoughts on advocacy planning *Architectural Forum* **128**, 72–5.

Heathcote, R. (1974) Drought in South Australia, in G.F. White *Natural Hazards* New York: Oxford University Press, 128–36.

Herbert, M. (1981) The land debate and the planning system *Town and Country Planning* **50**, 22–3.

Henderson, J. and Karn, V. (1986) *Race Class, and State Housing* Aldershot: Gower.

Herbert, D.T. and Johnston, R.J. (1976) *Social Areas in Cities* Chichester: Wiley.

Heskin, A. (1980) Crisis and response *Journal of the American Planning Association* **46**, 50–63.

Hicks, D. (1982) *Urban America in the Eighties* New Brunswick NJ: Transaction Books.

Hinshaw, M. and Allott, K. (1972) Environmental preferences of future housing consumers *Journal of the American Institute of Planners* **38**, 102–7.

Hodgart, R. (1978) Optimising access to public services *Progress in Human Geography* **2**, 17–48.

Holterman, S. (1975) Areas of urban deprivation in Great Britain *Social Trends* **6**, 33-47.

Holzer, T. and Johnson, A. (1985) Land subsidence caused by ground water withdrawal in urban areas *Geojournal* **11**, 245-55.

Holzer, T. *et al.* (1983) Faulting arrested by control of ground water withdrawal in Houston Texas *Earthquake Information Bulletin* **15**, 204-9.

Home, R. (1982) *Inner City Regeneration* London: Spon.

Horner, R. (1979) The Thames barrier project *Geographical Journal* **145**, 242-53.

Islington Borough Council (1980) *Islington Development Plan: Written Statement and Proposals Map* London: Islington B.C.

Ittelson, W. *et al.* (1974) *An Introduction to Environmental Psychology* New York: Rinehart and Winston.

Jackson, R. (1981) *Land use in America* London: Arnold.

James, F. (1980) The revitalization of older urban housing and neighbourhoods, in A. Solomon *The Prospective City* Cambridge MA: M.I.T. Press, 132-6.

Johnson, J. and Zeigler, D. (1983) Distinguishing human responses to radiological emergencies *Economic Geography* **59**, 386-402.

Johnston, R.J. (1979) *Political, Electoral and Spatial Systems* Oxford: Oxford University Press.

Johnston, R.J. (1981a) Applied geography, quantitative analysis and ideology *Applied Geography* **1**, 213-19.

Johnston, R.J. (1981b) The management and autonomy of the local state *Environment and Planning A* **13**, 1305-15.

Johnston, R.J. (1984) *Residential Segregation The State and Constitutional Conflict in American Urban Areas* London: Academic Press.

Johnston, R.J. (1986) *On Human Geography* Oxford: Blackwell.

Jovanis, P. (1981) Assessment of flextime potential to relieve highway facility congestion *Transportation Research Record* **816**, 19-27.

Kantor, A. and Nystuen, J. (1982) De facto redlining *Annals of the Association of American Geographers* **58**, 309-28.

Katz, S. and Mayer, M. (1985) Gimme shelter *International Journal of Urban and Regional Research* **9**, 15-46.

Keeble, D. (1978) Industrial decline in the inner city and conurbation *Transactions of the Institute of British Geographers* **3**, 101-14.

Kilroy, B. (1980) *The Financial Implications of Government Policies on Home Ownership* London: S.H.A.C.

Kilroy, B. (1982) The financial and economic implications of council house sales in J. English *The Future of Council Housing* London: Croom Helm.

Kirby, A. (1979) *Education, Health and Housing* Farnborough: Saxon House.

Kirby, D. (1976) The convenience store phenomenon *Retail and Distribution Management* **4**, 31-3.

Kirby, D. (1979) *Slum Housing and Residential Renewal* London: Longman.

Knox, P. (1978) The intra-urban ecology of primary medical care *Environment and Planning A* **10**, 415-35.

Knox, P. (1979) Medical deprivation and public policy *Social Science and Medicine* **13D**, 111-21.

Kraushaar, R. (1979) Pragmatic radicalism *International Journal of Urban and Regional Research* **3**, 61-80.

Krefetz, S. (1979) Low- and moderate-income housing in the suburbs *Policy Studies Journal* **8**, 288-99.

Krohn, J. and Slassen, J. (1976) Landslide potential in the United States *California Geology* **29**, 224-31.

Krumholz, N. *et al.* (1975) The Cleveland policy planning report *Journal of the American Institute of Planners* **41**, 298-304.

Krupat, E. (1985) *People in Cities* Cambridge: Cambridge University Press.

Ladd, F. (1972) Black youths view their environment *Environment and Behaviour* **2**, 74-99.

Lagana, G. *et al.* (1982) Urban social movements and urban restructuring in Turin, 1969-76 *International Journal of Urban and Regional Research* **6**, 223-45.

Lancourt, J. (1979) *Confront or Concede: the Alinsky Citizen-Action Organisations* Lexington MA: Lexington Books.

Lansing, J. and Marans, R. (1969) Evaluation of neighbourhood quality *Journal of the American Institute of Planners* **35**, 195-9.

Lansing, J. *et al.* (1970) *Planned Residential Environments* Ann Arbor MI: University of Michigan.

Lapping, M. (1974) Preserving agricultural lands *Town and Country Planning* **43**, 394-7.

Lasswell, H. (1958) *Who Gets What When How* Cleveland: World Publishing Company.

Lawless, P. (1986) *The Evolution of Spatial Policy* London: Pion.

Lazarus, R. and Cohen, J. (1977) Environmental stress, in A. Altman and J. Wohlwill *Human Behaviour and Environment* New York: Plenum, 90-127.

Leclerc, R. and Draffan, D. (1984) The Glasgow eastern area renewal project *Town Planning Review* **55**, 335-51.

Lee, J. (1963) *Social Leaders and Public Persons* London: Clarendon Press.

Levy, F. *et al.* (1974) *Urban Outcomes* Berkeley: University of California Press.

Lewis, J. (1985) Technical change in retailing *Environment and Planning B* **12**, 165-91.

Ley, D. (1980) Liberal ideology and the post–industrial city *Annals of the Association of American Geographers* **70**, 238-58.

Ley, D. (1981b) Inner city revitalisation in Canada *Canadian Geographer* **25**, 124-48.

Ley, D. (1983) *A Social Geography of the City* New York: Harper and Row.

Ley, D. and Cybriwsky, R. (1974) *Urban Graffiti as Territorial Markers* Association of American Geographers **64** 491-505.

Lineberry, R. (1977) *Equality and Urban Policy* Beverly Hills: Sage.

References

Lloyd, P. (1979) The components of industrial change for Merseyside inner areas *Urban Studies* **16**, 45–60.

Loo, C. (1980) Neighbourhood satisfaction and safety *Environment and Behaviour* **18**, 109–31.

Lorimer, J. (1972) *A Citizen's Guide to City Politics* Toronto: James Lewis and Samuel.

Lowe, S. (1986) *Urban Social Movements* London: Macmillan.

Lowry, M. (1973) Schools in transition *Annals of the Association of American Geographers* **63**, 167–80.

Lynch, K. (1960) *The Image of the City* Cambridge MA: M.I.T. Press.

Lynch, K. (1981) *A Theory of Good City Form* Cambridge MA: M.I.T. Press.

Lynch, K. (1984) Reconsidering the image of the city, in L. Rodwin and R. Hollister *Cities of the Mind* New York: Plenum, 151–61.

Macdonald, M. (1977) *Food Stamps and Income Maintenance* New York: Academic Press.

McIntosh, A. and Keddie, V. (1980) *Industry and Employment in the Inner City* Inner Cities Directorate, Department of the Environment London: H.M.S.O.

McLean, I. (1974) Popular protest and public order: Red Clydeside 1915–1919, in J. Stevenson and R. Quinault *Popular Protest and Public Order* London: Allen and Unwin, 215–42.

Mack, J. and Lansley, S. (1985) *Poor Britain* London: Allen and Unwin.

Mandelker, D. (1977) Racial discrimination and exclusionary zoning *Texas Law Review* **55**, 1217–53.

Marcuse, P. (1986) Abandonment, gentrification and displacement: the linkages in New York, in N. Smith and P. Williams *Gentrification of the City* London: Allen and Unwin, 153–77.

Maslow, A. (1970) *Motivation and Personality* New York: Harpe.

Masotti, L. (1973) Epilogue: suburbia in the seventies. . . and beyond, in L. Masotti and J. Hadden *The Urbanization of the Suburbs* Beverly Hills: Sage, 534–44.

Massey, D. (1980) Residential segregation and spatial distribution of a non-labour force population: the needy, elderly and disabled *Economic Geography* **56**, 190–200.

Massey, D. and Megan, R. (1976) *The Inner City and the International Competitiveness of British Industry* London: Centre for Environmental Studies.

Meehan, E. (1977) *A Decent Home and Environment* New York: Ballinger.

Merrett, S. (1979) *State Housing in Britain* London: Routledge and Kegan Paul.

Milgram, S. (1976) Psychological maps of Paris, in H. Proshansky *et al.* *Environmental Psychology* New York: Holt, Rinehart and Winston, 194–24.

Milgram, S. *et al.* (1972) A psychological map of New York City *American Scientist* **60**, 194–200.

Miller, D. *et al.* (1974) Windstorms, in G.F. White *Natural Hazards* New York: Oxford University Press, 80–6.

References

Miller, F. *et al.* (1980) Neighbourhood satisfaction among urban dwellers *Journal of Social Issues and the Family* **38**, 309–20.

Miller, J. (1974) *Aberfan – a disaster and its aftermath* London: Constable.

Ministry of Housing and Local Government (1955) Green belts *Circular No. 42/55* London: HMSO

Ministry of Transport (1964) *Road Pricing: the economic and technical possibilities* (the Smeed Report) London: H.M.S.O.

Mladenka, K. and Hill, K. (1977) The distribution of benefits in an urban environment *Urban Affairs Quarterly* **13**, 73–94.

Moore, C and Booth, S. (1986) Urban policy contradictions *Policy and Politics* **14** (3), 361–87.

Moore, V. (1983) The public control of land use, in J. Carr and E. Duensing *Land Use Issues of the 1980s* Rutgers: State University of New Jersey, 85–98.

Mukerjee, T. (1971) Economic analysis of natural hazards: a study of adjustments to earthquakes and their costs *Working Paper No. 17* Natural Hazards Research, University of Toronto.

Muller, P. (1976) Social transportation geography *Progress in Geography* **8**, 208–31.

Munton, R. (1981) Agricultural land use in the London green belt *Town and Country Planning* **49**, 17–19.

Munton, R. (1983) *London's Green Belt* London: Allen and Unwin.

Myers, P. (1982) UDAG and the urban environment *Journal of the American Planning Association* **48**, 99–109.

Nabarro, R. *et al.* (1980) *Wasteland* London: Methuen.

Nakano, T. (1975) Differing degrees of danger associated with earthquake disasters *Conference Series* **8** New Zealand Geographical Society, 335–43.

Nanetti, R. (1985) Neighbourhood institutions and policy outputs: the Italian case *International Journal of Urban and Regional Research* **9**, 113–35.

Nanetti, R. and Leonardi, G. (1979) Neighbourhoods and the implementation of city plans *Geoforum* **10**, 363–88.

National Community Development Project (1975) *The Poverty of the Improvement Programme* London: C.D.P. Information Unit.

National Economic Development Office (1970) *Urban Models in Shopping Studies* London: H.M.S.O.

Nelson, H. and Clark, W. (1976) The Los Angeles metropolitan experience, in J. Adams *Contemporary Metropolitan America* vol. 4 Cambridge MA: Ballinger, 227–86.

Nelson, R. (1980) *Zoning and Property Rights* Cambridge MA: M.I.T. Press.

Newby, P. and Shepherd, I. (1979) Brent Cross *Geography* **64**, 133–7.

Newman, I. and Mayo, M. (1981) Docklands *International Journal of Urban and Regional Research* **5**, 529–45.

Newman, O. (1972) *Defensible Space* New York: Macmillan.

Newman, O. (1980) *Community of Interest* New York: Anchor Press.

Newman, O. and Franck, K. (1982) The effects of building size on personal crime and fear of crime *Population and Environment* **5**, 204-20.

Newnham, R. (1980) Community enterprise *Occasional Paper* **No. 3** School of Planning Studies, University of Reading.

Nicholson, D (1984) The public ownership of vacant land *The Planner* **70**, 18-20.

Norcliffe, G. (1977) Discretionary aspects of scientific districting *Area* **9**, 240-6.

Nugent, N. (1979) The ratepayers, in R. Ring and N. Nugent *Respectable Rebels* London: Hodder and Stoughton, 23-45.

Pacione, M. (1980a) Redevelopment of a medium-sized central shopping area: a case study of Clydebank *Tijdschrift voor Economische en Sociale Géographie* **71**, 159-68.

Pacione, M. (1980b) Differential quality of life in a metropolitan village *Transactions of the Institute of British Geographers* **5**, 185-206.

Pacione, M. (1982a) Evaluating the quality of the residential environment in a deprived council estate *Geoforum* **13**, 45-55.

Pacione, M. (1982b) Retail redevelopment in the inner city: a case study of Springburn *Scottish Geographical Magazine* **98**, 166-77.

Pacione, M. (1982c) Neighbourhoods and public service boundaries in the city: a geographical analysis *Geoforum* **13**, 237-44.

Pacione, M. (1984) Local areas in the city, in D.T. Herbert and R.J. Johnston *Geography and the Urban Environment* vol. 6 Chichester: Wiley, 349-92.

Pacione, M. (1985a) Venice *Cities* **2**, 290-6.

Pacione, M. (1985b) Inner city regeneration: perspectives on the GEAR project *Planning Outlook* **28**, 65-9.

Pacione, M. (1986a) Quality of life in Glasgow: an applied geographical analysis *Environment and Planning A* **18**, 1499-1520.

Pacione, M. (1986b) The changing pattern of deprivation in Glasgow *Scottish Geographical Magazine* **102**, 97-109.

Pacione, M. (1987) The socio-spatial development of the south Italian city *Transactions of the Institute of British Geographers* **12**, 433-50.

Pacione, M. (1988) Public participation in neighbourhood change *Applied Geography* 8(3), 229-47.

Pacione, M. (1989) Access to urban services: the case of secondary schools in Glasgow *Scottish Geographical Magazine* **105**, 12-18.

Page, S. (1984) *Stigma* London: Routledge and Kegan Paul.

Palm, R. (1981) Public response to earthquake hazard information *Annals of the Association of American Geographers* **71**, 389-99.

Palm, R. (1982) Earthquake hazards information: the experience of mandated disclosure, in D.T. Herbert and R.J. Johnston *Geography and the Urban Environment* vol. 5, Chichester: Wiley, 241-77.

Parker, D. and Penning-Rowsell, E. (1982) Flood risk in the urban environment in D.T. Herbert and R.J. Johnston *Geography and the Urban Environment* vol. 5 Chichester: Wiley, 201-34.

Parry, M. (1979) Climate and town planning, in B. Goodall and A. Kirby *Resource and Planning* Oxford: Pergamon, 201-20.

Peltz, M. (1982) State legislation supports community economic development *Economic Development and Law Center Report* **12**, 11–20.

Perlman, J. (1976) Grassrooting the system *Social Policy* **1**, 4–20.

Pearlman, K. (1978) The closing door: the supreme court and residential segregation *Journal of the American Institute of Planners* **44**, 160–9.

Perry, A. (1981) *Environmental Hazards in the British Isles* London: Allen and Unwin.

Perry, C. (1929) *The Neighbourhood Unit, Regional Survey of New York and Its Environs* vol. 7 New York: Regional Plan Association.

Peterson, G. (1967) A model of preference *Journal of Regional Science* **7**, 19–31.

Petticrew, (1969) Racially separate or together? *Journal of Social Issues* **25**, 43–69.

Pinto–Duschinsky, M. (1977) Corruption in Britain *Political Studies* **25**, 274–84.

Plane, D. (1986) Urban transportation: policy alternatives in S. Hansen *The Geography of Urban Transportation* New York: Guildford Press, 386–14.

Platt, R. (1982) The Jackson flood of 1979 *Journal of the American Planning Association* **48**, 219–31.

Porteus, J. (1985) Smellscape *Progress in Human Geography* **9**, 356–78.

Porteous, J. and Mastin, J. (1985) Soundscape *Journal of Architectural and Planning Research* **2**, 169–86.

Pucher, J. (1981) Equity in transit finance *Journal of the American Planning Association* **47**, 387–407.

Pucher, J. (1982) Discrimination in mass transit *Journal of the American Planning Association* **48**, 315–26.

Rainwater, L. (1966) Fear and house-as-haven in the lower class *Journal of the American Institute of Planners* **32**, 23–31.

Rapkin, C. and Grigsby, W. (1960) *The Demand For Housing in Racially Mixed Areas* Berkeley: University of California Press.

Rapoport, A. (1977) *Human Aspects of Urban Form* Elmsford: Pergamon.

Redfern, P. (1982) Profile of our cities *Population Trends* **30**, 21–32.

Rees, G. and Lambert, J. (1985) *Cities in Crisis* London: Arnold.

Reidel, J. (1972) Citizen participation *Public Administration Review* **32**, 211–20.

Revelle, C. *et al.* (1970) An analysis of private and public sector location Models *Management Science* **16**, 692–702.

Revelle, C. *et al.* (1976) Applications of the location set–covering problem *Geographical Analysis* **8**, 65–76.

Reynolds, H. (1961) The human element in urban renewal *Public Welfare* **19**, 71–3.

Rich, R. (1979) Neglected issues in the study of urban service distributions *Urban Studies* **16**, 143–56.

Robertson, I. (1978) Planning the location of recreation centres in an urban area *Regional Studies* **12**, 419–27.

Robertson, K. (1983) Downtown retail activity in large American cities 1954–1977 *Geographical Review* **73**, 314–23.

Roistacher, E. (1984) A tale of two conservatives: housing policy under Reagan and Thatcher *Journal of the American Planning Association*

50, 485–92.

Rose, H. (1971) *The Black Ghetto* New York: McGraw Hill.

Rose, J. (1975) *Transfer of Development Rights* New Brunswick NJ: Rutgers University.

Rosenbloom, S. (1982) Federal policies to increase the mobility of the elderly and the handicapped *Journal of the American Planning Association* **48**, 335–50.

Rosencrantz, A. (1981) Economic approches to air pollution control *Environment* **23**, 25–30.

Rosow, I. (1964) *Social Integration of the Aged* New York: Free Press.

Rossum, R. (1980) The rise and fall of equalization litigation *Urban Interest* **2**, 2–10.

Rowntree, S. (1901) *Poverty* London: Macmillan.

Royal Commission on the Distribution of Income and Wealth (1975) Initial Report on the Standing Conference *Cmnd* **6171** London: H.M.S.O.

Rusbult, C. (1979) Crowding and human behaviour *Environment and Planning A* **11**, 23–44.

Savas, E. (1979) On equity in providing social services *Ekistics* **46**, 144–8.

Savas, E. (1982) *Privatising The Public Sector* New Jersey: Chatham House.

Schuster, R. (1978) Introduction in R. Schuster and R. Krizek *Landslides — Analysis and Control* Washington DC: National Research Council.

Schwartz, G. (1979) *Retrospect and Prospects: Urban Policy Profile for the United States* Columbus Ohio: Academy for Contemporary Problems.

Scott, A. and Roweiss, S. (1977) Urban planning in theory and practice *Environment and Planning* **2**, 1097–1111.

Scott, M. (1969) *American City Planning Since 1890* Berkeley: University of California Press.

Scottish Development Department (1974) *Community Councils* Edinburgh; H.M.S.O.

Seley, J. (1970) *Spatial Bias: the Kink in Nashville's 1–40* Department of Regional Science, University of Pennsylvania.

Selye, H. (1956) *The Stress of Life* New York: McGraw Hill.

Shearer, D. (1984) Citizen participation in local government *International Journal of Urban and Regional Research* **8**, 573–86.

Singh, A. (1977) U.K. industry and world economy *Cambridge Journal of Economics* **1**, 113–36.

Smith, B. (1977) Central area development: the German style. *Town and Country Planning* **45**, 362–5.

Smith, C. (1981) Urban structure and the development of natural support systems for service-dependent populations *Professional Geographer* **33**, 457–65.

Smith, D. (1981) Actual and potential flood damage *Applied Geography* **1**, 31–9.

Smith, D.M. (1977) *Human Geography: A Welfare Approach* London: Arnold.

Smith, N. and Williams, P. (1986) *Gentrification of the City* London: Allen and Unwin.

Sommer, R. (1972) *Design Awareness* San Francisco: Rinehart Press.

Squires, G. *et al.* (1979) Urban decline or disinvestment: uneven development, redlining and the role of the insurance industry *Social Problems* **27**, 79–95.

Stever, D. (1980) *Sealrock and the Nuclear Regulatory Commission* Hanover NH: University Press of New England.

Stungo, A. (1984) Public sector land *Estates Gazette* **269**, 291–5.

Susskind, L. and Elliott, M. (1981) Learning from citizen participation and citizen action in Western Europe *Journal of Applied Behavioural Science* **17**, 497–517.

Sutcliffe, C. and Board, J. (1986) Designing secondary school catchment areas using goal programming *Environment and Planning A* **18**, 661–75.

Suttles, G. (1972) *The Social Construction of Communities* Chicago: University of Chicago Press.

Sumka, H. (1983) Neighbourhood revitalisation and displacement, in M. Baldassare *Cities and Urban Living* New York: Columbia University Press, 144–64.

Tabb, W. (1978) The New York fiscal crisis, in W. Tabb and L. Sawers *Marxism and the Metropolis* New York: Oxford University Press, 241–66.

Taylor, F. and Brabb, E. (1972) Maps showing distribution and cost by counties of structurally damaging landslides in the San Francisco bay region, California, winter 1968–9 *US Geological Survey Miscellaneous Field Studies* MF-327.

Terwindt, J. (1983) Prediction of earthquake damage in the Tokyo bay area *Geojournal* **7**, 215.

Thomas, R. and Robson, B. (1984) The impact of falling school roles on the assignment of primary schoolchildren to secondary schools in Manchester, 1980–1985 *Environment and Planning A* **16**, 339–56.

Thompson, D. and Slocum, T. (1982) A geographic information system for political redistricting in Maryland *Proceedings of the Applied Geography Conferences* **5**, 21–35.

Thomson, J. (1977) *Great Cities and Their Traffic* Harmondsworth: Penguin.

Thornes, J. (1979) The best practicable means of air quality management in the European community *Progress in Physical Geography* **3**, 427–42.

Tietenberg, T. (1980) Transferable discharge permits and the control of stationary source air pollution *Land Economics* **56**, 391–416.

Tietz, M. (1968) Towards a theory of urban public facility location *Proceedings of the Regional Science Association* **31**, 35–44.

Tobin, G. (1982) Natural hazards and urban planning, in D.T. Herbert and R.J. Johnston *Geography and the Urban Environment* vol. 5 Chichester: Wiley, 157–99.

Townsend, P. (1979) *Poverty in the U.K.* Harmondsworth: Penguin.

Trowbridge, C. (1913) On fundamental methods of orientation and imagery maps *Science* **38**, 888–97.

Urban Land Institute (1980) *Downtown Development Handbook* Washington DC: Urban Land Institute.

U.S. Bureau of the Census (1984) Characteristics of the population below the poverty level: 1982 *Current Population Reports, Consumer Income, Series P-60* no. 144, Washington DC: Government Printing Office.

Vlassin, R. (1975) Food production and its implications for land resource conservation *Journal of Soil and Water Conservation* **30**, 2-7.

Walker, B. (1981) *Welfare Economics and Urban Problems* London: Hutchinson.

Wang, L. and Tan, T. (1981) Singapore, in M. Pacione *Problems and Planning in Third World Cities* London: Croom Helm, 218-49.

Warren, R. (1978) *The Community in America* Chicago: Rand McNally.

Warren, R. (1986) Equity and efficiency in urban service delivery, in M. Rosentraub *Urban Policy Problems* New York: Praeger, 218-52.

Washnis, G. (1972) *Municipal Decentralisation and Neighbourhood Resources* New York: Praeger.

Wates, N. and Wolmar, C. (1980) *Squatting* London: Bay Leaf Books.

Webber, M. (1963) Order in diversity: community without propinquity, in L. Wingo *Cities and Space* Baltimore: Johns Hopkins University Press.

Weicher, J. (1971) The allocation of police protection by income class *Urban Studies* **8**, 207-20.

Webster, B. (1982) Area management, in J. Stewart *Public Policy and Local Government* London: Allen and Unwin.

Weink, R. *et al.* (1979) *Measuring Racial Discrimination in American Housing Markets* Department of Housing and Urban Development Washington DC: U.S. Government Printing Office.

White, G.F. (1964) Choice of adjustment to floods *Research Paper* **No. 93** Department of Geography, University of Chicago.

Wilner, D. *et al.* (1962) *The Housing Environment and Family Life* Baltimore: Johns Hopkins Press.

Wilson, H. and Wormsley, L. (1977) *Change or Decay: Final Report of the Liverpool Inner Area Study* London: H.M.S.O.

Woodall, M. *et al.* (1980) The elimination of racially identifiable schools *Professional Geographer* **32**, 412-20.

Yancy, W. (1971) Architecture, interaction and social control *Environment and Behaviour* **3**, 3-18.

Yeung, Y. (1985) Cities that work: Hong Kong and Singapore *Occasional Paper* **No. 72** Department of Geography, Chinese University of Hong Kong.

Zehner, R. (1977) *Indicators of the Quality of Life in New Communities* Cambridge MA: Ballinger.

Zeisel, J. (1981) *Inquiry By Design* Monterey CA: Brooks/Cole.

Zeisel, J. *et al.* (1977) *Low Rise Housing For Older People* Washington DC: U.S. Government Printing Office.

Zimmerman, D. (1982) Small is beautiful, but: an appraisal of the optimum city *Humboldt Journal of Social Relations* **9**, 120-42.

Zukin, S. (1982) Loft living as historic compromise in the urban core *International Journal of Urban and Regional Research* **6**, 256-67.

Index

191

For Product Safety Concerns and Information please contact our EU
representative GPSR@taylorandfrancis.com
Taylor & Francis Verlag GmbH, Kaufingerstraße 24, 80331 München, Germany

www.ingramcontent.com/pod-product-compliance
Lightning Source LLC
Chambersburg PA
CBHW050441280326
41932CB00013BA/2192

9 7 8 0 4 1 5 7 0 7 6 6 4